The Hiker's Way

JOHN McKINNEY

The Hiker's Way

Hike Smart · Live Well · Go Green

OLYMPUS PRESS
SANTA BARBARA

THE HIKER'S WAY

Editor: Cheri Rae
Book design and typography: Jim Cook
Cover illustration and logo design: Mark Chumley
Research assistant: Carla Neufeldt

Manufactured in the United States of America
Published by Olympus Press, a division of
The Trailmaster Inc.
www.TheTrailmaster.com
Visit our website for a complete listing of our books and for ordering information.

Portions of this book have appeared previously in the *Los Angeles Times* and in *The Joy of Hiking.*

The Hiker's Way

Why You Need This Book / 7
PROLOGUE / 9

THE HIKER

The Hiker Redefined

1. Welcome to The Hiker's Way / 13
2. Hike Smart. Live Well. Go Green / 29

The Hiker Flourishes

3. In Good Health / 41
4. In Good Spirit / 51
5. In Harmony with Nature / 61

The Hiker Prepares

6. The Ten Essentials / 75
7. Food and Water / 83
8. Gearing Up / 95

THE WAY

Beginning The Way

9. All About Trails / 117
10. Choosing a Trail / 133
11. Planning a Hike / 141

Along The Way

12. On the Trail / 155
13. Finding The Way / 165
14. Cautions and Precautions / 179
15. Seasons / 199
16. Terrain / 219
17. Wildlife / 231

Sharing The Way

18. Companions and Going Solo / 239
19. Children / 249
20. Sharing the Experience / 265

Epilogue / 273
Resources / 274
Index / 280

WHY YOU NEED THIS BOOK

Q & A About The Hiker's Way

CHANCES ARE THAT, if you are active, love nature and getting away from it all, you are a hiker—you just haven't defined yourself that way. This is a book that treats hiking—and hikers—in a different way. Here are some of the most common doubts and resistances hikers have about trying a new approach:

If I already go hiking and have all the gear, what more do I need to learn?

To become a hiker. By reviewing what you know about hiking and learning new approaches, you'll improve your life on and off the trail.

You're not really thinking people are going to become hikers just by reading a book, are you?

This book will help you think, then act like a hiker; you'll become a hiker by hiking and by embracing certain core values of *The Hiker's Way* on and off the trail. We learn by doing, whether that's using the latest digital device or practicing yoga. Books inspire us, challenge us, motivate us, and at the very least help us learn what we don't know.

Hiking is just so simple; it's all about putting one foot in front of the other, right?

Well, not that simple. This book shares the basics—as well as a philosophy—to become a trail-wise hiker and learn ways to make the most of your time on the trail.

Do I have to be young and super-fit to be a hiker?

Absolutely not. This books helps hikers of any age get the most out of their time on the trail. As much as anything else, this book is about getting to know yourself as a hiker.

Doesn't hiking take a lot of time?

Some, not lots. If you're a hiker, not just someone who likes to hike once in a while, you'll find the time. You've got a busy life, perhaps too busy, but as a hiker you know the value of connecting/re-connecting with nature and with your fellow hikers. Each time you go hiking, you will remember just how good it feels to be out in the fresh air, getting some exercise and enjoying the wonders of nature.

PROLOGUE

It's time for a new way, The Hiker's Way.

FOR MANY of us these days, times are tough, the going is rough, and the trail ahead uncertain. Who better than an experienced hiker to lead the way across rugged terrain to safety?

The value of a hiker and hiker values has never been more apparent. A good hiker has a keen sense of direction, the ability to travel solo or with trusted companions, the knowledge and experience to face adversity and rapidly changing conditions.

This book was written in the Year of the Ox. Those born in this year, or during one of the 12-year cycles of animals highlighted by the Chinese Zodiac/Calendar, are said to be able to endure almost any hardship without complaint. Other ox-like qualities include fortitude, patience, hard work, common sense, calm dependability, and modesty.

God knows we need people with these qualities each year—and every year.

And this is a time, indeed a century, when we need more because we are living at a time when following in the footprints of the mammal ahead of us and plowing the same fields of endeavor is not enough. We cannot get to a new place by following the same trail.

As I write these words, it is the Year of the Tiger. Those born in this cycle of the Chinese calendar are said to be dramatic, quick, intense, and have a love for travel. Sierra Club outings groups describe their fastest hikers as "tigers."

We need hikers who emulate the ox and have their feet firmly planted on the ground. And we need hikers who are tigers, brave hearts who encourage us to pick up the pace.

We need a variety of hikers with strong spirits. Curious ones. Bold ones. Hikers born in the Year of the Dog and the Year of the Dragon, the Year of the Cat and the Year of the Rat.

This is the time in our history for everyone who hikes to share with the many who hike and the many more who do not what it means to be a hiker. And what better way to do this than by taking a friend or family member on a hike? Or by inviting a recent acquaintance, a child, or a co-worker to take a hike with you?

Share with your trail companions the health and wellness benefits of hiking. Help them achieve that wonderful perspective on the natural world gained by walking through it at two or three miles an hour. Be a good listener and know that hearing somebody out in the great outdoors is one of the greatest gifts one hiker can give another.

Now is the time for hikers to step up and share the best pathways, to advocate for the environment, to offer trail-tested advice and to inspire our companions with our words and example. It's a time to pare down and pack light, taking with us only what we need for the journey ahead.

Now is the time for hikers to share the way, the hiker's way, on this great pathway we call life.

JOHN MCKINNEY
Santa Barbara

The Hiker Redefined

1.

Welcome to The Hiker's Way

"Determine that the thing can and shall be done,
and then we shall find the way."
—Abraham Lincoln

What do you mean you're a hiker?

So John, what do you do?"

"I'm a hiker."

"Seriously, what's your real job?"

If I had a pound of trail mix for every time I've been asked that question, I'd have a ton of GORP.

The fact is, being a hiker is my job—and has been for more than two decades. I've hiked from youth to middle-age, and plan to continue hiking until I'm carried off the trail.

They say, "Do what you love and the money will follow."

Uh, not always, but I still feel blessed to be able to share my passion with countless hikers and would-be hikers. I wouldn't trade hiking for all the money in the world.

Answering "I'm a hiker" to one of society's most fundamental questions provokes some interesting responses.

Some questioners suspect they're being trifled with and stare right through me. Others figure I'm unemployed and don't want to talk about it or guess my last employer told me to take a hike and I must have taken this edict literally.

I admit I sometimes choose to avoid this line of conversation and answer the what-do-you-do question with the gig of the moment: "I'm writing a book about hiking in New England." Or "I'm working with the Leukemia and Lymphoma Society to train hike leaders for the group's fund-raising events."

"I'm a hiker" is my most frequent response though, and the most honest one.

I am a hiker. By temperament. By orientation. By choice.

After pronouncing, "I'm a hiker," I continue acting as provocateur on behalf of the hiking profession by asking a question of my own, one that helped me gain much insight into the minds and hearts of hikers: "Are *you* a hiker?"

I've been delighted by the responses to that question.

A small number of the most enthusiastic outdoors-goers answering in the affirmative declare, "Yes, I'm a hiker!"

Most responses, though, are more qualified, such as, "I like to hike sometimes. Wish I could get out more often." Or, "I like hiking the trails near my home." Most who like to hike like to talk about hiking, but few refer to themselves as hikers.

And that's just fine, in my book.

Interestingly, while individuals are reluctant to call themselves hikers, they show no such reluctance in attaching the appellation to others—mothers, fathers, sisters, brothers, kids, grandmas, friends and co-workers are hikers. Like hiking downhill on a gentle path, saying, "He's a hiker," or, "She's a hiker" is easy.

It was never my goal to become a hiker and, most likely, it's not yours either. People don't want to be hikers per se; they want to experience what hiking can give them—a connection with nature the opportunity to experience places that can only be reached on foot, good health, companionship on the trail; a measure of peace and tranquility.

Whether calling themselves hikers or not, a huge number of people say they like to hike. Advertisers—quick to capitalize on a lifestyle trend—increasingly use hiking as a theme to sell as diverse a set of products as cars, cereal, granola bars, crackers, allergy relief, wine and fine spirits.

The numbers of hikers per capita in North America, Europe

and Australia are substantial, with hiking topping the list of outdoors activities in countries around the globe. By all accounts, hiking is the most popular form of outdoor recreation among Americans.

- More than 60 million Americans a year go hiking. About 25 percent of these hikers say they hike at least thirty times a year.
- Among the fifty states in the U.S., Utah and Idaho have the highest per capita rate of participation for hiking, while California has by far the largest number of hikers.
- Californians lead the way down the trail. Repeated surveys report that Californians say hiking is their Number One outdoor sport.
- The U.S. Forest Service predicts steep increases in hiking, including an 80 percent increase in the Southern and Pacific Coast regions over the next fifty years.

Sources: American Recreation Coalition, American Hiking Society, Outdoor Industry Association, California State Parks, National Sporting Goods Association.

The Hiker Defined and Redefined

With so many people who like to hike, it's surprising that the word "hiker" lacks a widely accepted popular definition. This lack of a clear definition—much less a rich and transformative one—presents both a challenge and an opportunity.

A challenge to overcome is the sometimes negative, somewhat geeky, sometimes nonsensical defining of a hiker by the popular media. It's enough to convince any would-be hiker or hesitant hiker to stay home.

The huge opportunity—one presented in this book—is to redefine and to refine the definition of a hiker, illuminate the many pleasures available to one who hikes, and point out the benefits to the mind, body and spirit along the way.

If we who love to hike don't define what a hiker is, others (non-hikers to be sure) will do it for us. We've all seen hikers poorly portrayed in the various media—as goofy gals and macho guys, as crazed survivalists and tender-footed nincompoops. Even worse are the news reports that sensationalize stories about lost, injured or dead hikers. Rarely do these reports get the facts straight, and often those they characterize as "hikers" are often anything but: a family that wanders away from the RV campground; motorists stranded on a road to nowhere who have to walk back to civilization; the ill-prepared storm-forecast-ignoring urbanite whose only survival skill is dialing 911 on a cellphone that unfortunately has no reception in the wilderness; numbskulls who fail to heed park warning signs and step over ledges or get stomped by bison.

Most mainstream media pick right up on the fear factor and exploit it. CNN recently reported a hiker rescued from the depths of "treacherous" Temescal Canyon near a waterfall in the Santa Monica Mountains close to Los Angeles. Of course, my daughter hiked that canyon and made it under her own power to the waterfall when she was five years old.

Typical of this media fear-mongering was a news report from South Mountain Park in Phoenix: a hiker was attacked by bees, and then, while trying to escape, he fell 200 feet down a mountain into a patch of cholla cactus. The story was reported as if Mother Nature is out to get you: killer bees attack you, mountain slopes make you fall, and there's cactus out to stick it to you. The news report failed to mention that this so-called hiker decided to hike in 110-degree heat, on a record-breaking May day even for Phoenix, and he decided to leave a popular trail and head cross-country up a steep ravine.

The dictionary definition of a hiker is a simple one:

hiker one who hikes (especially frequently); a foot traveler; someone who goes on an extended walk in the mountains or country (for pleasure)

There is nothing wrong with the dictionary definition of a hiker—as far as it goes.

It just doesn't go very far or very deep.

Surely hiking and being a hiker means more. And in this book I'll expand upon and refine the definition of a hiker.

However, before moving on to an alternative or expanded view of the hiker, several words in the dictionary definition require closer examination. "Frequently" is frequently part of the definition, suggesting one must hike often in order to be a true hiker. I've known hikers who discuss—and a few who obsess about—the frequency of their hiking adventures. Most hikers wish to state confidently, "I hike frequently," rather than say wistfully, "I wish I could get out more frequently.

Both those who hike and those who don't assume that there is an unofficial requirement that a person must take a certain number of hikes over a particular time period in order to be a hiker or to remain a hiker in good standing. Of course no hiking expert knows the number of hikes a hiker "must" take for the honor and privilege of being a hiker. One hike per week? One per month? Twenty, thirty, or forty per year?

I'm certain that's its not a number at all. As if expressing little confidence that a hiker need hike "frequently" to be a hiker, dictionaries almost always put the word "frequently" in parentheses.

How often should a hiker hike?

"As often as possible" is one good answer. "Whenever and wherever you can" is another. It's definitely not a particular number of hikes taken in a particular time frame.

Like another activity that gets ten thousand times more attention, hiking feels good when we do it, the most natural thing in the world. After we do it, we wonder why we don't do it more often; unfortunately, it seems we're too busy and stressed out to do it with the frequency we like and, when we finally are in the mood to do it, there's no one around who will do it with us.

Another element of the dictionary definition of hiker that bears scrutiny is "extended." A walk extended from what? A longer than normal walk? What would be a normal walk and what would be a prolonged one?

I can live with the dictionary definition of a hike being an extended walk, and I suspect most hikers can as well. I'm guessing that non-hikers and those who dislike hiking would argue that the dictionary use a more pejorative term than extended, such as aimless, arduous, unnecessary, purposeless, or hellish.

Ah, some people fear what they do not know and do not know what they're missing. I say remove the parentheses from "for pleasure" in the definition of hiker. A hiker is one who hikes for pleasure not one who hikes (for pleasure). Let's not be tentative here. The pleasure for a hiker can range widely: the scent of wildflowers, companionship on the trail, overcoming a challenge, the chance to get away from it all,

I assure you, hiking doesn't have to be so hard. It really doesn't.

Is it correct to define a hiker as one who walks? Absolutely. Everyone who speaks of hiking routinely uses the words walk and hike interchangeably. But there's an important difference to remember: Every hike is a walk, but not every walk is a hike. There are many ways to shade the differences between a walk and a hike, but the most essential difference is in locale: To go hiking is to go green. A hiker walks "in the mountains or country" as the dictionary puts it. Hikers also walk along lakeshores, seashores, through forests and across prairies, and in many other natural environments. The point is a hiker walks in the natural world or at least a reasonable facsimile, such as a undeveloped park or botanical garden.

The Hiker's Way

The Hiker's Way narrates the rewarding path to becoming a hiker in ways far deeper than that of dictionary definition. It's a path through nature—and through human nature. To begin this journey, it's necessary to take a fresh look at hiking and, more important, at hikers, to determine where we're going, how we're going, why we're going, and who we really are.

I open each chapter with an anecdote or story, a way of illuminating the major theme or subject. As noted in more detail in Chapter 2, I switchback from the philosophical to the practical and back, zigzagging along toward the hiker's goal of getting the most from time on the trail.

Sometimes we'll contemplate a few of life's Big Questions from a trailside vantage point. Other times we'll keep our feet firmly on the ground, as it were, and review the fine points of choosing a good pair of hiking boots. It's all a part of the hiker's way.

The Hiker's Way answers many of the questions hikers have asked me—in the city and on the trail, online and on the air. Hiking is a vast subject area (witness the 7 million Google entries on the popular search engine) so I was compelled to narrow the field a bit.

The Hiker's Way will help you:

- Get to know yourself as a hiker
- Prepare for any hike
- Hike for good health
- Hike in good spirit
- Hike safely
- Hike in all kinds of weather
- Hike over all kinds of terrain
- Share the way with children and other hikers
- Hike smart. Live well. Go green.

Origins of *The Hiker's Way*

The title for this book, and my mission to write it, came a couple of years ago in Seattle when I met Sally Jewell, CEO of REI. The dynamic corporate leader (and avid hiker, camper, cyclist and kayaker) said that REI, even though the company had gross sales in excess of a billion dollars a year, was concerned about its future because so many Americans, especially younger ones, were not going outdoors in the same high percentages as their parents, or of even earlier generations. Fewer Americans hiking, camping, cycling and so on translates out into fewer Americans purchasing gear to pursue those activities.

Jewell said that REI, along with other outdoor industry stalwarts, commissioned a study to find out why Americans resist outdoor recreation. Hiking has long been, and still is, the most popular form of outdoor recreation; thus, the REI study is highly relevant to hikers and would-be hikers, parks and recreation departments, gear-makers and gear-sellers. The study found four basic reasons why Americans are reluctant to go outdoors:

1. Don't know where to go.
2. Don't know how to go. (lack outdoor skills and training)
3. Don't have anyone to go with
4. Too darn stressed out, distracted and overwhelmed by modern life.

It seems like with all those outdoors guides, including a number of my books about trails, and all those online accounts, "where-to-go-hiking" would not be one of the obstacles in the way of taking a hike, I suggested to Jewell.

REI's outdoors commander-in-chief agreed, and we concurred that the resistance to where to hike was the easiest challenge to address with more information and improved information delivery. The other reasons though, were more fundamental.

"Sounds like we have both an individual and societal problem," I offered, feeling a bit overwhelmed as the words crossed my lips.

Jewell and REI are all about "can-do" when it comes to getting people outdoors. Hikers need to be the leaders in countering these resistances, she explained, because hiking is the main portal to the outdoors

"We need more hikers," Sally Jewell told me. "You need to show them the way."

In more than twenty-five years of writing about hiking, I've advised readers where-to-hike and how-to-hike, why-hike and why-hike-more-often. I've lost count of the number of questions I've answered about basic hiking lore in public (on the radio and after giving talks and classes) and privately (one conversation, one phone call, one e-mail at a time).

Questions to The Trailmaster have by no means been confined to practical questions about destinations and techniques. I've fielded questions (or tried to) about relationships and spiritual growth and their connections to hiking.

Importantly, my relationship with my fellow hikers goes way beyond the narrow confines of Q&A and has been, and is, a lively and expansive two-way conversation. Hikers of all ages and abilities have offered tips ranging from the tastiest trail-mix recipes to hiking with llamas. Many have expressed what's on their mind and in their hearts on the trail, as well as their hopes and fears as hikers.

For this I am profoundly grateful. Input from hikers from all walks of life has made my writings, my talks and my own hikes immeasurably better.

I suppose I've taught hiking by various methods and media, though I've never looked at it that way. I have taken school children on hikes and, while letting them have fun in nature, have squeezed in some instruction. And I've recently written a couple of books about hiking for kids.

I use the same philosophy with adults when I lead them on hikes—keep them safe, let them have fun, and slip in a bit of instruction along the trail. I became more conscious of how to teach hiking when I helped create a hike leader's training manual and trained hike leaders at weekend seminars. The classroom instruction actually worked better than I had imagined, though it was not nearly as effective—or enjoyable—as getting out on the trail with my hike leader trainees.

I enjoy sharing the hiker's way with every kind of hiker: beginning and experienced, younger and older, male and female. Well, almost every kind. Given a choice between hikers who are Eeyores and those who are Tiggers, I'll take Tiggers every time.

Let me explain.

For best results, take to the trail like Tigger

In his wise, wry, poignant and triumphant *The Last Lecture,* Randy Pausch speaks of two very different characters in the children's classic, *Winnie-the-Pooh,* and the choice we have between assuming the world outlook of the optimistic Tigger or that of the pessimistic Eeyore. I agree with Pausch, and firmly believe there are only two kinds of hikers: Tiggers and Eeyores.

If it's been a while since you read—or were read to from—the Pooh stories by A.A. Milne, Tigger is the bouncy tiger and Eeyore the gloomy donkey. Tigger, literally and figuratively, has a bounce in his step, and is forever encouraging his fellow creatures: "Come on, Rabbit. Let's you and me bounce, huh?"

Tigger knows who he is and where he's going.

RABBIT: Tigger! But . . . you're supposed to be lost.

TIGGER: Aw, tiggers never get lost, Bunny boy.

Eeyore grumbles when it's hot and when it's cold. He complains when walking alone and complains about too much company on the trail: "Everybody crowds round so in this forest. There's no space. I never saw a more spreading lot of animals in my life, and in all the wrong places."

On the trail and off, we face all kinds of weather and challenges from those who share our ways and those who don't. And much of the time, we can choose to go with the flow and face the obstacles in our path with good cheer.

A few hikers are irreversibly Eeyores, and can find the one patch of thistles amidst the wide beautiful meadow or look at their reflections in the surface of the pond and think "pathetic." Most of us, though, have briefer periods of pessimism, our Eeyore moments.

Perhaps we can't always be as bouncy and relentlessly optimistic as Tigger, but we can start a hike and keep on hiking with the knowledge that hiking lifts our spirits. At the trailhead, a hiker can be Eeyore ("It's going to rain, we're going to get soaked") and a half-mile along the trail turn into Tigger. ("What a great time we're having in this little rainstorm—I hope we see a rainbow.")

My approach to *The Hiker's Way*

If, with a wave of a magic hiking stick, I could have my way, I'd hike with you, not write to you. The best way, the only way of becoming a hiker is by taking a hike.

It's been my pleasure to lead a diversity of hikers down the trail: First-graders on beach hikes, Rotary Club members on wildflower walks, middle-school students into the mountains. I've guided hikers, aged thirty-something to seventy-something, on weeklong hiking holidays. I've hiked politicos, VIPS, and big-time donors to conservation causes across lands endangered by development and/or bureaucratic ineptitude.

I plan to continue leading hikes for a very long time, but I can't take very many of you to very many places. Instead, we'll have to use our imaginations. I imagined you were with me on the trail as I wrote this book.

I imagined that I was taking you on one of my favorite hikes in the mountains near my home. I'd check to see if you had packed The Ten Essentials, snacks and lunch. We'd check the weather, and talk about layering and what to wear. We'd also talk about mileage, pace and the elements of a hike that you find most pleasing. Then we'd hike up Rattlesnake Canyon Trail, whose very name might prompt some questions about dangers on the trail. We'd enjoy companionship, as well as some solitary thoughts, as we hiked through a place far more inviting than its name. (Never judge a trail by its trailhead or by its name, we'd agree.)

About noon we'd reach what I call Lunch Rock, a large flat boulder in the middle of a frisky creek. We'd rest here, listening to the soothing sound of the cascades, eating our snacks and trail mix, letting our thoughts drift from trails past to this wonderful day to trails ahead. And we'd talk about what it means to be a hiker, how to return to our busy lives in the city with some of the serenity and knowledge gained from our time on the trail.

Join me now in these pages as we hike together to Lunch Rock and beyond. Blessings wherever and whenever you roam.

My Life as a Hiker

The Wonder Years My unusual career path began when I was a Boy Scout in Troop 441 in Downey, California. I lived for the monthly hikes in the mountains, deserts, and forests around California, and for weeklong summer hikes in the San Gabriel Mountains and the High Sierra. Hiking was far and away my favorite merit badge earned on my way to becoming an Eagle Scout. (It should have been a tip-off that I wasn't cut out to be a Wall Street mogul when I needed three tries to pass the test for the Personal Finances merit badge.)

When I was fourteen, my parents sat me down for what they characterized as a frank discussion about my future.

"John, your mother and I appreciate how fun this hiking-camping-outdoors stuff is for you," my father began. "But let's face it, you're not going to be doing this as an adult."

"When I'm a grown-up, I'm going to keep hiking," I declared.

"What your father's saying," my mother chimed in, "is nobody makes a living by hiking."

"You need to take up a sport that will help you in the business world," my father continued in the persuasive manner that garnered him salesman-of-the-year honors at the huge corporation he represented. "So we've decided to help you out by—"

"Not another tennis racket," I whined.

"No, you're going to be surprised," mother cautioned, as my father disappeared into the next room, soon re-emerging with—

"Golf clubs," I said glumly.

"And a certificate for eight lessons at the club," father enthused.

My heart sank. I had been hoping for a new backpack. I took the golf lessons to please my parents, but my heart wasn't in it. For me, golf was a good walk ruined, years before I ever heard of the Mark Twain quip.

Trails and Trojans My studies for a degree in broadcast journalism from the University of Southern California proved to be somewhat useful to my life's work; more so were my collegiate extracurricular activities. I helped found and lead hikes for the USC Hiking Club. While the cheerleaders for the football team looked good on TV, the coeds who hiked looked great on the trail—and that made them the most interesting and attractive on campus—at least to my way of thinking. The post-hike beers with my fellow hikers, when we talked about our next hikes and where our life paths may lead, I remember even now.

Hikes in the Hollywood Hills For a while, I did the Hollywood hustle, working as a location scout and nature-film writer by day, writing the Great American screenplay at night. (If you know a producer interested in a biopic about John Muir, *John of the Mountains* is a great script . . .) Between film screenings and pitch meetings, I went for hikes in the Hollywood Hills. I discerned that the hills are blanketed with a green-leaved, red-berried native plant called California holly—which gave Hollywood its name. I discovered that I greatly preferred being on top of hills and looking down at Hollywood than being in Hollywood and looking up at hills. What could this mean?

Trail Writer While the industry never came through with those six- and seven-figure offers I thought my screenplays deserved, I was pleasantly surprised to learn that magazine editors would pay me two, three, and four figures to write about hiking and the great outdoors. Readers of *California, Sunset,* and *Los Angeles Times* magazines enjoyed my hiking stories while *Islands* magazine sent me from Fiji to Kauai to Corfu to hike around the world's islands and write about them.

My articles about hiking caught the attention of legendary California publisher Noel Young and his Capra Press, who signed me to write *Day Hiker's Guide to Southern California.*

This title, now *Southern California: A Day Hiker's Guide,* and expanded from 50 trail accounts to 150, is still popular and remains a regional bestseller.

In 1986, a *Los Angeles Times* reporter interviewed me for a story he was writing about hiking. In mid-interview, he stopped and declared: "Hey, you should be writing about this subject. Let me introduce you to the editor."

So began my 18-year stint as the newspaper's hiking columnist. The weekly column proved tremendously popular. Maybe the Missing Persons song lyric, "Nobody walks in L.A.," is true; however, it seems most everybody hikes. Local parks had to assign extra staff on the weekends following some of my hike write-ups because so many hikers turned out to hit the trail.

My *Times* readers liked my accounts of regional hikes but soon requested that I go farther afield to detail hikes. So off I hiked, around the West, across the East, and to intriguing hiking locales all over the U.S. I compiled the trails I described for the *Times* and other publications into a dozen more guides, including *Day Hiker's Guide to California's State Parks, Great Walks of New England,* and *Great Walks of the Pacific Northwest.*

Hiking: Isn't it Romantic? Meanwhile, even my social life revolved around hiking. I must confess I took my dates on (sometimes too) rigorous hikes and I'm sure more than one woman not-so-fondly remembers not only a bad date but the hike from hell. Fortunately, I met a gal who could not only keep step with me on the trail, but surpasses me in every other way. Cheri and I have been together since our first hike, uh, date.

Pioneering the California Coastal Trail Of the many lands that have called to me, spoken to me, my home shoreline and coastal mountains have called the loudest. I answered the call by agreeing to the California Coastal Trail Foundation's request to pioneer the California Coastal Trail. And so I took a little walk—a 1,600-mile hike as it turned out—from the Mexican border to the Oregon border along California's diverse shore, through the coast range and redwood forest. It was a life-changing hike for me, as I transformed from a sportsman with something to prove to a traveler with something to learn—and share. I wrote a narrative, *A Walk Along Land's End,* that chronicled my adventures and the unique people and places I encountered.

Hiking Vacations An upscale walking vacation company headquartered in England asked me to set up a North American branch. I helped create weeklong hiking holidays from the Olympic Peninsula to Santa Fe to the coast of Maine, and led tours around Santa Barbara and Point Reyes north of San Francisco. I thoroughly enjoyed guiding hikers from all around the U.S. and Europe on some lovely paths, getting to know some wonderful people, and learning what goes on behind the scenes in this fun and rewarding part of the travel business.

Kids on the Trail These days I enjoy family hikes and sharing the trail with my daughter Sophia and son Daniel. I've learned as much from my children as they have from me, and I'm delighted by the opportunity to share what we've learned together in the "Hiking with Children" chapter of this book.

Recently I've been quite alarmed by the rise of what the outdoors recreation community calls "Nature Deficit Disorder," brought to our attention by author Richard Louv in his landmark book, *Last Child in the Woods.* I've been speaking out on that topic and writing books about hiking and outdoors skills for kids, including *Let's Go Geocaching!* and *Let's Go Hiking!*

Older, Wiser, The Trailmaster More than a decade ago, a California newspaper reporter, who shall be held blameless and left nameless, branded me "The Trailmaster" after interviewing me for a story he wrote about hiker safety. Shortly thereafter, a radio talk show host picked up on the name and invited listeners to call in with their questions about hiking for "The Trailmaster."

The name is easy to remember and is as good or better than any of the other names I've been called: "Trails expert," "Hike writer," and "Hiking spokesman" as well as less flattering terms—"eco-crank," "curmudgeon" and "coastal access extremist."

At a certain time in life, some of us feel a calling to share their calling. For me, that time is now. It's time to share the gospel of hiking, its rich tradition and its many benefits for body, mind and spirit.

I make no claims to be the smartest or most eloquent spokesman for hikers, but I do have one standout ability that helps me spread the good word: I can walk and talk at the same time.

Go on and scoff. But it's harder than you think to hike and impart hiking wisdom at the same time, particularly into microphones with TV cameras tracking your every move. To be sure it's an obscure talent, but one I'm delighted to use to share the hiker's way.

2

Hike Smart, Live Well, Go Green

"Me thinks that the moment my legs begin to move,
my thoughts begin to flow."
—Henry David Thoreau

The Tao of Back and Forth or Homage to Switchbacks

"WHAT'S wrong with this trail?" the perspiring young sportsman in the Boston Red Sox baseball cap complains to me as I catch up with him at the one-mile marker on Echo Mountain Trail. "It doesn't seem to be leading anywhere. And it's got too many of those . . . turning things, those—"

"Switchbacks," I offer.

"Don't you just hate them?"

Caught between the urge to lecture him and the urge to whack him with my hiking stick, I do neither, and simply stride past him with a smile. "I like switchbacks," I call out over my shoulder.

"Yeah, right," he mutters.

As I zigzag along on a perfect winter day, savoring the alternating vistas of mountains above and metropolis below, it occurs to me that lately I have encountered a great number of people who are unaware that the switchback is the hiker's best friend and one of the West's greatest inventions. Worse, increasing numbers of hikers like "Sox" who hate switchbacks.

Perhaps such bias arises from ignorance, I muse. While most hikers can define a switchback (a trail that follows a zigzag course on a steep incline) and know one when they see one, detractors don't grasp why the switchbacking way is so wonderful: it's lots easier zigzagging up the shoulder of a mountain than taking a straight line up it. California's recreation trails are ranked among the world's best, in part because they use so many switchbacks to reach so much beauty.

Ah, the beauty. Switchbacking up Saddle Peak in the lovely Santa Monica Mountains. Switchbacking up Mt. Whitney on those ninety-seven superbly graded switchbacks hewn out of granite—one of the finest examples in America of the trail builder's art—at sunrise when the switchbacks slowly turn pink, then a magnificent fiery orange . . .

The sound of a cellphone ringing ends my reverie and draws my attention down to Sox, two switchbacks below. As I zig north and he zags south, I overhear Sox tell his caller: "This crazy guy I met likes these *#$@!@% switchbacks."

Switchback-haters like Sox are divided into two camps: some would prefer to eliminate them altogether in favor of straight Point-A-to-Point-B-style pathways; others regard them as an unavoidable necessity that gets you up a mountain at a maddeningly slow pace. Sure you gain elevation, but so slowly that the trail becomes repetitive and the trudge becomes a drudge.

You don't know what you've got 'til it's gone and even I never fully appreciated the switchback until I hiked in the eastern U.S. A decade ago I was commissioned to write a book about the great hikes of New England and before I hit the trail wondered: After ascending the West's great mountains, how difficult could it be for me to summit a piddling, 3,000-foot peak?

Very difficult, I discovered, because New England trails lack switchbacks. In fact, New Englanders take a perverse pride in the steepness of a trail. I guess the region's diehard hiker think slogging up a trench-like trail eroded down to the bedrock straight up a mountain is true hiking because it's such hard work. Apparently, switchbacks would add ease and pleasure to the journey and run contrary to the Puritan ethic. Idle feet are the devil's playthings or something like that.

I feel blessed to have been born west of the Rockies, where trailblazers took a different approach. Many now-popular pathways were first prospectors' trails constructed with switchbacks for the use of pack animals. This switchbacking tradition continued when trail use changed from business to pleasure. Traditionally, western land has been cheap and there's been plenty of room to roam, so that a trail builder can afford "the luxury" of long, meandering switchbacks.

A few switchbacks from the top, my thoughts drift to friend and fellow Californian Greg Miller, now president of the American Hiking Society and stationed in Washington, D.C.

"I'm going through switchback withdrawal," he confessed. "Where are my beloved switchbacks? Philosophically speaking, what's wrong with hiking back and forth in a never-ending zigzag pattern?"

Yes, that's it, switchbacking is a philosophy. Sure I appreciate, more than anyone, the switchback, the noun, the thing, but it is switchbacking, the intransitive verb, the process that literally and figuratively gets my heart pumping. When we talk of the trail switchbacking over the mountain and hikers switchbacking up the trail, we are talking about a philosophy that values the journey as much as the destination.

You see, Sox, switchbacking is more than a better way to build trails; it's a philosophy, best studied and practiced in the West's wide-open spaces. California is all about creative movement—in the performing arts, on the football field with the West Coast Offense, and on the hiking trail.

Sox? Far, far below, I see Sox in rapid retreat back to the trailhead. Guess the switchbacks got to him.

Sox, you need an attitude adjustment. Switchbacks don't force you to see everything twice, they help you view the world from every point of the compass.

Switchbacking, like life itself, is not all about getting from one place to another as fast as possible; it's about getting there the best way possible.

Switchbacking Along with *The Hiker's Way*

I've learned that the best way to hike up a mountain is via a trail with switchbacks. Not only do you reach the summit in the most effective way possible, but you get a great perspective on where you're going and where you've come from as you zigzag along.

The Hiker's Way approaches the many aspects of hiking as if they are a series of switchbacks. They are better mastered by taking the time to meander back and forth from one to another rather than by doggedly marching in a straight line from Point A to Point B. Hiking a switchback trail allows for incremental, measurable progress—not too hard or too fast. Just the way I like it.

The Hiker's Way uses the switchback way. I will show you that zigzagging back and forth, from the practical to the philosophic, and from developing a skill set to developing a mindset, will make you a better, more confident hiker, one who will get more joy and satisfaction out of every hike.

At the core of *The Hiker's Way* are three goals for the hiker:

1. Hike Smart
2. Live Well
3. Go Green

The Way may not always seem to head in their direction, but trust me, switchbacking along will get you there.

Hike Smart Long before I took to the airwaves to spread the The Trailmaster gospel, I often gave talks and Power Point presentations (slide shows in the early days) such as "Hiking the Desert" or "Great Hikes of the Pacific Northwest" at outdoor retailers and bookstores. Sometimes my audience enthusiastically embraced the topic and our time together passed quickly; other times, the audience enjoyed the presentation all right, but had scores of questions about hiking that were far from the advertised topic of my talk.

One fine spring day, for example, I appeared at an REI store to talk about hiking in national parks. Realizing it was John Muir's birthday, I launched into an impromptu talk about the great naturalist's life and work, rhapsodized about the wonders of wilderness hiking in the High Sierra and figured I just about moved the audience to tears.

I figured wrong. When I opened the floor to questions, it was clear that my audience of (mostly) novice hikers was more interested in self preservation than in wilderness preservation.

First question: What are the best hiking boots so I don't get blisters?

Second question: Can I hike alone?

Third question: How sick will I get if a tick bites me?

I stayed for another hour, answering questions and improvising a "Hiking 101" class.

While writing *The Hiker's Way*, I got a call from a radio talk show producer who wanted to do a special program about outdoor safety. The theme of the show was a kind of emergency response to news of a half-dozen California hikers perishing within a month of exposure to cold, falls from cliffs, slips on icy slopes, and getting lost.

The talk-show host wanted to know why there were so many hiker accidents. "John, why are so many hikers getting hurt, even dying in the great outdoors?"

My answer was a simple two-part one.

"Millions of Americans say they like to hike. Unfortunately, more poorly prepared hikers are hitting the trail than ever before. Not everyone who goes hiking is a hiker in the truest sense of the word."

Most hiking accidents can be prevented. National Park Service studies of accidents that required the agency to launch a search and rescue operation determined that 99 percent of these accidents could be prevented by rudimentary outdoors knowledge, better preparations and the proper gear.

Stupid is as stupid does.

Especially in the great outdoors.

Despite the efforts of the National Park Service and veritable thickets of warning signs, this summer you can bet at least one RV owner will attempt to drive a twelve-foot-high vehicle under a ten-foot bridge; at least one warning-sign-disdaining visitor will test the temperature of a geyser to see if the water really is that hot; at least one hiker will start a midday hike in Death Valley; far too many visitors will feed the birds and bears.

Park rangers contrived the word "touron"(a combination of tourist and moron to describe these dummies. Origins of the term are uncertain, though rangers at Yellowstone National Park, which attracts more than its fair share of tourons, are sometimes credited with coming up with this word. The term has spread from coast to coast—at least among park personnel.

To avoid being branded a touron—or worse yet, stepping off a 2,000-foot cliff, carried out to sea by a riptide, or stomped to death by a bison—use some common sense and follow park rules.

Sad to say, but hikers account for a significant share of touronic activity in our national parks. Unprepared visitors get into big trouble on little hikes. Hiking is not an inherently dangerous activity, but a small number of casual hikers who abandon their common sense at the park entry station, who choose to tempt fate and break rules, give hikers a very bad name: tourons.

Hiking on a trail is one of the safest activities you can pursue as long as you hike smart—that is to say, plan well, know the practicalities and certain outdoor recreation skills, obey human and natural laws, and use common sense.

Almost every page in this book could be considered to offer some kind of safety advice because the more you know, the safer hiker you'll be. Master the basics and you'll be a confident (but not overly confident) hiker who stays safe in the woods, or wherever you hike.

Live Well Hiking is one of the most natural forms of exercise, a gregarious activity for those desiring companionship, and a contemplative one for those seeking solitude. I wrote *The Hiker's Way* to inspire, inform and entertain hikers of all ages and abilities, particularly newcomers, and to heighten awareness of the world around them. Hiking promotes increased awareness of the natural world and our moral obligation to become better stewards of it.

If the reason for taking a hike (if indeed a reason be necessary!) is the hope for mental-spiritual-physical rejuvenation, or to take time to contemplate where you've been and where you're going in this confusing world, then a hike in nature can help make sense of it all. Of course, a more simple reason for taking a hike is that it's fun to do.

At times I challenge you to reach inside yourselves and get more from your hikes. I've dropped in some inspirational quotes to help motivate, empower, amuse, uplift, and comfort hikers on this amazing path we call life. If you're a hiker, it's altogether natural for you to regard life as a long hike with ups and downs and points of interest along the way.

Another reason for writing *The Hiker's Way* was to share the health benefits of hiking: to inspire hikers of every interest and intention—from those embarking on weight-reduction or stress-management programs to already dedicated exercise walkers and gung-ho trekkers. Hiking can assist those recovering from illness—for individuals determined to "get back on their feet."

This book is encouragement for those taking their first steps toward a healthier lifestyle, coax the leg-weary, stressed, and fatigued, and reinforce the commitments of already devoted walkers and hikers.

A good hike is a tonic for our stressful lives. As French hikers put it: *Un jour de marche, huit jours de santé.* A day of walking, eight days of health.

Hiking, like life itself, is both an interior and exterior process. Our search for meaning and meaningful change requires seeing things in a new light. Hiking provides that new light by opening us up to the world. The great nature writer John Muir, who literally hiked across America, recognized that we have vast interior landscapes to discover and to study. "I only went out for a walk," wrote Muir, "and finally concluded to stay out till sundown, for going out, I found, was really going in."

A good hike is transcendent, enabling us to cross the bridge between the visible and invisible worlds—and back again. When we get back, we've seen things in a new light.

By picturing the ideal, we can transform it into the real. What we can sort out, we can work out. What we can configure, we can figure.

Artists call it chasing the muse, psychologists call it reaching the "Aha!" moment, business strategists call it getting to yes. I call it The Hiker's Way, an insightful way of hiking that allows our internal boundaries to expand with our external ones enabling us to have more creative and fulfilling lives.

Go Green Hiking has been, is, and always will be the greenest of activities. "Take a Hike" routinely appears as an action item on nearly every list advising how to go green. Hiking is always on those "Simple Things You Can Do to Save The Planet" or "Twenty Ways to Be Green" kinds of lists compiled by eco-experts.

Going for a hike is simply, and inarguably, part of going green. And no wonder. Talk about a low-carbon footprint; a hiker leaves no carbon footprint.

Daily we demonstrate our concern for the environment by recycling, carpooling, and turning down the thermostat. And we try to be green consumers in our purchases, celebrate green weddings and raise green babies, buy "green" wine and the greenest possible washing machines.

A hiker goes beyond the basics of green citizenship and environmental awareness and seeks a connection with nature, an awareness of the seasons, the phases of the moon, changes in the weather, touches and is touched by the earth in meaningful ways.

Hikers were "going green" for about a century prior to the coining of the phrase, before the term "ecology" came into popular use, and long before anyone could imagine anything as perilous to the planet as global warming.

Going green, as a hiker anyway, has long meant walking easy on the land: "Pack it in, pack it out" is one slogan that's been repeated for generations. "Take only pictures, leave only footprints" is another. Hiking, more than any other activity, has been the way into the natural world for the greatest number of people in Europe and North America and for nature-seekers in many other parts of the globe.

Hiking helps us connect (or reconnect if it's been a while since our last hike) with the green scene, the natural world, the way the world looked like and functioned before humans "improved" it.

In the department of everything-old-is-new-again, the "Green Exercise" movement is taking hold across the North American continent and worldwide. Finally, researchers have demonstrated conclusively that walking in the park, hiking in the countryside, and other exercise in the green world has greater health benefits than walking in the city and exercising indoors.

Going green by taking a hike not only strengthens the body, it can actively sharpen the mind. University of Michigan researchers conducted a study that asked one set of participants to take a walk in an urban setting and another set to walk in a natural setting. When participants returned from their respective walks, their memories and attention spans were tested. Those who walked in nature showed a 20 percent improvement on the tests, while urban walkers showed no improvement whatsoever.

Other recent studies have demonstrated the many health and wellness benefits offered by hiking in the green world. Hiking in the countryside demonstrably relieves symptoms of depression while walking in a mall actually increases feelings of depression. Hiking has been found to have great benefit to children with ADD (Attention Deficit Disorder).

Going green—literally getting into the green scene, the natural world—is the fundamental difference between a walk and a hike. Duration, distance, or level of difficulty can mark the differences between walking and hiking, but going green is the most important difference.

That being said, there is a gray area between walking and

hiking and going green. Is a walk in an undeveloped park really a hike? Is an "urban hike" or excursion along a suburban greenway really a walk?

"Go Green" is a goal, not an absolute. And on less defined hikes, or walks, by making a calculated effort to meander amidst as much green as a particular locale allows, you will get the maximum physical, mental and spiritual benefits from your outings.

To live a green life, talk the talk and walk the walk—or better yet, hike the hike.

If you're in a funk, simply walking outside into whatever greenery or nature is nearby can buoy your spirits. Getting outside has a way of putting whatever is pressing on your mind into perspective.

Various retreat centers across the U.S. and around the world, some in top resorts and many located in lovely places, offer nature therapy in the form of hiking programs. You can learn to walk with a quiet mind, find your inner child, and restore harmony and balance in your life. By all means, if you have the time and money, sign up for a week of "medicine walks" or a "vision quest."

But know that going green and enjoying the benefits of nature is something you can do on your own, whenever the spirit moves you, and is as easy as taking a hike.

The Hiker Flourishes

3

In Good Health

"Walk out the door and find good health.
There is no fever that a ten-mile hike can't cure."
—Garrison Keillor, host,
National Public Radio's Prairie Home Companion

"I have two doctors, my left leg and my right.
When body and mind are out of gear, I know that I shall have
only to call on my doctors and I shall be well again."
—George M. Trevelyan, historian

FROM William Wordsworth's poetry to the Boy Scout Hiking merit badge pamphlet, tramping through the countryside has long been considered a tonic for good health.

Millions of Americans who like to hike believe that hiking contributes to good physical and mental health. And yet, until recently, nearly all evidence offered for the benefits of taking a hike was anecdotal and very little hiking-specific scientific research supported that belief. Now hiking-specific research is showing that the health value of walking is amplified when that walk becomes a hike.

In 2005, Austrian researchers announced the results of an intriguing study demonstrating that different types of hiking have different influences on the fats and sugars in the blood. For the study, one group hiked up a ski-resort mountain in the Alps and descended by cable car, while the other group rode the cable car up, and hiked down. After two months of hiking, the groups switched hiking programs and repeated the experiment.

As expected, hiking uphill proved to be a great workout and provided measurable health benefits. Unexpectedly, researchers from the Vorarlberg Institute for Vascular Investigation and

Treatment discovered that hiking downhill also has unique benefits.

Both uphill and downhill hiking reduced LDL ("bad") cholesterol. Only hiking uphill reduced triglyceride levels. The study's surprise finding was that hiking downhill was nearly twice as effective as uphill hiking at removing blood sugars and improving glucose tolerance. A second study of uphill/downhill hiking was made in 2008, with similar results.

The American Hiking Society, a Washington, D.C.-based nonprofit that promotes hiking, produces a widely circulated fact sheet, "Health Benefits of Hiking." It relies on studies, mostly of walking, made by the august American Diabetes, American Heart, and American Lung associations to make the case. Hiking-specific research is likely to be of more value in linking hiking and good health than the general "Exercise is Good for You" studies long used by AHS and other advocacy groups, hiking experts say.

"Hiking for health is what we're all about so we're glad the benefits are getting quantified," declared Tracy Roseboom, senior national campaign manager for Team in Training Hiking Adventures, a program of the Leukemia & Lymphoma Society that offers its supporters in chapters nationwide an opportunity to train for, and take a hike in a spectacular location while raising money for cancer research.

Participants train and take practice hikes in their home locales for fourteen to sixteen weeks before embarking on a marquee hike in a natural wonderland such as the Grand Canyon, Yosemite or Maui. Most hikers look at the training as a way to get fit for the once-in-a-lifetime hike, as well as for better overall health and fitness. Roseboom says the health benefits of hiking have been a key selling point for the program since it began in 2006.

Whether or not the latest research is influencing public opinion, hiking for health appears to be an idea whose time has come. The message is on cereal boxes and granola bar wrappers and a popular subject in *Prevention*, and many other women's and health magazines. Glamour.com and Self.com even feature a Hiking Activity Calculator. Enter your weight, duration of your hike, the kind of hiking you're doing (backpacking, climbing hills, etc.) and learn how many calories you blast on the trail. And from the Devon Hiking Spa in Tucson, Arizona to the New Life Hiking Spa in Killington, Vermont, hiking spas are very popular these days with those who find combining hiking with all the usual health-resort activities makes for a stress-reducing, fitness building holiday.

Team in Training guiding light Roseboom says she's pleased by the new data that suggests hiking has health benefits beyond those of walking around the neighborhood, but the research doesn't surprise her. "I see hikers routinely make the connections between nature, themselves and good health. I'm glad the researchers are making the same connections."

Walking and Hiking to Good Health

"Walking is man's best medicine."
—Hippocrates

Walking and hiking promote healing. We often hear someone say, "I'm walking back to good health." Doctors urge hospital patients to get out of bed and walk as soon as they are able. A patient in a weakened state takes a childlike satisfaction in shuffling down the hospital corridor. Complete strangers will speak encouraging words to such patients, as they trail IVs and all manner of machines behind them. Sometimes we don't recognize the value of walking until we're ill and immobilized.

Walking is good medicine, the most prescribed exercise for post-operative patients, particularly for those recovering from a variety of heart ailments and from open heart surgery. Walking literally opens up new lines to the heart, cardiologists attest. A strong heart, in turn, promotes oxygen delivery to active muscles. Much of the unheralded work of returning blood back up to the heart is accomplished by the calf muscles, which squeeze the veins and force the blood upward against gravity as they expand and contract. Walking, because it works all the leg muscles, has an integral role in increasing circulation; for this reason, walking is often called the "second heart," by doctors and exercise physiologists.

Unfortunately, most Americans aren't following their doctors' orders to walk. When it comes to working hard, most Americans are the busiest of beavers but when it comes to exercising hard (or even moderately) most Americans are the most sedentary of sloths. According to a recent report by the U.S. Department of Health and Human Services, only a paltry 15 percent of U.S. adults engage in an adequate amount of physical activity.

The average American's apparent aversion to exercise is not for lack of information. Study after study, going back decades, has found that regular exercise, particularly walking, boosts a person's health and well-being and results in a longer life.

When people do walk, it pays off big-time. Thirty years ago, my father-in-law, an overweight over-stressed engineer, saved his life by following his doctor's orders to walk. In preparation for quintuple bypass surgery, his cardiologist advised him to lose 30 pounds and walk 30 minutes three times a week. He responded in his typical overachieving fashion by dropping 50 pounds and walking five miles a day. His heart doctors were amazed at the corollary arteries he grew and enlarged by his ambitious walking program. He now has several grandchildren he's lived to enjoy, and he's still walking every day.

Increasingly, we are learning other benefits for walking: mental flexibility, as well as emotional and spiritual strength.Walking, as all the latest scientific research has quantified, improves cardiovascular efficiency, burns calories and reduces stress.

As recently as the 1970s, walking was regarded as the exercise of last resort, fit only for those too unfit to do anything else. Now walking is the exercise of first choice—for health, for fitness, for exploring the world around us, far and wide. We just have to get more people out and about and take advantage of all that walking has to offer.

The Walking-Hiking Connection

Until the first decade of the twenty-first century, when conclusive data from scientific research demonstrated the health benefits of hiking, hikers relied on the voluminous research into the health benefits of walking to make the case. Since every hike is a walk, much of what has been learned from studies about walkers can be applied to hikers. Hikers can be grateful for all these studies of walking that have proven what a tonic it is to good health—not that most seasoned hikers ever had any doubts.

A significant body of research shows that a vigorous, even modest walk, three or four times a week for a half-hour to an hour is sufficient for an adult to enjoy many of the advantages that exercise offers for good physical and mental health. Now research suggests that adding a green component to the walk provides even more benefits.

Whether the hike you choose as part of your weekly exercise routine is a moderate one-hour ramble along a local greenway or through a park—or a more vigorous 30-minute hike with some elevation gain—hitting the trail means big-time benefits for your body and mind.

"Painful" and "boring" are the two most common excuses offered for not exercising. While I won't attempt to defend "go for the burn" 90-minute aerobic classes or treading a treadmill from the charges of causing pain and boredom, I can attest that few hikers ever encounter much pain or boredom on the trail.

Certainly the no-pain, no-gain philosophy of various sports and exercise regimens is also part of the hiking world. Anyone who's hiked a steep trail at high altitude knows the meaning of encountering some pain to get that elevation gain. With hiking, however, there is a reward beyond better muscle tone: a view from the top, a new perspective, satisfaction in the going there and getting there.

Hiking boring?

Not!

I suppose someone could take the same hike on the same trail at the same time and cover the same distance, day after day in an attempt to make hiking boring. But even here, hiking conspires against boredom. Seasons change and so does the natural world along the trail. Nearly every trail has an optional route; even hiking a loop trail backwards adds a new perspective.

Turn a Routine Walk into a Rewarding Hike

Boredom thwarts our best intentions to exercise—including going out for a walk. Taking the same neighborhood loop day in and day out can dull the motivation of even the most diehard walking enthusiast.

To keep the spring in your step, add a little green exercise and try a different route. You might be surprised what a little research might uncover in the way of greenery and scenery in your area. Reinvigorate your walking by relocating your usual walk and turning it into a hike. Here's some relocation advice:

A Walk in the Park. Away from the maddening crowd, city and suburban parks are islands of greenery and nature.

Meander Down by the Riverside. The sound of running water is particularly restful to us. De-stress by walking alongside a river.

Make Tracks. The Rails-to-Trails Conservancy, along with assorted governmental agencies has converted thousands of miles of out-of-use railroad tracks to walking paths. Check to find a trail near you.

Walk with the Animals. Nearby wildlife refuges, estuaries and bird-watching sites often have trails leading to, or around them.

Walk U. College campuses offer safe walkways, athletic tracks, fitness trails, even gardens and nature paths.

Busman's Holiday. Take a bus to the edge of the city and walk back or walk to the end of the bus line and bus back.

The Hiker's Way to Good Health

Hike Off Excess Weight Hitting the trail is a superb means of shedding weight and surely a more satisfying (if you keep at it) and permanent way to lose weight than going on a crash diet, the latest fad diet, or ingesting one of those available-only-at-this-toll-free-number chemical formulas.

I'm not dissing diets. Many of them work quite well for those who get on them and stay on them, even if those diet books on the *New York Times* bestseller list seem to offer contradictory advice. (Eat more meat! No, eat less meat!)

While diet and hike are just four-letter words to those who disdain both, a healthy diet with a hiking-centered exercise program can greatly assist losing weight and keeping it off. A 150-pound hiker, sauntering along the trail at a two-miles per hour pace, burns 240 calories in an hour according to the American Heart Association. Hiking with a ten- to fifteen-pound daypack increases the calories burned by 10 to 15 percent. Add some hill-climbing and pick up the pace, and you can increase the calorie burn even more.

Hike for a Stronger Heart Heart disease is caused by many more factors than inactivity, but the odds of falling victim to what is the leading cause of death in America (every half-minute or so another American dies from cardiovascular disease) can be significantly improved by taking regular walks or hikes.

Those who fail to walk, hike or exercise regularly are twice as likely to have coronary heart disease.

Hiking helps reduce cholesterol, a leading factor of heart disease. In addition, hiking increases high-density lipoprotein (HDL), the body's so-called "good cholesterol" which assists removing bad cholesterol from artery walls.

Hike for Lower Blood Pressure Hypertension (high blood pressure) affects millions of Americans. Physicians almost reflexively prescribe medications, some mild, some strong, many effective, some not. For some individuals there is an alternative to such medications in the form of regular exercise. A walking/hiking program has been shown to reduce systolic and diastolic blood pressure. Specifically hiking lowers a hiker's plasma norepinephrine which corresponds to a lowering of blood pressure.

Hike to Prevent Osteoporosis A bone disease caused by calcium deficiency, osteoporosis affects a large number of (mostly) older women. This calcium deficiency reduces bone density and makes bone more brittle and likely to break. Older Americans suffer some 1.5 million fractures a year associated with osteoporosis, resulting in more than $6 billion a year in medical care costs. Hiking can help stop, even reverse osteoporosis by slowing calcium loss and increasing bone density.

Hike to Prevent and Control Diabetes Hiking, as much or more than any other form of regular exercise, can help prevent diabetes and assist in the well-being of the large number of Americans who already have the disease (some 15.7 million Americans—nearly 6 percent of the population).

A program that includes a healthy diet and a walking/hiking regimen can reverse the course of diabetes for those with Type II (non-insulin dependent) diabetes. For those with Type I (insulin-dependent) diabetes, hiking can reduce the required amounts of insulin.

Hike to Reduce the Pain of Arthritis It seems like the most natural human response: if a body part hurts, don't move it. However, responding to arthritis pain by ceasing or decreasing movement is a bad move, and can worsen joint problems.

The muscle-strengthening benefits of walking/hiking are numerous, particularly for the legs. Stronger leg muscles assist arthritis sufferers in the knees and ankles because these muscles lessen the pain cause by bones rubbing against one another.

Hike to Relieve Lower Back Pain The alleviation or elimination of lower back pain is the most widely reported and best documented health benefit of walking/hiking. And for that reason alone, many former back-pain sufferers have become hiking advocates.

Not much of what we do in the workplace is very good for our backs, whether is standing in one position or sitting down (no matter how ergonomically designed is the chair and work station) all day in front of a computer monitor.

Jogging and many kinds of aerobic classes are high impact on the lower back; hiking, by contrast, is low impact, literally and figuratively.

Contact a physician before you decide to hike away your back problem because certain conditions could be aggravated, not helped, by hiking.

Hike to Slow the Aging Process Major declines in physical activity and strength—once commonly believed to be the inevitable results of growing old—need not accompany aging, the latest research tells us. Studies lasting more than 20 years followed middle-aged men who exercised and others who did not into their senior years and found that the active men lost only 13 percent of their aerobic capacity while the sedentary men lost more than 40 percent.

Those seniors who take a hike and declare "it feels good" and "it keeps me active" now have confirming evidence for their gut instincts: aging per se doesn't markedly decrease one's desire or ability to be active, strong and healthy. Alas the converse is true: inactivity actually accelerates the aging process.

Hike For Improved Mental Health

"To keep the body in good health is a duty . . . otherwise we shall not be able to keep our mind strong and clear."
—Buddha

Stressed? Depressed?

You could lie on a couch and talk to a psychiatrist.

Or you could take a hike. Hiking prompts the release of endorphins, soothing chemicals that serve to calm us.

Perhaps as a holdover from the early days of the human race when homo sapiens were *not* at the top of the food chain and often were chased by predators, our modern bodies still produce lots of adrenalin, which helps us with our fight-or-flight responses and in a less dramatic way assists us with getting through tense meetings and getting over tall mountains. Adrenaline, if not periodically released, accumulates, tensing muscles and contributing to feelings of anxiety.

A study commissioned by Mind, a leading British mental health charity, suggests hiking contributes to improved mental and emotional health. In that landmark study, researchers from the University of Essex compared the benefits of hiking a trail through the woods and around a lake in a nature park vs. walking in an indoor shopping center on people affected by depression. They found that the hikers realized far greater benefits than the mall-walkers; in fact, taking a hike in the countryside reduces depression whereas walking in a shopping center increases depression.

Results from the 2007 study showed that 71 percent reported decreased levels of depression after hiking while 22 percent of participants felt their depression increased after walking through an indoor shopping center. Ninety percent reported their self-esteem increased after the nature hike while 44 percent reported decreased self-esteem after walking around the shopping center. Eighty-eight percent of people reported improved mood after hiking while 44.5 percent of people reported feeling in a worse mood after the shopping center walk.

The concept of "ecopsychology" explores the innate human need to connect with the natural, rather than the built environment. This "getting back to nature" movement may provide the kind of peace of mind so many of us seek in today's über-industrialized world. All the research in that field, too, supports what hikers have known all along: taking a hike is good for both body and mind.

Do hikers really need scientific proof and academic explanation for the benefits of hiking?

Probably not. But there's something very satisfying to learn that hiking has measurable mental health benefits as well as so many immeasurable ones.

4

In Good Spirit

It is no use walking anywhere to preach
unless our walking is our preaching.
—St. Francis of Assisi

FRESH AIR, great exercise, communion with nature—hiking offers all this—and more. Some hikers have discovered that getting outward bound helps them with an inward journey.

If you want to learn about on-the-trail technique and gear—and hold off on any kind of cosmic discussion about the value hiking may have to your inner self, higher self or the world at large—skip this chapter and turn to the dozen that detail all the practicalities. This discussion can certainly wait. I hiked for many years before giving my interior world on the trail—or anyone else's—much consideration.

I began looking at hiking a bit differently after making a Pilgrimage with a capital P and hiking up, down, and around the Holy Mountain of Greece. Journeying to the remarkable Mt. Athos, home to twenty Orthodox Christian monasteries, where the monks live and work today as they did in the Middle Ages, was a profoundly moving experience: architectural treasures; trails that have been isolated from the world for a thousand years; the wisdom and the spirituality of monks; a place where no females are allowed. That fact alone focused my attention inward and to a contemplative place. Here was an other-worldly place that stirred my soul.

I feel very lucky and very blessed to have experienced such a remarkable place, but you certainly don't have to hike a holy mountain in Greece, Peru, Tibet, or anywhere else to lift your spirit and nourish it. Scores of hikers have told me how they've discovered a greater sense of spirituality on trails near their homes. I believe nearly every hike has the potential to be a mini-pilgrimage if approached in the right spirit.

One of the most powerful tools for spiritual renewal is so simple, it's frequently overlooked: hiking. To hike is to receive a continuous intake of new images which, in turn, prompt new thoughts and spark new feelings. Step by step, thought by thought, hiking shapes our bodies and souls, and helps create and alter our life paths. We can hike our way out of a problem and into a solution. We can hike from questions to answers. We can hike from "Can I?" to "I can," and to, "I will."

Walking is the exercise of choice for millions of Americans and also a scriptural term in many religions commonly used to describe an individual's earthly pilgrimage. Similarly, hiking is the outdoor recreation of choice for millions of Americans and one that also opens up new paths for growth.

A good hike can spiritually strengthen us in our three most important relationships:

- With a higher power
- With other people
- With nature

In short, hiking can be a form of meditation. A good hike is most enlightening—a merging of the visible and invisible worlds.

In Search of Hiking Wisdom

"Our walking is not a means to an end.
We walk for the sake of walking."
—Thich Nhat Hanh

I truly wish I could report that the impetus for looking at hiking and finding something more came to me while on a hike to some ancient holy shrine—or even on a nature trail in the local mountains—but in fact it came under the hot glare of the lights in a television studio.

While on a book tour, I was interviewed on "Life and Times," a talk show produced by KCET, the Los Angeles Public Broadcasting System affiliate. My earnest host, Will Swaim, asked questions about my book, *A Walk Along Land's End*, a narrative about my 1,600-mile hike up the California coast. I talked about both the great beauties and environmental atrocities I'd seen, and the intriguing wildlife and colorful characters I had encountered. For the first three-fourths of our book chat, I was in fine form. Most of my book tour had been completed by the time I appeared on this show. I had been interviewed more than three dozen times and felt confident that I had an easy answer or an amusing anecdote for any question. That is, until near the end of this particular interview when my interviewer threw me a question I'd never been asked and—worse—had not truly contemplated.

Swaim talked about how I seemed to have grown more philosophical toward the end of my long walk and then asked if I thought hiking could be considered a spiritual quest.

I froze. I was probably silent for only about five seconds, but it seemed like an eternity. (A friend later commented: "John, you looked like a deer caught in the headlights.")

I punted the question. "A long walk is a spiritual quest in many religions. Some people might discover something spiritual on a long hike."

Swaim was quick with a follow-up question. "But how is hiking a spiritual experience for you? Doesn't something happen out there that changes your way of thinking, of feeling?"

Another pause. I could feel the perspiration on my forehead, seeping through the studio makeup. I fumbled this question as badly as the first. "Well, you have to think about something on a 1,600-mile hike. Hiking brought me closer to nature, closer to the mountains and the sea . . . "

Two more questions of the spirit followed, which I handled no better than the first two, before time mercifully ran out on the interview.

After the interview, I stormed out of the studio, angry with myself, angry with my interrogator. In PR lingo, I had lost control of the interview. I kicked the tires on my truck, pounded the dashboard, and seethed as I inched along the congested freeway during the three-hour drive home.

Calmer heads soon prevailed and convinced me that I hadn't performed quite as poorly as I thought: My publicist gave me a B grade on my performance, and my editor a B-minus. And Will Swaim, far from being the talk show host from hell, turned out to be a very spiritual man, educated by Jesuits.

It was Swaim who showed me his copy of *A Walk Along Land's End,* with the more spiritual passages marked with a yellow highlight pen and margin notes. He suggested I begin preaching what I was already practicing: "John, you know the power of a good hike. Why don't you help hikers out with the process? Give them something to think about on their own hikes."

So that's how someone very slow on the spiritual uptake, who always figured he had better developed thighs than thoughts, began wondering how to get something more than fresh air from my time on the trail.

What do Hikers Want?

As a "hiking writer," as an acknowledged hiking expert, I thought I knew the answer to that question. I had dispensed my share of *how*-to-hike advice in the form of newspaper and magazine articles and I had provided way more than my share of *where*-to-hike advice via every kind of print and digital media.

Certainly a lot of other experts think they know what hikers want. Homebuilders and realtors report that the most commonly requested "amenity" in new subdivisions is a walking path; in fact, homebuyers prefer hiking trails and greenways to tennis courts and golf courses by a wide margin. Tour companies say the walking-vacation business has expanded exponentially during the last decade. Manufacturers and retailers view hiking footwear, apparel, and equipment as big business.

But while the consumer needs of hikers are certainly being met, what about their inner needs? Do hikers even have any inner needs? Are most hikers as out of touch with the meditative aspects of a hike as we so-called experts?

Apparently I had intended to explore for years, perhaps on a subconscious level, to explore this "What do hikers want?" question at some later date. I discovered in the depths of filing cabinets and on long-forgotten computer disks such intriguingly named files as "God," "Walk Back from Cancer," "Desert Monks," "Eco-rabbi," "Around the World on One Leg," "Christian Conservationists," "100-Year Old Hiker," and a few dozen more.

As my filing system illustrated, I had quite literally maintained a strict separation of church and state, the body and the spirit, in my work. But what I discovered is that while some separation of spirituality and practicality may indeed be necessary in our everyday lives and in our nation's governance, such separation on our hikes, is not necessary at all. In fact, hiking serves to integrate, not separate, the material and spiritual worlds.

While seeking hiking wisdom, I became acquainted with the writings and teaching of an array of walkers that included Charles Dickens, Jesus of Nazareth, Johann Goethe, Apostle Paul, Henry David Thoreau, Harry S. Truman, Johnny Appleseed, Buddha, Norman Cousins, Immanuel Kant, Jane Austen, Lao-tse, William O. Douglas, Ralph Waldo Emerson, Will Rogers, Mahatma Gandhi, Wolfgang Amadeus Mozart, Socrates, and dozens more. The Bible, both Old and New Testaments, proved to be a particularly rich source of walking wisdom, as well as the literature of Eastern religions and traditions.

Along with the great number of hikes I've taken to great destinations, I've managed to work in a few spiritual pilgrimages as well. In addition to my pilgrimage to the Holy Mountain of Greece, I've walked where the Transcendentalists walked in New England, and hiked with a Cistercian nun through a logging-threatened redwood grove that she and her order were attempting to save.

My parish priest, Fr. Simon of the St. Barbara Greek Orthodox Church, recalls that as a young man he decided to hike up

Yosemite's Half Dome on the weekend before boarding a plane to the East Coast and entering the seminary. "I wanted to connect with one of the loveliest spots on earth, make a kind of pilgrimage, before I began my studies for the priesthood," he explained.

I've often talked with other hikers, religious and not, about hiking in good spirit. Some hikers report that a good hike declutters the mind and lifts the heart, opening new avenues to faith or restoring existing ones.

Do you think anything spiritual on your hikes? Is there a point to hiking beyond getting from Point A to Point B?

Me, I'm getting better at answering those kinds of questions, though I still have far more questions than answers about sojourns of the spirit.

There are as many directions to travel as there are hikers. You'll find your own direction, your own path. One step at time.

Hiking: A Spiritual Path

From culture to culture, continent to continent, walking is an ancient and literal way of pursuing a spiritual path. English pilgrims sojourned to Canterbury; Native Americans walk to sacred places on vision quests; Australian aborigines wander into the outback on walkabouts. Jesus of Nazareth walked into the desert for forty days and forty nights to pray and to prepare for his future struggles.

But we don't have to hike to, or through, the Holy Land in order to make a pilgrimage. By combining the outward-bound momentum of our bodies with the inner voyaging of our souls, we have the makings of a mini-pilgrimage every time we step out the door.

Many great poets, those explorers of the soul, have been great walkers. One of William Wordsworth's biographers calculated that the English poet laureate walked some 185,000 miles (!) during his lifetime. Samuel Taylor Coleridge walked ten miles daily and Percy Bysshe Shelley often walked the thirty-two miles to London when he was a student at Oxford.

Truly, the rambling British bards of the nineteenth century and their ancient and modern counterparts would seem to have little to offer us today. And yet philosophically and historically viewed, I believe we can say of walking in the great outdoors that it can properly be considered as one of the fine arts. Walking, by its rhythmic nature, by awakening our senses, makes all of us poets. We see aspen leaves flicker in the wind, a squirrel scurry up a tree, a child run across a meadow. Life hums to us as we invite it in by venturing out into it.

Certainly beauty inspires, elevating a good walk to a great one, but we don't need to ramble the Cotswolds, hike the High Sierra, or saunter the beaches of Maui to draw inspiration from our environment.

Some may avoid hiking because it doesn't lead anywhere—except to better health perhaps. Sure it's good exercise, but it's dismissed as a mere pastime, a leisure-class luxury, an idle recreation.

Some very busy folks I know say: "Every week I hike up to Inspiration Point, come back home and nothing's changed except I got two hours of exercise."

To view hiking solely as a physical activity is to completely miss the point. And besides, hiking the same path again and again is like crossing and re-crossing the same stream; it's a different experience every time.

Hiking, at its most personally satisfying, is the body and mind together in motion. The two elements interact with each and foster creativity. Movement aids creativity and, when you channel your creativity on something, you prompt movement. Once in motion, roadblocks become apparent, alternate paths reveal themselves.

Such hiking is not "inner-hiking"—something of a contradiction of terms because hiking can never be only a mental process. Inner-hiking reduces hiking to mere metaphor—not our goal at all.

It is the combination of our unusual, two-legged upright mobility and the evolution of our capacious brain that makes us unique among mammals. Our curious bipedal locomotion dictates what we *can* do long-term for exercise and our big brains what we *will* do. It seems we may just be too smart to continue with unnatural boring activities for very long.

That's the beauty of hiking. It's never boring.

Hiking can encourage interactions with our subconscious, involving our senses and emotions in our great thoughts of the day. Hiking gives the intuitive side of the brain a chance to interact with the rational sides.

Sometimes the two sides seem at 180-degree opposites, destined never to intersect, much less interact. Ah, but if we keep hiking we discover that the right and left sides of our brains, like our right and left legs, provide not only energy, but synergy, creating a force more powerful than the sum of its parts.

Here's a recent "conversation" between my left brain and right brain that took place on a recent hike in the foothills near my home.

RATIONAL BRAIN: Interest rates are low, it looks like it's time to re-finance our house and get a reduced mortgage payment.

INTUITIVE BRAIN: Look at the mountain lilac in bloom. Clouds of blue blossoms floating atop the ridge.

RATIONAL BRAIN: If I go for a 15-year fixed loan instead of a 30, I'd save thousands in interest, but the payments would be more each month.

INTUITIVE BRAIN: The coastal fog is lifting, the foggy curtain is parting, just a glimpse of Santa Cruz Island floating on the horizon.

RATIONAL BRAIN: The loan application must be twenty pages, all those credit checks, taxes . . . the bank bureaucrats . . .

INTUITIVE BRAIN: What a pungent aroma! The black sage is really flowering this year. *(Sneeze!)*

Now at first glance, what possible linkage could there be between these two resolutely parallel dialogues going on inside my head?

Actually, as it turns out, a lot.

My walk helps me realize that home is not simply the old 1912-vintage Craftsman house that's located on a residential street near downtown, it's my whole environment: the mountains, ocean, churches, schools, malls, movie theaters, family, friends, neighbors, the Mediterranean flora, the foothills and the flatlands, the soft southern light. From the perspective of my hilltop vista, that bank building way down there no longer looks very intimidating. Put in perspective, I realize that a loan is but a necessary obstacle to hurdle in order to enjoy my hometown, home mountains, and home shore. The sights and sounds gathered while getting "the big picture" of my environment will strengthen me and help focus my mission as I do battle with the bank's loan examiners on the subjects of points, interest rates, and a far-from-perfect credit report.

Hiking, aerobics experts say, generates alpha waves which are distinguished by their creative nature. These creative ideas, these creative solutions to problems that these alpha waves seem to prompt, often seem superior to those ideas produced by ordinary thinking.

Truth is, the simple act of taking a hike can be a life-changing activity, one step at a time. For me, hiking is a path to increased serenity, creativity and physical well-being, as well as a connection to something far greater than myself.

It could be that kind of path for you, too.

Make a Pilgrimage

For thousands of years, the notion of a pilgrimage—a purposeful journey to a sacred center—has beckoned the spiritually oriented walker. Today, hikers venture to spiritually compelling places around the world, from New Mexico to Tibet, Israel to India.

Pilgrims journey to Ireland to make a *tura*, or circuit of holy wells and gravesites of Celtic saints. Hikers trek to Mayan sites in Mexico, and in Japan follow in the footsteps of the great seventeenth-century poet-pilgrim Matsuo Bashō.

One well-defined modern pilgrimage is along the Camino de Santiago in Spain. Since medieval times, pilgrims have journeyed to the legendary shrine of St. James the Apostle at Santiago de Compostela, located on Spain's northern coast. Some seekers hoped that the saint, known as a miracle-worker, would heal them while others believed in the transformational power of a challenging walk and constant prayer.

Departing pilgrims from all over Europe first received the blessing of their local priest, then assembled the traditional apparel: a wide-brimmed hat, "official" scallop-shell pilgrimage badge, a backpack called a *scrip*, and a walking stick.

Many a writer has chronicled the Camino, beginning with the twelfth-century guidebook, *The Pilgrim's Guide.* Actress Shirley MacLaine wrote *The Camino: A Journey of the Spirit,* a book that recounts her walk and a whole lot more—including intimate encounters with her soul-mate Charlemagne and visits to the lost city of Atlantis. Many readers were completely baffled at MacLaine's new-age ventures far off the trail, but we can thank the peripatetic entertainer for putting the spotlight on the Camino and celebrating the value of a pilgrimage.

Certainly the Camino can be enjoyed simply as a terrific walk through lovely countryside, with fine meals and lodging, and close-up views of a remarkable array of architectural and cultural treasures. Ah, but The Way of St. James has a way of inspiring and illuminating today's traveler, and transforming a hike into a pilgrimage.

Traveling to defined Buddhist, Hindu, Judaic, Islamic or Christian holy sites can indeed be a pilgrimage. However, it's the journey, not the destination that makes a pilgrimage. A hike, solo or in the company of fellow seekers, offers a chance to reflect, an opportunity to gather spiritual wisdom. For the traveler intrigued by the notion of walking in a beautiful place while simultaneously journeying inward, a pilgrimage is a special walk indeed.

5

In Harmony with Nature

"When we walk, we naturally go to the fields and woods: what would become of us, if we walked only in a garden or a mall!"
—Henry David Thoreau

WHEN I was eleven, it was the highest peak in the world. It was a place where eagles soared, mountain lions lurked, Chumash Indian spirits dwelled. Remote it was, and regal. The great shoulders of the mountain were perfumed with sage. A crown of red rock touched the heavens. Often the peak was enshrouded in fog, activating a Tenderfoot Scout's already over-active imagination. It was a big mountain and more than a little scary. During my first trip to the top I shivered in my brand-new hiking boots.

From the summit I could see the whole world: Mt. Hollywood and the Los Angeles Basin, the Channel Islands and the San Fernando Valley, the Santa Monica Mountains themselves from end to end, and much more geography that my Scoutmaster patiently helped me match to the map.

It was a cruel disappointment to me to learn that Sandstone Peak (elevation 3,111 feet) was not the highest peak in the world, or even in the Los Angeles city limits, and that I couldn't see the whole world, or even all of metro L.A., from the summit. By the time I was an experienced 14-year-old hiker and an Eagle Scout,

I had climbed 11,499-foot Mt. San Gorgonio, highest peak in Southern California, and many more two-mile high mountains. More than three decades of adult wanderings took me to the tops of peaks around North America and across Europe.

As the years passed, my memory of the mysterious peak hidden in the fog, and the long trail to the top of Sandstone faded away. Only the view stayed with me, a boy's view of a Southern California that had no limits, of a land big enough, empty enough to accommodate every dream.

It was this view, from Scout days, that I carried with me one spring day to the top of Sandstone Peak. I wanted to compare my boyhood view with a view of today. I wanted to see how my part of the planet had changed.

As I hike up Mishe Mokwa Trail, the soft colors of the high chaparral—black sage, golden yarrow, red shank, woolly blue curls—bring back memories as surely as faded photos.

My spirits lift as I continue up the trail. Unlike so many mountain scenes from my boyhood memory that have been destroyed by the hand of man, this one has remained intact. I pass a striking red volcanic formation we scouts called Balanced Rock and a pyramid-like rock we called Egyptian Rock.

I push on to Sandstone Peak. Funny thing about that name; the summit is actually granite.

As I scramble up the rocks to the summit, I spot a blue flag. To my delight, floating in the Pacific breeze at the very top is an Earth Day flag—a portrait of planet earth as seen from outer space etched on a blue banner.

My view of the earth isn't quite the cosmic one on the flag, but it's mighty impressive. To the east is snow-capped Mt. Baldy towering over Los Angeles. I can see the sandy sweep of Santa Monica Bay, Palos Verdes Peninsula, Catalina Island. And I can see the San Fernando Valley, two national forests, the Channel Islands, and of course the mountains.

My mountains, the Santa Monica Mountains.

I was born on the other side of the Santa Monica Mountains; in a quite literal way, these mountains are home for me. I've lived in the most urban section of the Santa Monica Mountains—the Hollywood Hills—and in one of the most rural parts—Topanga Canyon.

I often take my son and daughter hiking on the mountain trails. Children talk to you on the trail, confide in parents in a way they don't back home. Every time I take kids on a hike I'm reminded that nature is nurture, a classroom without walls, and that even the youngest spirits sometimes need the restorative powers only nature can bring. I have no doubt that scientists will eventually discover that human nature is linked to the natural world in ways more powerful and profound than we currently recognize or even imagine.

From Sandstone Peak, I can see my shore, the Santa Monica Bay, some 40 miles of coastline. Half mountain man, half beach boy that I am, it's always given me a charge to look down from a mountain at the home shore.

From Sandstone Peak I can see my valley, the San Fernando Valley, a 24-mile long, 12-mile wide rectangle that has been almost completely urbanized and suburbanized.

As seen from Sandstone Peak, my islands, the Channel Islands—Anacapa, Santa Cruz, Santa Rosa, and San Miguel—are a series of blue-tinged mountains floating on the Pacific horizon.

I sure like the view from Sandstone Peak, but I guess if I lived in another of the planet's great cities, I would hike up whatever mountain was nearby to get a view of the world near my home.

But Sandstone Peak is my place to view the home mountains, home shore, home valley, home islands.

Surely one of nature's greatest benefits is the room, the space it gives us to think about—well, nature. Here I am at the Sandstone Peak Think Tank and Environmental Research Center. Hiking to the edge of the city and beyond reminds us that there is another way: Nature's way.

When you're eleven years old, you think every peak is the highest in the world. You think you can see the whole world from a place like Sandstone Peak.

Maybe you still can.

The Nature of Hiking

Hiking is defined, literally and figuratively, by its connection to nature. A walk must be in nature (usually termed the "countryside" in dictionaries) in order for it to be considered a hike.

Hiking is often literally linked to nature on the back covers of books about hiking. In order to display the books so that customers can find them, booksellers require publishers to categorize their books by subject areas. Hiking books are commonly categorized by both "Nature" and "Hiking."

There's no accepted standard of how to categorize this kind of title, so book publishers choose the best way to position their books in the marketplace. You'll find Nature/Hiking, Hiking/Nature, Outdoor Recreation/Hiking/Nature,Travel/Hiking/Nature, Pennsylvania/Nature/Hiking and many more variations on the backs of books.

Most books about hiking, particularly guidebooks, promote the natural wonders reached by trail with back-cover blurbs. Getting into nature is inseparable from hitting the trail.

During a long tenure as the *Los Angeles Times* hiking columnist, my weekly column, titled "Hiking," ran in three different sections of the newspaper: first, in View (California lifestyle) on Thursdays; next, Calendar (what's happening around town) on Fridays ; and finally, Travel on Sundays.

Editors for each section made the case that hiking "belonged" in that part of the paper. Hiking is definitely part of the California lifestyle, a good fit for the View section. Hiking is an excellent weekend activity and should be highlighted along with the many arts and culture opportunities in the Calendar section. Hiking is a great, low-cost and green way to travel near and far and appeals to readers of the Travel Section.

Over the years editors of all these sections of the paper explained why hiking could fit into their particular purview: readers want to get out into nature.

One *Los Angeles Times* editor, though, was dead certain he didn't want Hiking in his section.

"No way is hiking a sport," long-time *Times* sports editor Bill Dwyre told me. "A sport has to have competition."

Doubtless most sports writers and sportscasters, along with most fans of the major sports, would agree with the old-school sports columnist, though the word "competition" is nowhere to be found in the dictionary definition of sport. In fact, with sport usually defined as "any activity that gives enjoyment or recreation," hiking is a sport according to Webster's and other dictionaries.

Sport or not, admittedly, there's little competition in hiking. Hikers sometimes race each other up a mountain. But that's really trail-running, which is really running which, at its most competitive, is definitely a sport. Likely there are record-holders for completing various trails in the fewest number of hours or days, but neither hikers nor anyone else pays any attention to such feats.

"Sports take place on fields and courts and so on that are made by man," Dwyre explained, spelling out the difference between "real sports" and a recreation like hiking. "There aren't any spectators for hiking like there are for most sports. Hiking is something you do way out there in nature."

Out in nature is where readers of my hiking column, where every hiker wants to be. The most impassioned responses to my trail dispatches in the newspaper came from those readers who took to the trail and were sufficiently moved by their experiences in the natural world that they took time to write me a letter or post a comment online.

Sure, readers liked my directions and step-by-step trail accounts and the clear maps that accompanied my prose, but they loved my nature notes and, more to the point, loved their own hikes into nature.

Perhaps the most satisfying part of that trail-writing job was reporting on what I discovered in nature: finding a chocolate lily, wandering through fields of purple lupine, meandering along solemn colonnades of redwoods. And then there were the sightings of creatures great and small: Roosevelt elk and bighorn sheep, fringe-toed lizards and banana slugs.

I make no claims to be anything but the most amateur of naturalists. I've written about stands of Douglas fir that were actually big cone spruce. I've misunderstood and mischaracterized the mating habits of elephant seals. I've lost track of geologic time, confusing the Cenozoic and Mesozoic eras. (Hey, what's a couple of million years anyway on the grand scheme of things?)

And one time out of the thousand pieces about hiking and nature that I wrote for the *Los Angeles Times,* I blew it big-time. Early in my hike-writing career, on a fateful day in mid-March (not that I'm superstitious, but it was the Ides of March) I took a hike out in the desert at the Antelope Valley California Poppy Reserve. It was rainy and very cold on my hike with the park ranger, who pointed out the multitude of poppy buds, sure to put on a spectacular show in a few weeks—waves of orange flowers as far as the eye could see.

My column about the joys of hiking through wondrous fields of poppies ran a month later. Scores of readers drove out to the desert to delight in the pathways through the poppies.

Two weeks before publication, the poppies were popping up in all their glory; unfortunately, a long and searing heat wave occurred a couple of days before my hiking column appeared and toasted just about every poppy in the reserve. Readers who made the long trek found brown hills instead of orange ones, desiccation instead of lush beauty. Some hikers were understanding about the vicissitudes of nature and took it in stride; others wanted to boil me in poppy-seed oil and demanded I be fired from my position for wasting their time. Thankfully, my editor realized I had no control over nature and kept me on the trail.

What a young writer learned from that experience is that nature is nothing if not ever-changing and that I had better qualify my observations to avoid future miscues. So I began to write of seasonal creeks, meadows seasonally sprinkled in wildflowers, and migratory birds that are sometimes observed in winter at the lagoon.

More important, I learned of the powerful attraction hikers

have for nature. And it's been my pleasure, for many years, to be in a position to share my sense of wonder and curiosity as well as the delights of discovering nature reached by footpaths.

I've been labeled a "hiking writer," a "nature writer," and a "writer about nature and hiking."

Any of these labels is just fine with me, as long as I make the connection—and others make the connection—between nature and hiking.

Nature Nurtures

As writer Lorraine Anderson puts it: "Nature has been for me, for as long as I remember, a source of solace, inspiration, adventure, and delight; a home, a teacher, a companion."

I couldn't agree more.

Sauntering by a burbling brook, napping by a lakeshore, and meditating upon a mountain are among the many ways hikers find peace, tranquility, and so much more in nature.

Those who like to categorize our positive orientation toward the natural world make distinctions among nature appreciation, nature awareness and nature inspiration.

Nature appreciation, broadly, is spending time outdoors enjoying the natural world. Educators would likely add that, in order to truly appreciate nature, one must learn all about it. Hence the nature museum, nature trail, nature talks, and nature walks.

Nature awareness comes in two flavors: old school and New Age. Traditional use of the term is an awareness of the natural world gained by keen observation and tracking, and by learning to identify plants and animals. More recently, nature awareness refers to a kind of therapy useful for assisting people coping with depression, loss, or other life challenges.

Nature inspiration is obvious to those who write, paint, or photograph. And nature inspires in many other ways as well, beginning with delight in the beauties of nature and the resultant good feelings and uplift in spirit engendered by reconnecting with nature.

Man vs. Nature and other Conflicts

While hiking lacks the kind of competition common to most sports, it's not all "Kumbaya" and "Happy Trails." Hikers come into conflict with nature, with each other, and with their own limitations.

Remember learning about the kinds of conflict in your high school and college English classes? Conflict is a necessary element of fiction, crucial to a good story. The greater the conflict, the more difficult it is for the protagonist to triumph, and the more value there is in the drama.

When boomer and older generations learned about them, the three major conflicts were listed as Man vs. Man, Man vs. Nature and Man against Himself. These days the conflicts are usually presented in the classroom as Human vs. Human, Human vs. Nature and Human vs. Self. And add one more conflict to a list that's held steady since the time of the ancient Greeks: Human vs. Technology.

Human vs. Human conflicts among hikers might include: a bullying hike leader who berates hikers who fall behind his ridiculously fast pace; teenagers tussling on one of those wilderness backpacking programs designed for troubled youth; well-to-do guests sniping at each other on an upscale walking vacation. I believe there were times, as an eleven-year-old Boy Scout gasping for breath as I labored up a steep wilderness trail, that I wanted to throw a rock at my Scoutmaster, particularly when he repeated: "What doesn't kill you, will make you stronger."

Human vs. Nature is surely a conflict faced by hikers. Hikers don't have an inherently adversarial relationship with nature, but the power of nature is considerable and humans, not nature, must do the accommodating. Hikers must deal with the many challenges to travel in nature in the form of animals (bears, mountain lions, rattlesnakes), terrain, and ever-changing weather.

Human vs. Self is a common, even constant, conflict for many hikers. Can I make it to the top? Can I overcome the effects of an illness? A disability? A broken heart?

Overcoming physical, mental, or emotional challenges is part of life—on and off the trail.

Hiking: Green Exercise at its Best

The term "green exercise" refers to physical activities that give participants the benefits of exercise and direct exposure to nature.

A growing body of green exercise research shows that interacting with nature while exercising can positively influence health and well-being, relieve stress, and promote concentration and clear thinking. In other words, walking city streets is okay, but not as beneficial to mind-body-spirit as hiking through a park, greenbelt, or nature preserve, recent studies demonstrate.

Hikers, whether they know it or not—and I suspect most don't—are the chief practitioners of green exercise, also practiced by kayakers, surfers, and cross-country skiers.

Research conducted at the University of Essex identified four principal reasons why people enjoy green exercise:

- Natural and social connections—being with friends and family, bonding with pets, watching wildlife, stimulating spiritual feelings
- Sensory stimulation—noting colors and sounds from nature's diversity, breathing fresh air, being exposed to weather, experiencing a sense of adventure, excitement, fun, enjoying an escape from pollution
- Activity—learning physical skills, achieving challenging tasks, enjoying the energy of physical activities
- Escape from modern life—having time to think and reflect/clear the head, getting away from pressures and stress, recharging batteries

Make Time for Nature

We're just too busy to hike into nature. Sure, Henry David Thoreau and John Muir found great measures of intrigue and inspiration, peace and tranquility in nature, but that was then and this is now, and the idea of spending time in nature is so over, so nineteenth century.

Or is it?

In my observation, a healthy dose of nature—call it Latter Day Transcendentalism or just Time on the Trail—does wonders. I've witnessed scores of hikers, after an hour's hike in nature, transform from feeling stressed to feeling blessed.

Scientists are quantifying exactly how we benefit from nature in terms of improved mental and physical health. This is nice to know, but exactly how nature benefits us is not as important to know as the fact that it does benefit us.

Of course, if we have long known anecdotally what's now proven scientifically—that going into nature can heal us physically, emotionally, or spiritually—then why aren't we hitting the trail in greater numbers?

Well, I'll have to leave that question up for discussion with my fellow hikers, or try to answer it in another venue.

Or not. Reading books and watching nature programs are fine ways to learn about nature, but the best way to reconnect with nature is by getting into it. Taking a hike and reconnecting with nature also can help the minds and hearts of hiker and help them reconnect to friends, family, spirit, and self.

And while enjoying the many benefits of nature, hikers often feel moved to embrace the responsibilities of caring for it.

While on the trail, hikers can't help but note the multitude of irreplaceable benefits nature provides. Often this realization prompts an increased commitment to the stewardship of trails and the terrain they cross, as well as to the earth itself—perhaps only one small part of creation, but certainly the only place where we can take a hike.

Hikers have an important role to play in helping humankind find its place in nature before that place is lost. We spend more time closer to the land than most—and we have an imperative to help our city-bound friends return to the pleasures of the natural world.

The Hiker's Land Ethic

Environmentally unsound construction is evident all over America. The forces of Cut & Fill and Grade & Pave each year engulf more and more open space. There are still places that remain inviolate from the earthmover and the cement mixer, but these places grow fewer each year. As the twenty-first century version of the good life creeps into our backcountry, it may be time to ask ourselves, "What color is paradise?"

I think it's green.

A change in our land ethic begins with a change in perception and a change in perception begins with you. It's not a difficult change to make; in fact, hiking can provoke it. The change I'm suggesting requires only that you open your eyes a little wider and see the natural world from a different perspective.

Perception is a funny thing. Did you ever notice the change in pitch of a train whistle as it goes away from you? A nineteenth-century Austrian physicist, Christian Doppler, figured that sound waves varied with the relative velocity of the source and the observer. He applied his Doppler effect to light waves, as well. He saw that, as the position of observer and light source change, the colors of light will shift.

Hikers can notice a Doppler effect of their own. Looking up at Mt. Baldy rising above the Los Angeles basin, the hiker sees a snowy peak rising above the smog. From the top of Old Baldy, the hiker often looks down on a yellow-brown inversion layer topping the sprawling metropolis. Quite a difference in views between the bottom of the Basin and the top of the mountain! Seattle hikers have similar contrasting views when looking up at Mt. Rainier from city sidewalks and looking down at that metropolis from trails on the mighty mountain.

Everywhere, there are profound differences in vistas between looking out at the natural world from the city and looking back at the city from the natural world. In a few special places there's not a profound difference between the human-built and natural environments, but all too often there is.

To hike is to alter your perceptions, to see things in a new light. You see where you are and what you left behind, and you realize that the two are closer together than you had imagined. The distinction between "out there" and "right here" blurs; when that happens, you've become a conservationist. As a conservationist, you'll perceive that our boulevards, our wilderness, and we ourselves are part of a fragile island. The future of the island depends on your perceptions and your actions.

With global warming threats clouding our future and our increasing awareness of the interconnectedness of the wondrous web of life on this fragile planet, getting onto The Hiker's Way is taking steps in the right direction to appreciate and protect the green spaces and natural places that nurture our bodies and souls.

The Hiker Prepares

6

The Ten Essentials

"There is an intense but simple thrill in setting off in the morning on a mountain trail, knowing that everything you need is on your back. It is a confidence in having left the inessentials behind and of entering a world of natural beauty that has not been violated, where money has no value, and possessions are a dead weight. The person with the fewest possessions is the freest. Thoreau was right."
—Paul Theroux

BY NOW, on one hike or another, I've forgotten each and every one of the Ten Essentials. And always regretted it.

I've left the trail map in the car and grabbed a bag of hamster food off the kitchen counter instead of a bag of trail mix. I can't seem to remember to check the freshness of the batteries for my head-lamp, and I forget to replenish the supplies in my first-aid kit. When airport security confiscated my trusty Swiss Army knife out of my daypack, I assured myself I could do without a pocket knife for a week of day hiking. (Naturally, I needed it several times.)

How many essentials are there in the Ten Essentials?

No, this isn't a whimsical question, like "Who's buried in Grant's tomb?"

Some hiking experts count twelve or even fourteen essentials. And what about the daypack, essential to carry those essentials, shouldn't that count as an essential? New hikers argue that a cellphone should be the eleventh essential while veterans insist it should be "common sense." Some Ten Essentials lists include matches and fire starter as two separate essentials, some count them as one essential. Some lists include water, some don't.

Items that usually finish just out of the top ten but that are considered essential by some hikers include signaling devices (whistle and mirror) and insect repellant.

A Ten Essentials list was first circulated in the 1930s by The Mountaineers, an outings club located in Seattle. Since then it has become a kind of gospel among hikers and an essential teaching tool in outdoor education programs.

1. Map

Even if you're positive about where you're headed and how to get there, it's wise to bring a map with you on the trail. GPS maps are great, but the wise hiker has a paper map back-up.

You can find good trail maps at specialty outdoors stores, travel bookstores and a number of on-line outlets. Use care when you select a map off the rack. Many maps sold to tourists are okay for sightseeing in the city, but unfortunately they simply don't show the backcountry in the kind of detail hikers require for getting onto the trail.

Maps in trail guidebooks and from local and regional park authorities vary in quality from great to abysmal. Funky hand-drawn maps or poor-quality reproductions are indicators that you should purchase additional maps of the region in which you intend to hike.

Forest Service maps are available at ranger stations and various commercial outlets for a small fee. They're general maps, showing roads, rivers, and trails. The Forest Service usually keeps its maps fairly up-to-date.

Topographic maps show terrain (elevations, waterways, vegetation and improvements) in great detail.

(More about maps in the chapter, "Finding Your Way")

2. Compass

A compass and map go hand-in-hand. Once you figure out how to use them together, you'll find yourself hiking around the backcountry with increased confidence. Add (but do not substitute) a GPS unit to your hiker navigation system.

Some of the features to look for in a good compass:

- One that registers 0 to 360 degrees with two-degree increments
- Liquid filled to protect the magnetic needle and reduce fluctuation
- Adjustable declination to adjust for the difference between magnetic north and true north
- A base plate that can be used as a straight-edge for determining distances on maps
- A pop-up mirror for making sightings

3. Water

"Drink before you're thirsty" should be the hiker's mantra. Bring plenty of water for your hike, plus some extra. And drink it! As ridiculous as it sounds, The Trailmaster has observed many hikers who remember to pack water, but don't take the time to drink it.

Try to bring your entire water supply for the day with you so that you don't have to rely on trailside streams. It's still possible in some locales to drink from a very select number of back-country creeks and springs without ill effect, but each individual water source should be carefully scrutinized.

With a few exceptions, I reluctantly advise: Don't drink untreated water. Many hikers assume water is pure, and then, 48 hours later, get that queasy feeling that tells them their assumption was wrong. Even clear-looking waters may harbor *Giardia lamblia,* one of the causes of "traveler's diarrhea." Treat back-country water with purification tablets and/or a quality filter.

4. Extra Food

Bring more food than you think you might eat. Your hunger—or the day's plans—may surprise you, and you'll want to be prepared.

On a day hike, weight is rarely an issue, so you can pack whatever you wish. Remember to pack out what you pack in. The day you hike is not the day to diet. Calorie counters rejoice: There's a lot of calorie-burning on a hike and quite an energy cost. You'll need all your strength, particularly on steep grades. Energy bars and trail mix with fruit, nuts, and M&Ms are good, high-octane fuels. A sandwich, fruit, and cookies make a lunch. A continental spread featuring sourdough bread, a fine cheese, and a splash of chardonnay is also nice.

Snack regularly and avoid a big lunch. Exertion afterward sets up a competition between your stomach and your legs and your legs lose, leading to weakness and indigestion.

5. Extra Clothes

Wherever you travel, there's a good chance you'll encounter some old-timer who loves the old adage, "If you don't like the weather in [pick a region], then wait five minutes and it will change." It almost doesn't matter where you're hiking, the weather often changes quickly and with little warning. The trick is to be prepared. If you start out on a warm sunny morning, dress accordingly (T-shirt, shorts), but bring along a long-sleeved button-down shirt, pullover, and a pair of lightweight pants. Vice-versa, of course, if it's cold. The extra shirt is especially nice when stopping or sitting down to rest on the trail. It's surprising how chilly you can get when you stop moving, particularly when you're in dry weather, windy places, or at high altitude.

Extra clothes also come in handy after an unexpected fall into a creek or on a wet, muddy trail. Depending on the climate, dry clothes might be the key to saving an otherwise lousy hike.

6. First-Aid Kit

While you don't need to lug along your entire medicine cabinet, there are a few essential items that will make any trip much safer and more comfortable. It's important to be prepared for a range of mishaps: blisters, cuts, scrapes, and sprained ankles.

- A small assortment of adhesive bandages in various sizes.
- Antiseptic towelettes
- Antibiotic ointment
- Sterile dressing a small roll of adhesive tape for larger cuts
- Antihistamine and ibuprofen tablets for allergies and aches

- Anti-diarrheal tablets (not a necessity, but if you need them will make your trip a whole lot more pleasant)
- Moleskin, for blisters
- Ace bandage—really helpful in the event of a sprained ankle
- A couple of safety pins. These can help with the oddest of medical and non-medical mishaps—a torn T-shirt, a broken zipper, you name it.
- Some hikers swear by homeopathic products such as Rescue Remedy cream, tincture, or tablets, and arnica for aches and bruises.

Larger injuries are less common on the trail, and for those, I suggest you consult a more comprehensive first-aid manual. Hike leaders and those with advanced first-aid training will carry larger kits.

7. Pocket Knife

From slicing salami to cutting an Ace bandage to rigging emergency shelter, a pocket knife is an indispensable tool on any hike. Knives really run the gamut of price, utility and style, and you can find yourself paying as little as $5 or as much as $70 for one of these gadgets. Almost any pocket knife will do on a day hike, as long as you keep these criteria in mind: your knife must be clean, sturdy, and sharp.

Few know basic wilderness preparedness as well as the Boy Scouts—and *The Official Boy Scout Handbook* offers guidelines for caring for your knife that are worth noting:

- Keep your knife clean, dry and sharp at all times
- Never use it on things that will dull or break it
- Keep it off the ground. Moisture and dirt will ruin it.
- Wipe the blade clean after using it
- Treat the joints to an occasional drop of machine oil so that the blades will keep opening easily.

Keep your knife sharp by using a sharpening stone, which you can find at most hardware stores. Sharpening a knife is not rocket science; learn how to maintain a sharp blade and keep this vital hiker's tool in tiptop shape.

8. Sun Protection

No matter where you live, or what season it is, hikers need to take precautions against the hazards of the sun's rays. Overexposure can leave you fatigued, dehydrated, and painfully burned. A combination of a hat, sunglasses, sunscreen, and the right clothing can keep you properly protected from the dangers of too much sun.

It's important to be extra sun-savvy when hiking in high altitudes, long stretches of un-shaded or reflective terrain (on sand dunes or near water, for example), and when the sun is at its most intense—roughly between the hours of 10 and 2.

9. Flashlight

Although you may have no intention to stick around on the trail past sunset, it's still a good idea to carry a flashlight or headlamp every time you head out for a hike. It's easy to underestimate just how long a particular hike might take, and you might find yourself scrambling down the mountain as dusk approaches. Without a light source, you're far more likely to lose your way, take a fall, or worse, panic.

Many seasoned hikers have stories about getting stuck on the trail after dark. And most will tell you that packing a flashlight is a classic case of "better safe than sorry."

It's easy to bring one with you. A light can be inexpensive, lightweight, and—if you bring along a set of extra batteries—pretty reliable. Headlamps are now more popular than ever. They're just as good (or better) than regular flashlights, and they have the added benefit of allowing hands-free illumination.

Because of vastly improved battery technology and capacity, as well as compact and powerful electronics, the flashlight is one "essential" that's been greatly improved over the years.

Be sure the flashlight selected throws a beam strong enough to light up a trail in total darkness. Check with store clerks (or read-up online) about beam-strength. Many cheaper lights may be great for night-time reading, but won't help you navigate a dark trail. Some lights boast a high-intensity beam that can adjust from "spot" to "flood" or from a bright, focused point of light to a wider, slightly dimmer beam—kind of like the zoom lens on a camera.

Select one that's waterproof. While you may never get stuck in the dark when it's raining (cross your fingers), it's worth the extra expense.

10. Matches and Fire-starter

Fire-starter is foolproof kindling for starting emergency fires in the wilderness. Anything from rolled-up newspaper, pinecones dipped in paraffin, to store-bought sawdust "nuggets" work to get flames going in a jiffy. Some old-school, hardcore backpacker do-it-yourselfers go with petroleum-jelly-saturated cotton balls—birthday candles, and paraffin-covered dryer lint, while most day hikers will just purchase an inexpensive packaged fire-starter found in the camping section of sporting goods stores.

More than likely, you'll never use it, but it's an important item to bring along in case of an emergency. Keep fire-starter in a dry corner of your pack, and forget about it.

A handy—and necessary—fire-starter companion is, of course, a box of matches. It's best to buy the waterproof or "stormproof" variety for trips on the trail. Camping-supply stores carry them. Keep your matches wrapped up, toss them into your pack with your fire-starter, and you're set for any day trip—and unforeseen emergency.

7

Food and Water

"We sit, we eat, and we walk."
—Buddha

"'I think,' said Christopher Robin, 'that we ought to eat all our provisions now, so we shan't have so much to carry.' "
—A.A. Milne, *Winnie-the-Pooh*

"THE Great Trail Mix Taste Test" was the first (and last) publicity stunt I ever cooked up. Here was the plan:

To promote my new hiking guide detailing the wild side of L.A., I would take the sports reporter for KFI, a major metro news-talk station, on a hike in the wilds of Griffith Park. Rich Morada good naturedly agreed, as well as to judge which trail mix tasted best. The four trail mix contenders were three store-bought brands and my wife Cheri's special homemade blend, which I figured would win the contest easily.

The hike went very well, with birds singing and astonishing (for Los Angeles) clear-day panoramas from the mountains to the sparkling blue Pacific, and live, lively dispatches from cell-phone back to the morning talk-show host. We reached Amir's Garden, sat down at a picnic table and Rich began to taste-test the trail mixes. That's when the trouble began.

"I like the simple kind," the sports reporter began, giving high marks to a just-raisins-and-peanuts variety.

Uh-oh. If Cheri's trail mix doesn't win I'll never hear the end of it. She will have been humiliated on the city's most popular drive-time radio show.

"I don't know about this one with all the stuff in it."

Enter Amir Dialameh, who tended his namesake garden on the slopes of Mt. Hollywood for three decades. "This is the best one," he says, savoring Cheri's mix.

"What's this weird thing—papaya or something?"

"Mango, and it's quite delicious. Try the butterscotch chips."

"Okay, I'll defer to Amir on this one. We have a winner. What brand is it, John?"

"Amir, Rich, you have good taste. That's my wife Cheri's secret recipe, which I will reveal to your listeners. First she takes. . . ."

That was close.

Whether you're a traditionalist or an experimental gourmand, you're sure to enjoy eating on the trail.

Day hikers have a multitude of options when it comes to snacking on the trail. Depending on palate and budget, the hiker can pack away anything from power bars and water to fancy imported cheeses and fine wine. I know of a guy who actually packed a watermelon on a long day hike in the High Sierra. How carried away you get is really up to you and your taste buds, wallet, and in some cases, physical ability.

Most people I know tend to go pretty simple with their food on the trail. Hiking makes everything taste delicious (well, almost). Peanut butter and crackers, a snack of last resort at home, combine for a tasty feast on the trail.

Use common sense with your menu selections. Don't bring anything on the hike that is prone to quick spoilage, especially if you are hiking in the heat. For example, a mayonnaise-laden tuna sandwich would be a really poor choice for a hot desert hike. When in doubt, leave it out—or pack a frozen gel pack to keep it cool.

It's important not to pack large meals, but rather, put together a variety of snacks that can be eaten throughout the day. Eating too much at one sitting can make you feel bloated and sluggish.

Part of the fun of hiking is stopping to enjoy your favorite trail treats, and sharing them with companions. Thanks to the miracles of modern packaging—and much government regulation—you can review a snack's ingredients, nutritional value, and calorie count.

Favorite Trail Foods

Dried fruit Grocery stores seem to be stocking a greater selection of dried fruit these days. Places like Trader Joe's, Whole Foods, and even Costco carry your basic banana chips and prunes, and also sell more exotic dried fare like strawberries, mangoes, pineapples, and blueberries. Yum. Dried fruit is easy to pack, high in carbohydrates (a good thing when you're climbing hills all day), won't spoil in the heat, and tastes great.

Jerky Meat and meat alternatives have also gotten swept up in the dehydration frenzy. In addition to the old standby, beef jerky, some stores and online catalogs now carry turkey, pork, clam, salmon, elk, buffalo, and tofu jerky. Yikes. You never know what they'll come up with next. Jerky, whatever its pedigree, boasts a lot of protein and offers the hiker a kind of Early Man experience: the chance to gnaw away at dried meat in the middle of the woods.

Cheese and crackers A satisfying protein-carbohydrate-fat combination, and a cinch to prepare and carry. Hard cheeses pack much better than the softer ones, and can withstand a surprising amount of heat. Whole-grain crackers, flatbread, or even a hunk of your favorite sourdough bread are all easy to pack and great to eat.

Chocolate It tastes great at home, even better on a mountain top. But be forewarned: chocolate melts in the heat, and can turn into a gooey mess. (Many would argue that it tastes better that way.) M&Ms deliver chocolate satisfaction with minimal melt-down.

Fresh fruit Apples and oranges are among the easiest to carry with you. They round out a meal of peanut butter sandwiches or crackers rather nicely. Fruits like bananas, cherries, and peaches tend to bruise easily, get mushy in your pack and are best left at the trailhead for a post-hike snack.

Veggies Consider cut-up or baby carrots and celery. For a more exotic taste treat, try sweet red peppers or jicama.

Bars Energy bars, granola bars, protein bars, power bars, whatever you want to call them. Bar fever has hit the outdoor recreation industry like nothing else, and everyone seems to have a favorite brand and flavor. Keep a few in your pack. If you don't eat them that day, they can keep for the next hike. They're also a superb emergency-food source.

Ants on a log A favorite in every kindergarten classroom, this tasty snack is also great on the trail. If you missed out on ants on a log in childhood, fear not! They are simple to make. Cut up a bunch of celery, fill stalks with peanut butter, and sprinkle with raisins. They're a great source of protein, carbohydrates, fat, fiber, and flavor.

GORP "Good Old Raisins and Peanuts," or trail mix, has been a part of the hiking experience for generations. But if GORP really consisted of only raisins and peanuts, it wouldn't be nearly as popular as it is. Hikers have added all kinds of great stuff to it over the years, and now things like M&Ms, almonds, chopped-up dried fruit, and coconut have become GORP mainstays.

Making your own GORP at home is a cinch, and it allows you to throw together foods and flavors you really love.

Begin with these basic GORP recipes and customize to your heart's desire.

Tasty Trail Mix

1 cup dry cereal (pick your favorite!)
1 cup peanuts
1 cup raisins
1 cup dried fruit
1 cup yogurt-covered almonds or peanuts
1 cup sunflower seeds
1 cup pretzels
Put all ingredients in a large Ziploc bag. Shake to mix.

Healthy (and tasty!) Trail Mix

½ cup roasted soy nuts, plain or seasoned depending on your tastes
½ cup flaked coconut
¼ cup carob chips
1 cup mixed dried fruit (tropical mixes that include bananas, mango, and pineapple are a good choices)
¼ cup shelled sunflower seeds
Mix ingredients in a Ziploc bag.

Fuel for the Trail

"Fat," "calories," and "carbohydrates" have become dirty words these days. And for good reason. Obesity has become a widespread problem in this country, and many agree that high-calorie diets are the major culprits.

But a large part of the problem is lack of exercise. In fact, doctors frequently point to walking and hiking as two of the best ways to improve health and lose weight.

If we think of our bodies as complex machines, we need food to fuel us along. When we place strenuous demands on the body—exercise, heavy labor, cold weather activity—we burn more fuel then we may otherwise need.

Hiking is more physically taxing then many of us might think. Unlike ordinary walking, hiking often involves steep uphill climbs, rugged terrain, a heavy load, and battles with the elements. These demands on the body call for higher-calorie foods, particularly carbohydrates and fats.

With that in mind, however, hiking every now and again shouldn't be excuse to constantly pig-out. It is important to balance how much you consume with how much you exercise.

How Much Do We Really Use?

It's difficult to estimate how many calories a given person expends while hiking. The pace of the hike, incline, outdoor temperature, size of the hiker, and amount of weight carried are all factors that affect how the body uses "fuel."

That said, many agree that a 150-pound person hiking 2 mph and carrying a 20-pound pack is likely to burn about 300 calories per hour. Bigger hikers burn more calories, as do hikers who maintain a faster clip, carry more weight, or hike in cold weather. While estimates vary tremendously, this can give you a rough idea why hikers get so darned hungry. So eat up!

Nutrition Basics

Carbohydrates have the most immediate effect on a hiker's energy level. They provide roughly 100 calories per ounce, and are immediately absorbed into the body as blood sugar. Simple sugars (like candy, juice, or fruit) digest more quickly than complex carbohydrates (whole-grain bread and crackers), which take a couple of hours. Both have their place in a hiker's diet: choose simple carbs for quick energy and complex carbs for pre-hike breakfasts or sit-down lunches. The longer you're on the trail, the more carbohydrates you'll need to keep your energy up throughout the day.

Fat, despite its notorious reputation, is essential to any diet. By themselves, carbohydrates offer a high jolt of energy, and then cause us to crash. Packing about 200 calories per ounce, fats digest more slowly than carbohydrates and help to even out the highs and lows from blood sugar fluctuation.

Protein is a critical part of any diet. Like fat, it digests slowly, and is a great complement to high-carbohydrate consumption, and provides roughly 80 calories per ounce. Nuts, cheeses, jerky and lean meats are all great sources of protein on the trail.

Salt is hard to avoid. These days, most packaged and processed foods are loaded with salt, and many people are advised to drastically cut down on their sodium intake. It is worth mentioning here, nonetheless. Because we lose sodium and other minerals during periods of strenuous exercise, eating a few salty snacks (along with ample water) can help to keep the body's mineral balance intact.

Water 101

Hiking without sufficient water intake can be extremely uncomfortable, and potentially disastrous.

Individuals are constantly losing water, even at rest, through respiration, urination and perspiration—all part of basic day-to-day functioning. When out on the trail, hikers invariably sweat more and breathe harder than usual; this increased activity accelerates water loss, especially in hot, dry climates and in high altitudes. Long hikes in hot weather can cause a body to lose up to two gallons of water per day.

Keeping yourself hydrated is easy. Drink plenty of water before and after the hike, and while on the trail. People have managed to over-hydrate, but that's almost impossible. For most people, the only downside to drinking excessive fluids is frequent trips to the bathroom. Or the bushes.

Many experts recommend drinking one-half to one quart of water for every hour you're on the trail. I'd say this amount is likely to be excessive for cool, low-altitude hikes, so think realistically about the location and duration of your hike.

Hikers should not, however, wait until thirsty to gulp down fluids. Thirst is a sign of mild dehydration, which at best, decreases stamina and increases sluggishness. At its most severe, dehydration can impair judgment, cause nausea and headaches and, in extreme cases, lead to death. A grim thought, indeed.

Signs of dehydration include:

- thirst
- dizziness
- confusion
- fatigue
- dry mouth
- less-frequent urination
- dry skin
- headache
- light-headedness
- increased heart rate

During exercise, fluids and valuable electrolytes are lost. Electrolytes contain high concentrations of sodium, potassium, and other minerals, and are critical to healthy cell functioning. Some people swear by electrolyte replacement drinks (Gatorade, Powerade, etc.) to stay hydrated. Sports drinks come in crazy colors and have cool names like "Glacier Freeze" or "Riptide Rush," as well as being quite tasty and refreshing.

Fortunately, the kidneys were designed to keep electrolyte levels pretty well regulated. Although sports drink manufacturers might have you believing otherwise, humans managed to survive tens of thousands of years before the invention of Gatorade.

These days, a whole new generation of super-sugared and caffeinated drinks are marketed to sporty types—but don't fall for their energetic promises that are more hype than help up the trail.

The good news for day hikers is that tap water works just fine—or bottled water if you're a purist. Never drink untreated water from trailside water sources (more about this later in the chapter).

Water Bottles

Reusable water bottles come in all shapes and sizes: wide mouth with screw-top lids and narrow mouth with stoppers. While the simple cylinder is still popular, time and bottle design march on. Some bottles feature so-called ergonomic designs with textured rubber grips and there are squeeze bottles that when squeezed gush forth fluid at a rate faster than anyone can swallow. Some bottle-makers list bottle capacity measured in liters and half liters while others, mostly American made brands, stick to ounces.

Water bottles come in a variety of colors; if you're a hiker who likes to know what your water really looks like, beware that it's becoming increasingly more difficult to find a clear plastic bottle. Many outdoor retailers, as well as outdoors gear and apparel makers market their own branded water bottles with logo, company name, and inspirational slogan.

I spotted one hiker with a hunter safety-orange bottle made by industry stalwart Nalgene, which sported the label: "Don't shoot, I'm a hiker!"

To each his own taste in water bottles.

Considering the other chotchkies and crapola for sale in gift shops in popular hiking areas, a water bottle inscribed with a place name is an excellent souvenir purchase. You could do a lot worse than a "Yosemite National Park" or "Appalachian Trail" water bottle. The half-liter size bottles are great souvenirs for kids.

With so many makes and models, selecting a reusable water bottle can be a challenge. But do get one instead of stopping by the local convenience store prior to a hike to buy disposable sports bottles filled with what is labeled "mountain spring water." Economics is one reason to avoid disposable water bottles; store-bought water for your hike costs more per ounce than the gasoline for your drive to the trailhead!

Environmental concern is another reason to shun disposables; Americans throw away more than 60 million plastic water bottles a day. And plastic bottles, when exposed to warm temperatures, taint the water with that plastic taste from trace amounts of BPA (Bisphenol), a chemical that studies have linked to numerous health issues. Most heavy-duty hiker water bottles made these days are labeled "BPA free" and you need not worry about the chemical!

For many hikers, going green means forgetting about plastic altogether and getting an aluminum or stainless steel water bottle: no plastic aftertaste, and such bottles last a very long time.

Hydration Packs

A hydration pack is a small backpack that can hold anywhere from 50 to 100 ounces of water in a plastic "bladder" that slides right into a sleeve in the back of the pack. A tube extends from the bladder to the outside of the pack, and can be kept right at chest or shoulder level—so you can easily turn your head for a quick sip. Some models of hydration packs tap into excellent, user-friendly water bottle like reservoirs, while others are more complicated to access and a challenge to clean.

Hydration packs vary widely in price from about $50 to as much as $200. Be careful about picking one in this category that's too small. The Ten Essentials and various personal items must fit in the pack.

Bladder packs come in many models of sizes, so try on a few varieties to see what you think and what fits well. Some of the packs I've tested out I found to be a little skimpy for long day hikes, but perfect for shorter trips. Some of these packs are big enough to carry your refrigerator (well, almost), while others can hold little more than a granola bar and band-aids.

The challenge with these packs is to keep the entire thing impeccably clean. Don't bother getting one unless you're committed to maintaining it.

Backcountry Water Treatment

Hikers often encounter beautiful lakes, ponds, streams, or rivers. No matter how crystal-clear they might appear—DON'T drink from them. The likelihood of ingesting *giardia, cryptosporidium,* or other nasty parasites is high, and the risk just isn't worth it. The symptoms of both giardiasis and cryptosporidiosis (the diseases caused by these respective pathogens) don't often show up right away, but they certainly aren't subtle. Cramping, diarrhea, and vomiting are the most common effects, and must be treated by a doctor.

If enough water can't be carried, you'll need to pack a water filter or water-treatment chemical like iodine. Pump-action microfilters have gotten lighter—and cheaper—over the years, and are a cinch to use. Some of the big-time filter manufacturers claim that their products can eliminate *giardia,* fungi, parasites, cholera, typhoid, *cryptosporidium,* and salmonella from even the most foul water.

These filters can clog, and become so annoyingly slow and difficult that you'll want to hurl them at a nearby tree. Remember to carry replacement filter cartridges and other parts that are prone to clogging, breaking or getting lost.

A less technical option is to treat your water with chlorine or iodine. Hiker-friendly tablets and drops are relatively cheap and easy to use. Iodine and bleach can even be used as is to treat water, but I'd go with the pros, and buy a bottle of purification tablets specially made to treat backcountry water. Overdoing it with the chemicals can be disastrous.

When used properly, chlorine and chlorine-based products kill all water pests: viruses, bacteria, you name it. Iodine, however, is ineffective against *cryptosporidium*, and should never be used by pregnant women or people with thyroid problems. Although chemicals and filters may treat water so it's safe to drink, it may still look and smell, well, unpalatable.

8

Gearing Up

"He who would travel happily must travel light."
—Antoine-Marie-Roger de Saint-Exupery

I HAVE LEARNED to never judge a hiker's ability by what he or she wears or carries on the trail. I once went on a week-long hiking holiday with a tour group that included a gentleman named Minor Bishop, a 73-year-old architect from Manhattan. It was a difficult week of tramping across England on the Coast to Coast route.

I was shocked when Minor appeared in "hiking" garb that included dress slacks, a trench coat and slip-on loafers. He proved to be a cheerful companion who never missed a step, even on some rigorous 15-mile-long days with lots of ups and downs. When it rained, Minor pulled an umbrella from his coat, as well as a pair of what he called "rubbers" (waterproof coverings for his street shoes). He pulled more gadgets from his trench coat, including a vintage 1960s-era Polaroid camera, with which he recorded the hike's highlights and shared them with fellow hikers at our evening communal dinners.

I share the story of Minor Bishop and his hundred-mile hike with the worst apparel and accessories I've ever seen on the trail, not as an endorsement of his particular hiking gear philosophy, but as a cautionary tale for all of us who take this matter of choosing gear a little too seriously.

Most hikers I know who regularly take to the trail have accumulated a collection of apparel and accessories that was carefully purchased and has been field-tested. These hikers know what they like and what works for them.

Gear Philosophy 101

Good gear—hiking apparel and accessories—makes an important, even critical, contribution to a hiker's well-being and safety. While good gear alone doesn't ensure a good hiking experience, it certainly can enhance the experience.

Obviously you'll enjoy a hike—even a hike in the rain—if you're warm and dry rather than cold and miserable; the difference between the two is sometimes the difference between quality and inferior rainwear.

Apparel makers and equipment manufacturers have made tremendous strides in the evolution of fabrics, weight reduction, weatherproofing and waterproofing. Clothing and products available to the hiker today are significantly better than they were twenty years ago—even five years ago. As a hiker who's suffered with more than my share of uncomfortable daypacks, leaky rain gear and flimsy footwear, I salute the gear makers who've worked so hard to evolve their products over the years. My comfort and that of millions of hikers has increased immeasurably thanks to their efforts.

Not only has the quality of products increased, so has the quantity. For example, a couple of decades ago only about a half-dozen brands of lightweight hiking boots were on the market; today, several hundred models are available.

Of course, when is there too much variety, too much to choose from? Only in America can a hiker visit a large outdoor retail store and find four different tick-removers for sale, each brand with a slightly different magnifying system to find the little buggers and a different extractor system for removing them.

My concerns about gear are less about the gear itself than how it's marketed. Advertisers and the editors of the national outdoors-themed magazines target a 24-year-old male searching for high-intensity adventure. Look for the ads for hiking products and apparel sandwiched between snowboards and SUVs with mud all over them.

This youngest-demographic-possible obsession of outdoors magazines leaves the huge majority of hikers behind. Words and images are for the most part wholly unrepresentative of the people who hike. Apparently the twentysomething male hikers never become fortysomething or sixtysomething, never get married, become parents or grandparents. What we see in the ads and stories is a natural world without children, trails without the kind of people we know use them every day—seniors, a mom with two kids, hikers with wrinkles.

Good gear—particularly apparel—can be expensive, but it doesn't have to be. If cost is no object—or nothing but the highest end garments will do, spend $25 on a pair of hiking socks, $90 for a sun hat and $600 for a parka. Just know you don't have to spend that much. Know that a hiker doesn't have to spend like a skier or a golfer to get equipped for a good time outdoors.

When it comes to gear, hikers tend to separate by personality into two categories: Early Adapters and Late Adapters. In other words, some hikers like to get clothes made of the latest miracle fabric and the latest electronic gizmos. Others wear out their clothes before buying new ones, and the most modern electronic accessory they tote is a vintage 1988 pocket flashlight.

You'll find The Trailmaster just a bit over the line into the Late Adaptor category. While I do try out new stuff fairly soon after it comes on the market, I tend to be very slow and conservative about replacing my trail-tested items with something new.

I still carry a map and compass and sometimes bring a GPS. I carry a cellphone (turned off) for emergency use and average but two calls a year from the trail. I own bladder-style packs but prefer carrying a water bottle in my conventional daypack. I'd rather stop and drink from a bottle than sip through plastic on the run.

While leaning toward Thoreau ("Beware of enterprises requiring new clothes."), I nevertheless do have my weak moments when I crave the latest gear, particularly after receiving an e-mail blast or enticing color catalog in the mail, or walking into the hiking section of an outdoor retailer during the holiday season. I particularly like purchasing hiking apparel and accessories as gifts for friends and family members.

I look forward to *Outside* magazine's annual Gear Issue. The magazine's reviews are to the point; they explain a product's technical features well, and are often quite entertaining. I browse a number of websites to view the coolest in gear and gadgets, and like to read gear reviews online, among them The Gear Junkie.

Just as getting into uniforms helps team members increase their concentration on their game, hikers who dress well for the outdoors and carry the right equipment show a certain healthy respect for the elements.

If you're going gear-shopping first, before you go out on the trail, you might get lucky and get exactly what you need, but I highly doubt it. Don't try to buy everything before you hit the trail. Ask experienced hikers what they like to wear and carry. Evaluate gear and apparel one item at a time.

The Daypack Evolves

Call me Pack-Man, a guy gobbling up miles and miles of trail, always with a daypack on my back.

All too often, my aching back.

For years and years, on hikes around the world, as soon as I reached the top of that peak or that beautiful lake, I literally tossed off my pack in relief. (Some brands were so badly designed I was tempted to throw them off the mountain or into the lake.)

Manufacturers have sent The Trailmaster an array of low-tech, ill-conceived daypacks, hardly more evolved than the rucksacks I carried during my Boy Scout days, and my response has always been the same: "Hey, hiking is not supposed to hurt."

I don't know why daypack design lagged so far behind innovations in outerwear and footwear for so long, but it did. Maybe pack-makers thought that by adding pouches, pockets, and an outdoorsy logo to a flimsy book-bag, they'd fool us into thinking we're purchasing a great daypack.

More recently, though, some excellent daypacks have come on the market and outdoor retailers often carry a wide selection. If you know what to look for in a good pack, you'll select one that will be a welcome companion, not an albatross around your neck, or on your back.

Choosing a Daypack

A daypack is a soft, frameless pack that attaches to your shoulders and usually includes a hip band or waist belt for support. A good one will last a lifetime.

High-quality daypacks are made specifically for hiking so there's no need to settle for a bike-bag, book-bag, laptop computer backpack or a pack fashioned for another sport. It's best to purchase one at a specialty outdoors store.

Padding is crucial to a comfortable daypack. Padded shoulder pads are an absolute must, and go a long way in keeping the spring in your step. A good daypack has a padded back, as well. A wide, padded lumbar belt is important, too, because you want to try and put the weight on your hips, away from your neck and shoulder muscles.

Features of a good daypack

- Durable weather-proof fabric
- One-piece body construction
- Padded shoulder straps
- Padded back
- Wide, padded lumbar belt
- Sufficient pockets and compartments to suit your needs
- Side pouch for water bottle
- Strong buckles and straps
- Storm flap-covered zippers
- Strong top grab handle

Before you purchase a pack, put a little weight inside it and walk around the store. Check to be sure it really fits your frame.

We hikers come in all shapes and size—and there are major body differences between men and women regardless of size—so be assured that there's no such thing as a one-size-fits-all daypack.

A modest-sized daypack measures about 16 inches high, 12 inches wide and about 6 inches deep. A larger daypack can be as much as 18 inches or more in length, 14 inches wide and more than 6 inches deep.

Daypack capacity is measured in cubic inches, with 1,000 to 1,500 cubic inches sufficient for most all-day adventures. If you're the designated donkey in your hiking group, or a parent toting gear for several kids, consider investing in a "weekend" daypack, one with a capacity of 2,000 to 3,000 cubic inches. (Europeans and other hikers around the world measure daypack capacity in liters. A typical daypack has between 15 and 30 liters of cargo room.)

With the Ten Essentials, extra clothing, food, water, and a camera, figure that you'll be toting 10 to 15 pounds of gear on a day hike. Sure you and the pack *can* carry more weight, but remember you're going day-hiking not backpacking. Remember that the suspension systems of most daypacks are not designed to support heavy loads, so if you put too much weight in a daypack, that load will pull on your neck and shoulders and stress your frame.

As a general rule, you can comfortably carry 10 percent of your body weight in a well-designed daypack. Consider 15 percent of your body weight or 25 pounds as an absolute maximum load, even with a superior daypack.

Some day hikers, particularly those who hike in warm weather, prefer packs with a built-in hydration system. Remember that you'll be giving up some storage capacity and have to pack around the pack's built-in bladder sleeve. Some hydration packs are all bladder and no backpack—with minimal carrying capacity for anything but fluids. Other hydration packs are a better balance between water and cargo toting capacities.

Fanny packs have their fans among day hikers. Buy a good

one with ample padding and storage. Look for rugged, covered zippers and easy access to pouches. Be sure the pack you choose comfortably carries water bottles.

Packing a Daypack

Let's not over-complicate a simple procedure. Remember just two rules about packing a daypack:

- Pack items you'll most likely use on the hike in the most accessible place.
- Pack the heaviest items at the bottom of the pack, the lightest ones toward the top.

Main compartment Put heavier items that you won't need to instantly access (extra food and water, first aid kit) in the bottom.

Sub-compartment Some clothing, lighter items and cellphone go here.

Top pocket Store, maps, guidebook, binoculars, insect repellant, sunscreen and other items here for ready access on the trail.

Side pockets Mesh ones are particularly good for holding a water bottle. Easy access for snacks and a compact camera.

Clothing: The Importance of Layering

Although meteorologists are getting better and better at predicting the weather, hikers can often be caught off guard if they rely on the weather report alone. It's critical that you wear and bring clothing that can accommodate changes in weather, and the inevitable changes in body temperature from alternating between steep ascents and periods of rest.

Outdoor pros can get pretty scientific when it comes to dressing for the trail, but it doesn't have to be terribly complicated if you understand some basic principles of layering. In some respects, layering is just like it sounds—you add layers of clothing as you cool off, and you peel them off as you cool down.

What makes the concept seem so complex, however, is the dizzying array of fabrics, weaves, and types of clothing available to hikers. From polypropylene to Thermax, Polartech 100 to Capilene and polyester, there are so many synthetic fabrics on the market now, it's enough to intimidate almost anyone from taking a hike.

When not complicating your life, these new fabrics work together to provide lightweight insulation and breathability—a combination that was unheard of twenty or thirty years ago. Historically, the price you paid for staying warm was to wear heavy, bulky clothing. And to keep dry, plastic ponchos did the trick—until you started to move, of course. Once you began to sweat, you became a walking, sweat-trapped sauna. Yuck.

The quick-drying fabric is an especially welcome feature when hiking in the rain, or when resting after a long uphill climb. Cotton is a great fabric to wear if you want to stay cool (on desert hikes, for instance), but, because it holds moisture, it is useless as an insulator. "Cotton kills," some outdoors experts warn.

On all hikes, it's best to start out a little cool and keep extra clothing layers in your pack for later. You'll start to heat up as you get moving. And, if you're taking an early morning hike, chances are that outside temperatures will heat up as the day wears on.

Clothing for Clear, Mild Days

While weather may be fickle, most of us have a pretty good idea of the seasonal changes where we live and are likely to hike. If you are hiking in mild, sunny weather, it's silly to prepare for a blizzard (though strange things do happen!). For mild hikes, it's often good to wear lightweight synthetic shorts. Some hikers swear by lightweight pants with legs that can zip off. This is a really cool feature if you want to keep yourself especially prepared.

T-shirt A synthetic T-shirt is a good first layer on top. More and more companies are making great synthetic alternatives to the traditional cotton T-shirt. A good outdoors retailer will stock several styles and colors.

Long-sleeved shirt Wear or bring along a long-sleeved shirt to wear on top. One that zips or buttons is best for temperature control—but it's really up to you.

Extra pants are also a good idea, if you aren't wearing "convertible" pants/shorts. I sometimes forget about keeping my legs covered until I reach a windy summit, and I wish I'd brought along a pair of synthetic pants to pull over my shorts.

On warm, sunny hikes, wear a **broad-brimmed hat** to keep you shaded from the sun. Light colored hats reflect the sunlight better than darker ones, and will keep you cooler. Nylon hats with mesh around the crown of the head are especially nice on a hot day. Very fair, sun-sensitive hikers might opt for the expedition-type hat with a long flap that extends over the neck, offering extra protection from the sun.

No matter where or when you're hiking, it's wise to keep a **lightweight rain jacket/windbreaker** in your pack. Likely it will come in handy when you least expect it.

Clothing for Cold and Windy Days

Layering takes on new meaning when temperatures drop. On chilly days, your first layer should fit snugly against your skin. Depending on the weather and temperature, your first layer can range from lightweight Capilene pants and top to heavy wool long underwear. The job of the first layer is to keep you warm and dry. A snug fit gives the fabric a better chance to do its job, and will likely make for a more comfortable hike.

Your second layer is your major insulator. Warm fleece pants and top work well, and an extra wool hat and sweater will keep you even warmer.

No matter what the weather, it's important to bring a hat along with you. Wool or fleece hats help keep you warm, since most body heat is lost through the head.

Rainwear

If you dress properly, a little rain shouldn't put a damper on an otherwise great hike. In many regions of the country, rain can sneak up very quickly, which is why it's so critical to keep basic rain gear with you at all times. Many manufacturers make lightweight jackets and pants that live up to the claim of being waterproof and breathable in drizzly weather. Gore-Tex is now so ubiquitous that you can find rain gear that keeps you pretty comfy and dry in anything from summer showers to chilly autumn rain.

Rain jackets No jacket is completely waterproof, but many will protect you from getting soaked for an entire day. Always keep your rain jacket in your daypack.

Rain pants not only keep your legs dry, but your feet as well. If they're cut a bit long (that's the proper fit for rain pants), they'll extend over the top of your boots; rather than trickling down your pants into your boots, the rainwater will flow toward the more waterproof sides of your boots.

Rain hats While rain hits the top of our heads first, hikers often think of keeping our heads dry last. Partly that's because we rely on the hood of rain jacket—which works pretty well most of the time. Some rain hats come with a wide brim (geeky but effective) and offer excellent protection in wet conditions. Other models (remember, we're not talking style here) are bucket-shaped or fedora-like and offer 360-degree protection. The better hats are quite waterproof, breathable, and weigh-in at only a couple of ounces. They double as sun hats, too.

Demystifying the Primary Fabrics

Unlike cotton, synthetic fabrics don't leave you soaked in sweat. Most are designed to "wick" moisture away from your skin so you stay relatively dry. While cotton is great for hot desert hikes (where a sweaty cotton T-shirt helps to keep you cool), synthetics are better for most other climates. When the wind picks up, or after you stop to rest after a long climb, you'll be thankful for your dry shirt.

Polypropylene One of the first to come out on the synthetic market, polypro (as it's referred to among folks in the outdoor biz) is cheap and a good, basic insulator. It's main drawback, however, is that it doesn't do very well at "wicking" moisture away from your skin. Without an absorbent layer over it, it has the same effect as the plastic poncho.

Properly combined with other synthetics, or even under a wool shirt or pants, polypro is pretty good at keeping you nice and toasty on the trail. Also, be forewarned. It can retain odor (usually the "been on the trail too long" kind), and you can't throw it in the dryer—it shrinks and bunches up, and is hard to pull apart.

Gore-Tex Invented by a guy with the last name Gore (not the brainy, eco-conscious former U.S. vice president), this stuff is pretty neat. And it's all over the place. Boots, jackets, pants, backpacks, hats, you name it. The reason it's so popular is that it is—at its best—breathable and waterproof. The company claims that this is due to "patented membrane technology." What this appears to mean is that Gore-Tex consists of two (or more) layers of fabric. The outer layer is impermeable, the inner layer is semi-permeable.

In theory, Gore-Tex works like a charm. I've found that I stay a little damp in my Gore-Tex jacket, nevertheless. The jacket does "breathe" reasonably well. Hiking in the pouring rain in Gore-Tex outerwear has been pleasant enough—I've stayed warm and dry. Gore-Tex sure beats a lot of the alternatives—heavy slickers, or leaky, sauna-like nylon jackets, for instance.

Wool Unless you grew up on a small, isolated tropical island, you've likely encountered this timeless fabric. It's always been a great insulator. Historically, only the heartiest of folks could tolerate wool's scratchiness right next to the skin. Wool is still mostly used in socks and sweaters, but several companies have been able to soften the material up a bit (blending it with synthetics, among other things) and now offer sensitive-skin-friendly long underwear. It's a good insulation choice if you're wary about modern fabrics.

Polyester While leisure suits never became popular on the trail, a lot of great outdoor clothing is made of polyester and polyester-blend fabrics. Polyester itself is useless, but manufacturers have found ways to chemically treat the fabric so that it wicks away moisture so that you stay nice and dry. There are dozens of brands and blends out there—CoolMax is one of the most popular variations.

Capilene This is one of the more sophisticated insulating fabrics out there, and Patagonia's own brand. It can be washed and dried (in a dryer!) a million times, holds up well, and—if reasonably cared for—doesn't get stinky. The downside is that it's a lot pricier than some of the other fabrics.

Footwear

A good pair of hiking boots can keep you on the trail for years, and a bad pair may march you right back to the store.

Before you even think about buying, be sure to be clear about how your boots will be used. What kind of terrain are you planning to encounter? Hikes in the muddy Northwest require something a little different that desert walks do, for instance.

Not only should you take weather and terrain into consideration, but it's critical that you realistically evaluate the intensity and duration of your hikes. Boots made for extended backpacking trips are more durable, but much heavier than boots intended for day hiking.

Never rely on shoe size alone to determine what you should buy. Online boot shopping is a mistake, unless you are ordering a pair that is identical to boots you already own—right down to the size, brand, and model. I'm sure it's not news to anyone to report that footwear has one of the highest customer return rates in the mail-order biz.

Boots can vary quite a bit in terms of their construction, comfort, and durability. Until about the 1980s, most hiking boots were made of leather. Now boot-makers offer leather-synthetic combos and all-synthetic models.

Don't expect hiking boots to last all that much longer than running shoes. Some lightweight boots on the feet of aggressive hikers offer only 300 or so miles of wear. The uppers often can go several hundred miles more, but soles lose their tread and can eventually start splitting from the rest of the boot. These days, stuff is meant to be worn out, and then thrown out.

Per mile, it can cost less to keep an economy car running than to walk in hiking boots. (Let's see, if a $90 pair of boots goes 300 miles, operating cost would be 30 cents per mile. Hmmm . . .)

If you are as averse to getting rid of things as I am, you can always look into resoling your boots—for the heavier varieties, not the lightweights. It's also a nice way to keep an otherwise sturdy pair around a whole lot longer.

Manufacturers can have you believing that you need a different pair of shoes for every kind of terrain you encounter. This is certainly true in some cases—warm beach walks and snowy mountain hikes each require different features to keep both you reasonably comfortable and your boots in good shape. But as a rule, hiking is hiking, and a boot either fits or it doesn't.

The other caveat, however, is to consider how likely it is that you'll be hiking in the rain and mud. A wet hike wearing "breathable" nylon mesh and split-grain leather boots will make you utterly miserable.

Boots generally are categorized as follows:

Lightweight These are made to be worn on day hikes and light overnight trips. Also included in this category are trail-running and all other low-top trail shoes. Lightweight trail shoes/boots are usually a combination of split-grain leather and nylon mesh, and have a thinner sole than heavier boots. As a result, they don't last nearly as long as the others, but are a great choice for both novice and expert day hikers because they aren't at all cumbersome and require little to no break-in time.

Midweight These are designed for backpacking trips or off-trail day hiking. They typically require some breaking in. If you have injury-prone ankles, midweight boots are also a good choice for lighter day hikes because they provide ankle support and are sturdier (but heavier) than their lightweight counterparts. The ankle support offered by mid- and high-topped boots is an especially welcome feature when traveling unstable terrain.

Heavyweight or Mountaineering These are what the big-time backpackers and mountaineers wear. Almost always made of full-grain leather, they feel like stiff cement blocks when you first put them on. Needless to say, they are very heavy, extremely durable, and take a long time to be broken in.

Breaking Them In

Experts warn not to wear boots on the trail that haven't been broken in. It's an odd piece of advice—after all, don't you need to wear them hiking in order to break them in?

The answer is, "it depends." Lots of hikers wear new, lightweight hiking boots straight out of the box and onto the trail. Low-top lightweight boots are especially trail-ready. Generally this works out fine, and if the boots are a good fit, you'll start out and stay blister-free.

The more heavy-duty your boots, the more you'll need to prep them for a hike. Thick, full-grain leather mountaineering boots, for example, need a lot of break-in time before they can comfortably carry you down the trail.

Start breaking-in your boots by taking short walks around the block. Walk up and down hilly streets. Wear them and stand on your toes several times. Wear them around the house and yard, on shopping trips.

If the Shoe Fits . . .

- You have room to wiggle your toes, but the boots won't be so loose that you feel like you're floating in them. Tightness in the toe box can eventually lead to extreme discomfort later on, especially when hiking down steep down hills.
- Your heel won't slide up and down when you walk, and stays put without feeling pinched.
- You should be wearing the type of socks that you'd wear on the trail. This helps ensure a good fit.
- You've tested several pairs already, even though the pair you choose may have been the first you tried on. It's a good idea to get a feel for fit from several different boots.
- You've walked around in each pair through the store and up and down an incline (most shoe stores that carry hiking boots have these).

Socks

The time-honored two-sock tradition is still a useful one for hikers. A thin, inner liner sock of synthetic material, such as polypropylene or Capilene is coupled with an outer layer of rag wool. This tandem reduces friction and thus the odds of developing blisters.

Ah, but time and sock technology marches on.

For many years now, I and a whole lot of other hikers have opted to one-sock it. I prefer wearing hiking-specific socks, such as those made by Thorlo, a company that weaves and markets a line of socks specifically for hikers, and even for specific kinds of hiking. I've appreciated the company's usage suggestions (i.e. "light hiking") and found these recommendations to be right on target.

A good-fitting sock should be snug, but not tight. Bring your hiking boots with you when you sock shop (and bring your hiking socks with you when you boot shop). Sock thickness can bump up your boot size a half-size or more.

Many hikers are prepared to spend the money for a good pair of boots but go into sticker shock when they see the cost of quality hiking socks. Nevertheless, don't skimp on socks. Wearing cotton gym socks with your new hiking boots is almost guaranteed to make your feet—and hike—very unhappy. SmartWool socks are well worth their price—superior to the scratchy rag wool socks of the past.

Carefully check sock sizes on the package. Don't know your hiking sock size? Not to worry, neither does anybody else. (The way sock-makers size socks is truly bizarre.) Some quality European brand socks have Euro-sizes and correlating Euro shoes sizes printed on the package in much larger print than the American sizes. If your sock size is anywhere close to falling "between sizes" try the pair on! One manufacturer's size medium might be another manufacturer's large. Other sock makers put the "M" and "W" for Men and Women in a type size so small you need a magnifying glass to see it.

Fresh feet are happy feet. On any day hike longer than half a day, consider bringing an extra pair of socks. Change socks at midday and hang your damp pair on the back of your daypack to dry.

Hiking Sandals

Okay, I admit it—I'm more comfortable wearing hiking boots than any other footwear, and that includes running shoes, dress shoes, sandals, and, worst of all for me, being barefoot.

Many of my fellow Californians, and others who live in warmer climes, would prefer to wear sandals most of the time. They almost have to be coaxed into lacing up their hiking boots, and would prefer to be barefoot almost every day.

For them, and other like-minded hikers, the introduction of hiking sandals has solved a real problem. Originally designed for river-running, these new-generation sandals designed for hiking feature shock-absorbing soles and well-designed strap systems. Several boot manufacturers have gotten into the act with sandals that offer both support and protection.

Some fresh-air fiends and hikers who just prefer the freedom offered by this approach to footwear swear by these high-tech hiking sandals, especially for beach walks or streamside hikes, rambles with many creek-crossings, or simply on very hot days. But for me, it's socks and boots on every hike.

Walking Sticks

Hikers who carry walking sticks may not look like the toughest guys on the trails, but they are doing their muscles and joints a gigantic favor. Walking sticks and hiking poles help with balance, absorb shock, and provide much-welcomed leverage for steep ascents.

While I don't consider a staff or pole an absolute hiking "essential," I'm convinced that its utility is highly underrated.

Several terms identify products that serve (essentially) the same function: walking stick, hiking stick, walking staff, hiking pole, trekking pole. In my discussion, I'll used the terms interchangeably; the differences between the terms are highly debatable, if they even exist at all.

Walking sticks help a great deal with balance. Having a third, or even fourth "leg" to lean on can increase your confidence on the trail tremendously. And this added balance is especially critical when you're hiking over uneven terrain, on winding, narrow trails, and when crossing streams and rivers.

Walking sticks also redistribute weight from your lower body to your arms and shoulders, easing up the strain on your knees, hips, ankles and lower back. They are a blessing for those prone to aching joints. Walking sticks help improve posture, too, which makes breathing much less labored, especially when climbing steep terrain. And better breathing increases endurance.

Hiking sticks help you

- Ease your knees on steep descents
- As a "third leg" for balance while traversing uneven terrain
- Cross fast-flowing streams
- Scare away menacing dogs
- Support an impromptu rain shelter
- Clear spider webs overhanging trails
- Probe areas where snakes are suspected

Some hikers enjoy collecting the metal medallions made to affix to a wooden hiking stick. Hint: if you do a lot of hiking, fasten those medallions you purchased at park visitor centers from around the country on a second hiking stick—creating an *objet d'art* that you can proudly display at home.

My own children felt they had truly arrived as full-fledged hikers when I purchased each of them a hiking stick. Nimble and very-well balanced without a stick, they nevertheless like carrying a stick and poking at things along the trail.

Depending on your physical and aesthetic preferences, there are (like so many hiking gadgets!) a wide variety of poles, staffs, and sticks out there.

Wooden staffs are the true classic in this arena. Not only are they functional on the trail, but they've held a prominent place in human history—as primitive weapons and as travel aids. Greek gods were often depicted with large wooden staffs. Shepherds wouldn't be shepherds without their telltale staffs, and Egyptian hieroglyphs include countless images of travelers with walking sticks in hand. And what about the story of Moses parting the Red Sea? Or the one about drawing water from a stone?

It's unlikely that you'll be able to use your staff to get water from a rock, but it will help to negotiate steep descents and winding trails.

Walking sticks can be made from many different kinds of wood—willow, maple, dogwood, hawthorn, hickory, oak, you name it. Hardwood sticks have greater lasting power than their softwood counterparts, which have a tendency to splinter and fall apart, especially at the bottom where the stick comes into contact with the ground.

You can make a walking stick yourself (if you have the carving skills), or buy them (probably the better bet for most of us). They are sometimes difficult to find in outdoor retail stores, but several places online offer—and even specialize in—walking sticks.

The downside to buying walking sticks online is that you can't test them out to see how they feel or be sure of the fit.

All the benefits of a great stick are lost when hiking with one that is either too long, or too short. The perfect walking stick should be about 6 inches higher than your elbow. Any shorter, and you'll find yourself hunching over; any longer, and you'll find it awkward to climb even small hills.

The benefits of choosing wooden over aluminum hiking sticks are largely aesthetic. Some people simply prefer the rustic charm of a hand carved wooden walking stick to a straight-as-an arrow mass-produced metal one. Cost is another factor to consider when comparing the two: sticks start at less than half the price of metal poles, and require fewer parts and accessories.

More and more people are turning to aluminum or titanium "trekking poles" for support on the trail, and understandably so.

Trekking poles are lightweight (compared with their wooden counterparts), sturdy, and (best of all) adjustable.

Most trekking poles are made from aluminum or a titanium alloy, so they are extremely lightweight. Many of the newer poles weigh as little as 9 or 10 ounces apiece, and are usually sold in pairs.

One of the neatest things about poles is that they're collapsible. Usually two or three sections make up the pole shaft. These sections telescope neatly into one another, and make storage and travel a breeze. Three-section poles are the easiest to carry or store, but are more prone to breaking than two-section poles, which have fewer parts and longer pole sections. For hikers boarding a plane, clearly a collapsible pole is the only choice.

Virtually all poles have handles, which protect you from the cold metal of the pole shaft, and keep your hand from slipping on warm days. The most common handle materials are rubber and cork, and there are benefits to each. Cork can absorb moisture more easily than rubber, but rubber will prove far more durable in the long run.

The most important factor to keep in mind when evaluating walking sticks or hiking poles is comfort. And the only person who can determine what feels good to you is, well, you. Like other products mentioned in this book, it's extremely important that you test them out for yourself.

Beginning The Way

9
All About Trails

"The laying of a trail . . . becomes not only a pleasure in itself, but an inducement to plan a better way of life, to contact worthwhile things, or to weave a better product in the loom of our being."
—Earle Amos Brooks, *A Handbook for the Outdoors*

LET US now acknowledge trail-builders, of this generation, generations past and generations to come. Not all hikers appreciate the trail at their feet—but to my way of thinking, they should. Trails are a thing of beauty and a joy to behold, especially considering the time, effort, expense and, increasingly, the mastery of bureaucracy required to build one these days.

The trail-builder's art—and it is an art as well as a science—is vastly under-appreciated, even by seasoned hikers. Who blazed the first trails? Who builds trails today? How are they built?

Trail-builders themselves, most volunteer, some professional, are very special, dedicated people. I've watched trail-builder Ron Webster practice his craft all over the mountains of Southern California for decades, and come to admire what he does, and the kind of dedication required, and the kind of person he is for making trail work a major part of his life's work. Webster brings solid contractual and people skills to the job, including the ability to do cost-breakdowns and construction estimates for trails, and to manage crews from a diversity of backgrounds. He's good at working with trail crews composed of at-risk youth, at teaching young men and women to be part of a team, to take pride in their work and to master many other social skills that will benefit them in their work and personal lives.

I particularly admire how the master trail-builder designs the route for a trail. After spending many, many hours on the slopes to be crossed by a new trail, he goes into what he calls "alignment," in which he envisions the trail upon the mountain. It's a combination of a Zen state and a construction blueprint.

Some modern-day trail-builders have a philosophic approach as they plan and construct the way. "A trail route is not a route from here to there. It is a place to reconnect," states Robert Searns, founding owner of Urban Edges, Inc., a planning and development firm based in Denver, Colorado.

"In building trails, we need to think about the trail experience," Searns explains. "What does the trail look like? What does it smell like, taste and sound like? Does the experience challenge the mind? Does it touch a chord that resonates the soul? A good trail will do that."

I love a hand-built trail, one that goes easy on the land, one that seems almost as much a part of the geography as a streambed. A good trail is like a good guide, subtly pointing things out and picking the very best route from place to place.

"Of trail-making there are three stages: there is the dreaming of the trail, there is prospecting the trail, there is making the trail," explained trail-builder Nathaniel Goodrich to the New England Trails Council in 1917. "Of the first, one can say nothing—dreams are fragile, intangible. Prospecting the trail—there lies perhaps the greatest joys of trail work. Making trails is more plodding work; yet it has reliefs and pleasures of its own."

The idea of a grizzled old ranger with pick and shovel and mule, heading into the wilderness to scratch out a new trail, is romantic and colorful, but not how trails are made these days. Sophisticated trails advocates press their case in the strange speech of the land-use planner, a jargon sprinkled with terms like viewsheds, visitor-use days, greenbelts, and easements.

To assist trails-ignorant urban planners, enthusiasts sometimes refer to main trails as "freeways" and narrower connector trails as "on-ramps." The modern trail-blazer cuts deals with local politicians and isn't afraid to go eyeball-to-eyeball with developers to demand paths.

A good trail is enduring, on the ground and in our hearts. As trail expert Robert Searns puts it: "In a world of constant change and flux, where being in the moment seems increasingly harder to attain, there is something about the notion of traveling along a pathway—under our own power—that reconnects us, and indeed binds together all humanity."

Early Trails

The first trail-makers were wild animals, breaking down brush as they journeyed to and from water. Prospectors used bear trails to get over the mountains, and many of today's best trails are superimposed over miner trails, picked out by old bruin long ago.

Native Americans used game trails and fashioned new ones for trade and travel. Such trails rarely climbed via switchbacks; instead, they took the steepest and direct route. In what would become the Southwest part of the United States, the Spanish blazed few new trails, contenting themselves with Indian pathways.

American pioneers were tireless trail-makers. They hurried into the mountains to dig for metals, graze cattle, and chop trees. They needed trails and they needed them right away. Trees were felled and brush cleared. Gunpowder was rammed in holes drilled into rock and the most immovable granite was blown to smithereens.

The period between 1890 and 1930 was such a wonderful time to hit the trail that historians in some parts of the country refer to it as "The Great Hiking Era." Trail camps, fishing camps, and resorts were established and soon the mountainous regions were crisscrossed with trails.

An astonishing number of miles of local trails were built by the young men enrolled in the Civilian Conservation Corps between 1933 and 1942. The Corps completed trail and conservation work that would be valued today at many hundreds of millions, if not billions, of dollars.

Trails Today

"If there's one essential ingredient to creating trails and trail systems, it's people. All the land and financing in the world won't blaze a trail if there aren't people championing the project."
—Bay Area Ridge Trail Council, *In Support of Trails: A Guide to Successful Trail Advocacy*

Trails, to the modern trail-builder/planner, are no longer solely the lonely wilderness path of the mountain man. Nature trails, urban promenades, suburban greenways and historical paths are a few of the more popular trail projects. Some trails groups are busy converting abandoned rail lines to trails while others are working to provide trails for the physically challenged.

Trails are not an end in themselves, trails advocates emphasize. They must be viewed within the broader context of the environment through which they pass, whether that environment is a remote wilderness or an urban gateway. And any cost of the path must be measured against what is lost by losing the trail *and* the land.

Often it's not just the path that's endangered, but the whole damn place. In addition to providing an obvious recreational value, a trail is often an indicator of environmental conditions. When people hike a streamside, oceanside, or mountainside trail, they likely form a constituency that cares about the past, present, and future of the land this trail crosses. Conversely, when people can no longer walk a trail, it's likely some land misuse or abuse has occurred or will soon follow.

Trails are a precious resource, and we shouldn't shy away from the cost of building and maintaining them. They're a way for people to get out of the traffic and into our green spaces and wilderness. Most important of all, trails help keep a little green on the map.

The Art and Science of Trail-building

The science of trail-building is better known than the art. Trail construction and re-construction projects are accomplished by professional trail-builders under contract with government agencies, and also by equally talented and efficient volunteer trail-builders.

The ranks of volunteer trail-builders seem swollen by engineers and those from the building trades—people who like to build things. In Pasadena, California, employees of JPL (Jet Propulsion Laboratory) are avid hikers and turn out to help the trail system in the mountains next to their workplace—the San Gabriel Mountains. Yes, even rocket scientists like to help out here on earth.

Certainly there is a science to trail-building. I've read the contractor's specifications for building new trails and was surprised at how exact they are—spelling out the regulation tread width, grade, and much more. Governmental agencies often conduct exhaustive environmental studies before allowing a shovel to hit the ground.

There is an art to trail-building, too. A well-designed trail is a kind of living sculpture. Some modern trail-designers practice *feng shui,* the Chinese art of arranging elements (indoors or outdoors) in order to create flow and harmony.

True, few trails were designed with *feng shui,* but many of the best trails have it—a harmony with the landscape, its features and attractions, a pleasing arrangement of color and texture, form and lines.

A hand-built trail goes easy on the land. Even if it's just been completed, a hand-built trail has a way of looking like it's always been there.

A good trail designer has the eye of a landscape painter—or at least a landscape architect. Landscape, at least the way a trail designer uses the word, means the sum total of an area's characteristics, particularly those that distinguish it from another area. A landscape's distinguishing patterns include its natural features—geography and flora—and may include its cultural features and structures as well. These landscape features combine with such basic elements as color, texture, form and line to create an area's landscape character, which distinguishes it from its immediate surroundings.

Hikers are a visually oriented bunch. What you see on a trail is what you get, and what you get from the hiking experience is often determined by what you see. And exactly what a hiker sees on a trail is often created by the trail designer.

One element of view is called sight lines—the forward view and rear view seen by a hiker on a given part of the trail. A good trail has good sight lines—that is to say, the path, real or imagined, that a hiker's eye follows when perceiving changes and contrasts in color, texture and form. A landscape itself has lines in it in the form of ridgetops, city skyline, the border between floral communities or between the natural and built worlds.

How the trail designer shapes the trail can shape a hiker's experience. For example, a trail designed to contour around a slope and one designed to switchback up and down it will give the hiker two different hiking experiences.

Workin' on the Trail

Most hikers take trails for granted. They figure some governmental agency is in charge of keeping pathways maintained. But in most cases, it's not park employees but trail-users themselves who have "adopted" trails and the responsibility for their upkeep.

A trail (as well as those who hike it) benefits enormously if an organization, sometimes known in the hiking community as "Friends of the Trail," assumes stewardship for a path. Some Friends are informal hiking clubs while others are private non-profit organizations. Such groups advocate for a trail during the political process or when it's in the grasp of a government bureaucracy and also gather work parties to construct or maintain a trail. Sometimes a Friends of the Trail group will have full responsibility for a trail, while in other instances Friends supplement or support the trail's management by a public agency.

Trails need repair for two chief reasons: brush and erosion. In many regions of the country, brush or various forest "understory" plants grow quickly and can crowd the sides of a trail until the way becomes first narrow, then impassable.

Two of the worst hazards for both trail-users and trail-workers are poison ivy and poison oak. These three-leafed menaces can quickly close down a trail, at least to those bipeds allergic to them.

Erosion is another enemy of trails and affects what is called the "tread"—that part of the path trod by hiking boots. Under compaction by boots, hooves, and mountain-bike tires, the tread becomes so hard that it can't absorb surface water and erosion begins. Water travels about 15 times farther and faster on a compacted trail than natural soil; the resulting rivulets tear the trail and wash away the surface. Erosion then is what causes a trail to become rocky, dusty and scarred by deep gullies.

The trail-builder fights erosion by building water bars that drain trails and keep water from puddling up or running down the trail.

Logs, rock piles, and railroad ties are used to prop up the trail. A good trail has good drainage. Often trails are built with lots of switchbacks in order to fight erosion.

Trail work is hard work. Volunteers work on the trail tread with pick and shovel, cut back brush with pruning shears. Workers construct and clean waterbars, paint trail markers, build bridges and rock walls.

The trail-builder's tools of the trade include the pick, pry bar, axe, mattock, shears, and shovel. Other tools are the weed cutter (weed whip, swizzle stick, slingblade) and the come-along, a strong cable fitted with a ratchet used to gain mechanical advantage for moving heavy objects over the ground. It's often used in trail work to move large rocks.

The McLeod looks like an over-sized hoe with tines on the opposite blade; it's used to smooth the tread on the trail. The cyclometer (measuring wheel) and clinometer, a hand-held instrument used for measuring percent of trail grade, are important measuring tools.

The Pulaski combines an axe bit with a hoe and is a very popular tool among trail-builders. During the early 1900s, U.S.

Forest Service Ranger Edward Pulaski of Idaho needed a good tool for clearing ground and chopping brush to build fire lines, so he welded the blade of a pick to the back of an axe head and created what has come to be known as the "Pulaski."

Some workers like the social aspect of trail-building: volunteers come from all walks of life and are usually a friendly, conservation-minded bunch.

Above all, the volunteer trail-builder learns about the environment and how to respect it. The hiker who works half a day with a hoe repairing an erosion-damaged path will never shortcut a switchback or an S-curve again.

As an investment in the future of our forests and parklands, and as a commitment to ensuring that the next generation has the opportunity to hike to the same places that you now enjoy, volunteer a little time to help build or maintain a trail.

Trail Days

By some hikers' reckoning, Trail Days, at least how we think of them now, began in California's Santa Cruz Mountains. Skyline to the Sea Trail, a gem of a 35-mile footpath that travels across redwood-forested slopes and through fern-filled canyons to the great blue Pacific, needed some maintenance and, as it turned out, this gem of a trail had many friends.

During one weekend in 1969, dedicated members of the Sempervirens Fund and the Santa Cruz Trails Association turned out more than 2,000 volunteers to dig, clear, prune, and otherwise improve the path. Area volunteers put together an annual Trails Day that became a model for trails organization through the state and planted the seed for a National Trails Day.

The American Hiking Society sponsors and promotes National Trails Day, an annual celebration held in June with some 3,000 events across the U.S. to encourage hikers and newcomers to appreciate, preserve and maintain their local trails.

Kinds of Trails

access trail: Any trail that connects the main trail to a town, road, or another trail system.

backcountry trail: A primitive trail (can be open to motorized or nonmotorized users) in an area where there are no maintained roads or permanent buildings.

connecting or side trail: Provides additional points of access to major trails.

destination trail: A trail that connects two distinct points (a trailhead and a point of interest) the destination.

directional use trail: A path designed in such a way as to encourage hikers to travel in one direction.

feeder trail: Designed to connect local facilities, neighborhoods, campgrounds, etc. to a main trail.

extended trail: Trails over 100 miles in length (as defined in the National Trails System Act).

hiker-biker trail: An urban paved trail designed for use by pedestrians and bicyclists.

hiking trail: Moderate to long-distance trail with the primary function of providing long-distance walking of a mile or more (often much more).

interpretive trail (nature trail): Short to moderate length trail (usually ¼ mile to 1½ miles long) with the primary function of providing an opportunity to walk and study plants or natural features at user's pleasure. Interpretive signs or numbers corresponding to descriptions in a pamphlet often provide information about features found en route.

fire road: Unimproved dirt road that allows fire fighting and ranger vehicles access to the backcountry.

frontcountry trail: Less emphasis is put on minimizing contact with signs of the civilized world. The main objective is to provide enjoyable trail experiences within the vicinity of developed areas.

long distance trail: In general a trail best characterized by length (more than 50 miles), linearity (follows a

	linear feature), and diversity (geographic and political).
loop trail:	Trail designed so that the route is a closed circuit connecting a number of points of interest, giving hikers the option of not traveling the same section of trail more than once on a trip.
multiple-use (multi-use) trail:	A trail that permits more than one user group at a time (equestrian, hiker, mountain bicyclist, etc.).
out-and-back trail:	A one-way trail on which you travel to a destination then backtrack to the trailhead.
rail-trail:	A multi-purpose public path (paved or natural) created along an inactive rail corridor.
recreation trail:	A trail that is designed to provide a recreational experience.
side trail:	A dead-end trails that leads to features near the main trail.
single-track trail:	A trail only wide enough for one user to travel. Requires one user to yield the trail to allow another user to pass.
single-use trail:	One that is designed and constructed for only one intended use (i.e. hiking only).
spur trail:	A trail that leads from primary, secondary, or main trails to points of interest such viewpoints and campsites.
trail:	Route on land with protected status and public access for recreation or transportation, such as walking, jogging, hiking, bicycling, horseback riding, mountain biking, and backpacking.
way trail (social trail):	Unplanned/unauthorized trail that develops informally from use and not designated or maintained by a governmental agency. A good way trail might lead to a pleasant off-the-main trail surprise; a bad way trail is one made by hikers who cut switchbacks.

Trail Sign Language

A trail sign is a board or a post of wood, metal, or some kind of synthetic material that displays written, pictorial, or symbolic information about the trail and/or the surrounding area.

A good trail sign boosts a hiker's safety and peace of mind. An unclear or misleading sign can stress, mislead, even endanger a hiker. A bad sign is worse than no sign at all.

To most hikers, a sign is a sign is a sign, but others in the field—trail-builders, park designers, pathway policy wonks—distinguish among five different kinds of signs, each having a distinct purpose.

Directional signs help the hiker navigate from Point A to Point B. They provide the names of points-of-interest or destinations, as well as the mileage to those destinations. The way mileage is expressed varies by park agency and geography. Older signs tend to express mileage in fractions (Deer Meadow 2¼) while newer ones use decimals and tenths (Deer Meadow 2.2). When fractions are used, quarter-mile increments are usually the smallest trail measurement, though occasionally eighths and even tenths are used. When trail distances are expressed with decimals, the smallest measure is usually 0.1 (one-tenth of a mile), though a few signs use one-hundredth of a mile increment (Deer Meadow 2.25).

Cautionary signs warn of potential trail hazards such as poison ivy, bears or errant golf balls.

Regulatory signs are the do-this and don't-do-that placards that encourage certain behaviors (Obtain Wilderness Permit) and discourage others (No Bicycle Riding).

Interpretive signs explain a natural or historical site (World's Tallest Lodgepole Pine, Three-Fingered Jack's Cabin) along the trail or near it.

Objective signs give information about trail conditions (Trail not Maintained) including the type of trail surface or warn about obstacles (Bridge Out, 1.5 miles).

Cosmic signs are definitely not yet acknowledged by park officials and sign-makers, but I'd like to see them added. If, for example, lightning strikes a tree in front of you, that's the universe telling you to get off the mountain. Cosmic Signs can also arise from cosmic thoughts and be put on signs, just like mileage markers. God, Mother Nature, great authors, and poets often provide inspiration for cosmic signs. My friend Glen Owens, a dedicated steward of the land, occasionally puts up a sign (i.e. *Take care of the land: Someday you'll be part of it*) deep in the Angeles National Forest that makes hikers stop and think beyond themselves and their everyday concerns.

Marking the Trail

Modern trail way-marking divides into at least two camps with plenty of hikers in the middle. Safety-first trail-markers believe in lots of signs. Their mission is to keep hikers on the trail so the more markers the better. Trail-marking minimalists insist too many markers detract from the hiking experience. Sign only a few crucial junctions and call it a day, they say. Some of the most radical wilderness travelers advocate for the removal of all signs, for knocking down all cairns, and for letting each hiker find his or her own way.

Blazes Thankfully, and increasingly, rare, a blaze is cut (usually by an axe—ouch!) into a tree to indicate the trail route. Blazes are cut on both sides of the tree trunk so the hiker can see them coming and going. Woodsmen of earlier eras used blazes (most likely to be spotted these days along old trails) to mark paths in the eastern U.S. and Canada.

Cairns, ducks, monuments Stacking rocks along a treeless, rock-covered route guides hikers over terrain when a trail is not visible and placing a sign impossible. Often cairns are used above tree-line on high slopes and mountain passes. Duck-placing is an art. A strategically placed cairn must be seen by both ascending and descending hikers. Too many ducks in a row makes hiking look like child's play and takes all the challenge out of route-finding, while too few can lead hikers astray.

Paint, Ugh! Paint on rocks and trees waymarks the trail in some U.S. and European parks and forests. Hues are often color coordinated to particular trails. Instead of following the yellow brick road, you follow the orange paint blazes. Blazes can be squares, circles, triangles or a simple brush stroke.

Discs Modern markers of metal or plastic are affixed to trees, sometimes to rocks. Used sparingly, they're not too intrusive and keep hikers on the trail at confusing junctions and show where to cross a stream and where to rejoin the trail on the other side.

Trail Right of Way

You've probably seen those triangular yield signs posted at the trailhead for a multi-use trail. Arrows go around the triangle from symbols of a hiker to a horse to a bicycle.

It's a common symbolic presentation of trail right-of-way-rules: Hikers yield to equestrians, bicyclists yield to both equestrians and hikers.

The same rules apply when different users encounter each other going uphill or down. When two trail users from the same group—two hikers, for example—the uphill traveler yields to the downhill one. (Most uphill hikers are happy to pause to let descending hikers pass—if only for the opportunity to catch their breath.)

On Mountain Bikes

I'm often asked to weigh-in on the hikers-versus-mountain-bikers issue. I wish it wasn't a one camp versus another situation. But all too often it is. And I wish it wasn't such a hot button emotional issue. But it is.

It's even a hot button issue for me when I recall the half-dozen times my companions and I have had brushes (literally) with careening mountain bikers. I try to remember that the great majority of mountain bicyclists aren't speed-crazy morons hell-bent on tearing up the terrain.

How big a deal is mountain bike use of the trail anyway?

It certainly varies greatly from park to park, mountain to mountain, path to path. On a wide, flat dirt road, no big deal. On a steep, narrow path—a very big deal.

The happiest trails for me—and judging by the amount of correspondence I've received about this issue—for most hikers, are those free of mountain bikes. I totally support the creation of more trails for everyone—for hikers, horseback riders, for cyclists, for walkers, for the disabled. But favoring trails for everyone doesn't mean I support everyone using the same trail.

Have I had happy hiking on multi-user paths? Of course. Many, many miles of it. Have I ever gone mountain biking? Yep. Our family of four owns four of them, and we go cycling on dirt roads and bike paths. Mountain biking is a great recreational activity, a fine family outing.

Some trails can accommodate hikers and cyclists—or even hikers, mountain bicyclists, and equestrians. Provided that these multi-user trails are designed for, and can handle different users, they have my full support. But multi-user trails are not hiking trails because the recreational experience offered by these trails is different from—and usually incompatible with—that of a hiking trail.

A hiker's pace, far slower than that of mountain bicyclist, is in tune with the rhythms of nature. Hiking is a silent, low-impact entry into the natural world—one free of machinery, including mountain bikes. Pathways designed for foot travel should be for foot travel only.

I support the American Hiking Society's philosophy, policies, and positions in regard to mountain bikes.

- Hiking trails, or foot-only trails, are pathways developed and managed for quiet, slow travel and the enjoyment of nature away from mechanical conveyances, including bicycles.
- Trails should be managed for the primary purposes for which they are designated.
- No mountain biking in designated wilderness areas and areas under consideration for wilderness designation.
- Current National Park Service policy restricting off-road bicycle travel in national parks should continue.

Accessibility

A few years ago, when I was signing my newest hiking book at a book festival, a young man in a wheelchair quietly waited his turn. Shyly he said, "I used to love to hike, but since my accident I can't get out on the trail. Do you have any suggestions about wheelchair accessible trails?"

It was one of the few times I've felt uninformed and unable to help someone interested in hiking.

"Well, I saw a guy with a wheelchair on a trail in one park—let me remember where that was," I began. "I know there are some accessible trails, but I'm not sure where."

I'll never forget the look of disappointment on his face.

"You might try some nature trails," I added lamely.

I ended up picking a half-dozen or so trails out of one of my guidebooks that I figured that a fit individual in a sports wheelchair could negotiate. Still, this man was a true hiker and needed some trail advice I couldn't provide very well.

Since then, I've learned about a modest—and growing—number of trail offerings to differently enabled hikers. Some 53 million Americans have disabilities, so an acute need exists for accessible trails. Such trails are crucial to ensure quality recreational opportunities for these many individuals.

Many local, state, and national parks—including such crown jewels as Grand Canyon, Rocky Mountain, Yellowstone, and Yosemite—have accessible trails. The free Golden Access Passport is available to permanently disabled individuals and their families.

Thanks to technological advances and good old ingenuity, beach wheelchairs have recently been introduced, allowing disabled individuals access to beaches, coastal paths, and shorelines. They have been extremely popular wherever they've been put into use.

The U.S. Access Board is the federal agency that established guidelines and standards for accessible environments. Guidelines include provisions for the types of surfaces required for accessible trails, an unobstructed width of at least 36 inches and many more specifications.

Many state and private nonprofit groups push for improved outdoor recreation opportunities. Recreational Outdoor Accessibility for the Disabled (ROAD) mainstreams people with disabilities into Sierra Club activities, teaches outdoors skills to people with disabilities, tests accessibility of trails, and recommends improvements. It also teaches club members how to assists people with disabilities on outings and educates the general public.

Along with pushing for more and better accessible pathways, we should all—challenged by a disability or not—work to ensure that everyone gets a chance to hit the trail and enjoy the pleasures of the great outdoors.

10

Choosing a Trail

"Find a path or make one."
—Seneca

"To have his path made clear for him is the aspiration of every human being in our beclouded and tempestuous existence."
—Joseph Conrad

AS SELF-APPOINTED president and sole member of the Brotherhood of Trail-guide Writers, with a lifetime of experience and more than a dozen guidebooks to my credit, I hereby order you to buy a shelf-full of guides. And you need to understand that the price of a pound of trail mix has risen faster than the cost of a gallon of gas, and that our publishers never pay our royalties on time, so my fellow hiking scribes and I need you to stock up on guidebooks. Buy a guidebook for every trail you plan to hike.

Nah, I'm just pulling your leg. Consulting a guidebook (and I'll explain how to choose and use a good one) and searching online are two ways to choose a trail to take.

The web is great for gathering information about trails, but don't stop with a download. I've discovered several lost souls on the trail scratching their heads at poor maps and Chamber of Commerce descriptions downloaded from a web site that inadequately detailed a particular hike.

After your web research, follow up with a call to park authorities or to hiking organizations to get the true story behind a trail. Often the enthusiastic employees at an outdoor retail store will have some great tips about local trails.

Choosing a Great Hike

What's a great trail? It's a question as difficult to answer, as unanswerable perhaps, as "What is great art?" or "What is great music?" Objectivity in these matters is impossible, statistical analysis inappropriate, a rating system downright ridiculous.

Insight into what comprises a great trail comes from my range of field experience. I've hiked considerably more than a thousand trails in America, plus many pathways abroad, from the perspective of both a "hiking writer" and "writing hiker." Most of these trails had one or more distinctly pleasurable sights and, at the very least, offered some good exercise.

I've also discussed the notion of a great trail at some length with dozens of trail-builders, fitness consultants, park service professionals, and experienced hikers. No two experts agreed what defined a great trail, of course, but some common themes emerged.

Elements contributing to a great hike are:

- Unusual landforms
- Forests, ancient or at least mature.
- Wildflowers, intriguing flora
- Splendid views
- Lakes, rivers, ocean shores
- Tranquility and solitude
- Wildlife watching
- Cultural or historical interest

To help pick the best trails in a region, I rely heavily on the advice of National Park Service rangers, Forest Service naturalists, Sierra Club outings group leaders, nature center directors, professional tour leaders, and many local hikers. Nevertheless, I always make it clear that the final selection of the hikes included in my guidebooks is mine and the many outdoors consultants who aided me should be thanked for their invaluable expertise and be held blameless for my admittedly subjective decision-making process.

Choose Your Hiking Experience

Quite apart from not-very-scientific criteria of trails, what makes a great hike often depends on what a hiker brings on the hike. No, I'm not referring to a hiker's daypack packed with trail mix and water bottle, but rather to the point-of-view a hiker brings to the great outdoors. Some hikers are looking for romance, some for trout, some for leg-stretchers to break up a vacation drive, some for a week-long hike that's a vacation from driving.

A great hike for a family might be one in which baby can come along, perched happily in a backpack; or one that tires out a four-year old so he'll nap in the car during the two-hour drive back to the motel; or a stirring sojourn that puts a smile on the face of even the most sullen teenager.

Choosing what kind of experience you wish to have on the trail—is just as important as selecting a trail to hike. Ask yourself these questions:

- What kind of social experience am I looking for—solitude, first date, male-bonding, girlfriend gabbing, grandparent-grandchild nurturing, romance?
- Is watching wildlife a goal? Want to photograph a moose, or identify a dozen species of water birds?
- What's my interest level in flora and flowering plants?
- How out there do I want to get? How remote a trail do you want to hike?
- How far, how long do I want to travel to the trailhead?
- What ancillary activities do I enjoy on the trail—swimming, fishing, photography, rock scrambling?

Selecting a Guidebook

Guidebook publishers have left almost no trail uncharted in North America, Europe, and in many other parts of the world. Trails are bundled into books in increments of 30, 50, 60, 75, 100, and 150 hikes and into categories such as Best Hikes, Short

Hikes, and Best Short Hikes—not to mention Best Hikes with Children and Best Hikes with Dogs.

When selecting a guidebook, check to see if it highlights the best hikes in a region or tries to detail all of them. I use the term "guidebook" in the broad sense of the word to include standard paperback trail guides, as well as trail accounts available online, downloadable for free or for a fee.

When I write where-to-hike guidebooks, my goal is to increase the odds for my readers to have a great day in the great outdoors, so I leave out many walkable but not-so-wonderful trails. As you might imagine, a "professional" hiker like myself encounters a lot of turkey trails; that is to say, paths that start nowhere and go nowhere, trails battered by nature or neglected by park officials to the point where I decided that they are too unsafe for my readers to use.

Even if the guidebook author is an enthusiastic field-tester and updates frequently with the help of park authorities, perfection is not possible. Trails change over time. Like every hiker, I hate seeing a good trail go bad, but regrettably it happens. The ravages of fire and flood, rampant real estate development, and bureaucratic neglect can ruin a favorite path.

While you're out hiking, if you happen across a neglected, hazardous, or overgrown trail, please report it to the relevant ranger or administrator. Only if you make your concerns known will conditions improve. It's up to all of us to preserve our trails—and the precious wild lands they help us explore.

Of course in selecting a guidebook it helps first to decide where you want to hike. A palm oasis? An alpine meadow? A deserted beach? Consult an area map. Once you've narrowed down a locale that you want to explore on foot, look through the guidebook to see if it has interesting hiking trails in your geographical area of interest, then turn to the corresponding hike description in the main body of the book.

If the guidebook tells you what you want to know about where you want to hike, buy it.

Getting the Most from a Trail Guidebook

Every hike in a guidebook has a soul and a goal. You provide the soul; the guide will provide the goals. Let's face it, we're a goal-oriented society and we hikers are no exception. We hike for majestic views or for the best fishing spot, not just to be out there. Some day hikers collect peaks or make it a point to hike every trail in a park or mountain range.

Most guidebooks list **mileage**, expressed in roundtrip figures, at the top of the page beneath the hike name or trail name. Hikes in most day-hiking guides range from 1 to 20 miles, with the majority in the 3- to 10-mile range. Gain or loss in elevation usually follows the mileage. In matching a hike to your ability, you'll want to consider both mileage and elevation as well as condition of the trail, terrain, and season. Hot, exposed slopes or miles of boulder-hopping can make a short hike seem long.

You may wish to use the following guideline: A hike suitable for beginners and children would be less than 5 miles with an elevation gain of less than 700 to 800 feet. A moderate hike is considered a hike in the 5- to 10-mile range, with under a 2,000-foot elevation gain. You should be reasonably fit for these. Preteens sometimes find the going difficult. Hikes over 10 miles, and those with more than a 2,000-foot gain are for experienced hikers in top form.

Season is the next item to consider. Guidebooks often offer seasonal recommendations or suggestions by the month: "Best from May through October." Seasonal recommendations are based partly on hiker safety, comfort, and perhaps even for legal restrictions, such as wildfire season closure or access restrictions because of endangered birds nesting near the trail.

After the just-the-facts introduction, the best guidebooks offer an **introduction** to each hike that describes what you'll see along the trail: plants, animals, panoramic views. You'll also learn about the geologic and human history of the region.

Directions to trailhead take you from the nearest major highway to trailhead parking. For trails having two desirable trailheads, directions to each should be given. A few trails can be hiked one way, with the possibility of a car shuttle. Suggested car shuttle points should be noted.

After the directions to the trailhead, you'll read a description of **the hike**. Important junctions and major sights are usually pointed out, along with options allowing you the choice to climb higher or farther or take a different route back to the trailhead.

Maps in hiking guides vary greatly in quality, level of detail, and accuracy. My preference is for simple maps that show the recommended hike along with various side trails and optional routes. A bonus is a map that includes the roads closest to the trailhead, to help the hiker find the beginning of the hike.

Guidebook **narratives** also vary greatly in quality, level of detail and accuracy. The best guidebooks have that basic accuracy and also provide nature notes, colorful local histories, and evoke the spirit of a particular trail. If you're an avid reader or one who admires a well-crafted description you'll appreciate the difference in prose style between a writer who hikes and a hiker who writes.

The Paths Less Taken

Oh, those demanding editors. As the *Los Angeles Times* hiking columnist, I wrote about my favorite subject every week for 18 years. A typical column detailed a hike, the majority of the time in California, as well as enticing destinations in other states and even in other countries.

Was that enough?

Nooooooo.

This was a newspaper, my editors reminded me. Give us something new. What's new about hiking?

With these directives, I began searching out special-interest trails and experiences that might be new to my readers. Some readers responded by saying they were perfectly happy hiking the same kind of trail in the same way time after time—just tell us what so great about this hike and give us directions to the trailhead. Other readers were pleased to hear about something new.

I always got plenty of reader feedback about my stories detailing new twists on the hiking experience so it wasn't hard to determine what worked and what didn't. Stories about snowshoeing ("that's not hiking") and multi-sport adventures ("If I want to hike, I'll hike, if I want to bike, I'll bike; it's ridiculous to try to do both.") turned out to be two ways to go that did not resonate with my readers. Other kinds of hiking adventures proved considerably more popular and I share them in this chapter.

Trails are where you find them. Most of us look for trails in all the right places—national parks and renowned hiking locales, plus the rest of what our hometowns and home mountains have to offer.

More hiking opportunities are available beyond the obvious. With a little sleuthing, the sojourner afoot can locate some out-of-the-way trails to hike. Here are some ways to discover new trails.

Join a trailwork party I don't know why they call them parties—at least during the day when you're working on a trail. At night around the campfire, it might be a different story. The Sierra Club and other conservation organizations sponsor low-cost and no-cost weekend and week-long activities.

For example, you might join a backpack into the Rocky Mountains, work on a remote length of trail or clean up and restore a long abandoned camp. The sponsoring organizations want to be sure volunteers have some fun, so they usually plan hikes to secret spots, talks by naturalists, special meals and more.

Get a lift from a ski lift American ski resorts have been very slow to learn from the Swiss, who transform their winter wonderland into a hiker's paradise by operating all the country's gondolas and funiculars during the summer months. However, some resorts, from world-class to funky, are getting the message. Whistler, often ranked as the number-one ski resort in North America, encourages summer hikers to ride the western Canada's Blackcomb or Whistler Mountains ski lifts to several trailheads.

Rails to Trails: Take a hike on the Reading? An abandoned rail line has big-time trail potential: an already existing right-of-way, a usually very well engineered route, a de facto conservation corridor. Add the advantages of cultural and historical preservation and the contribution to physical fitness a rail converted to a trail makes, and the future seems bright for thousands of miles of disused railway to be put to good use.

Founded in 1986, the Rails-to-Trails Conservancy (RTC) aims to enrich America's communities and countryside with the conversion of abandoned private rail lines into public recreation trails. The Washington, D.C.-based group envisions a nationwide network of public trails from former rail lines. As the Rails-to-Trails Conservancy tells it, the rail-trail movement began in the Midwest during the 1960s as railroad companies, big and small, in response to competition from the trucking industry, began pulling up tracks. Curious history buffs and the odd recreational walker began exploring these abandoned lines.

A lot of people began asking the same question at the same time: Why not convert these rail lines to recreation paths? Some of these railway corridors were paved for walkways and bicycle paths while others were graded and left with a natural surface.

Every time I walk a rail-trail I enjoy it and wonder why someone didn't come up with the notion earlier. With some exceptions, I've found many of the trails are best suited for bicycling, though walkers in urban areas certainly make good use of them.

I like to integrate a rail-trail into my travel plans. The 25-mile-long Cape Cod Rail Trail is an excellent connection to the beaches and resort towns of the Cape, and the 18-mile-long Mt. Vernon Trail that extends along the Potomac River to George Washington's estate offers a healthful way to absorb American history.

Thanks to the leadership of the Rails-to-Trails Conservancy and countless local governments and park agencies that know a good thing when they see it, America's trail system boasts more than 12,000 miles of rail-trail used by more than 100 million happy hikers, walkers, and cyclists per year.

11

Planning a Hike

"It takes as much energy to wish as it does to plan."
—Eleanor Roosevelt

ONE OF my all-time favorite journeys to the trailhead took place far from home, on the Greek island of Crete. Getting to the trailhead at the top of Samaria Gorge, Europe's deepest and longest gorge, definitely required some advance planning.

The trail through the gorge begins high in the White Mountains and drops 4,000 feet to the sea. What that means is the hiker must arrange two long bus rides and one boat ride, available as a package deal from tour operators or by arranging transport on your own.

I first tried mastering Crete's bus and ferry schedules and making separate arrangements for each, but possibly saving a few euros wasn't worth the trouble. (Besides, Greek buses run on Greek time; which is to say, don't set your watch by them.) I then started talking to tour operators, but some of the vital details of the hike and the ride to the trailhead were getting lost in translation.

And then my common sense kicked in. I decided to plan the way to Samaria Gorge in a manner similar to the way I plan a hike in the U.S. I contacted the Greek national park office, obtained a hiking map, weather report, and trail information from the very helpful staff, and got a ranger-recommendation of the best transport company.

The adventure began in the coastal city of Hania, where I boarded an early (5 A.M.) bus with other hikers from all over Europe, Japan, and Australia. We stopped for breakfast (delicious, thick, creamy yogurt topped with the island honey, fresh orange juice, and strong Greek coffee), then continued into the dramatic White Mountains.

The hike through the gorge was terrific. White cyclamen, pink rock rose, and golden dandelions splashed color on the mountainsides. Riding the thermals along the gorge walls were great birds, including the hawk, golden eagle, and the bearded vulture. I was lucky enough to glimpse an elusive agrimi, the Cretan ibex, an agile goat-like creature with large, bow-like horns.

The trail squeezed through the famous Sideroportes, "Iron gates," where the gorge is at its narrowest (about 9 feet across). This narrow passage, where the Tarraios River becomes a raging torrent in winter, is the main reason why Samaria Gorge is closed during the rainy season.

The path emerged on a sandy plain at the mouth of the gorge. Here I found food and refreshment at the village of Ayia Roumeli on the Libyan Sea. While waiting for the ferry, I took a dip and napped at the lovely beach.

A scenic, one-hour ferry ride along the spectacular south shore of Crete brought me to the port of Hora Spakion, where I boarded a bus and crossed the island back to the population centers on the north coast of the island.

Hiking Samaria Gorge was a very long day, one I'll long remember. The planning, as well as getting there and getting back, was very much a part of that great day.

Planning Ahead

Planning ahead is the first rule of backcountry travel. Study maps and know where you're going. Become informed about weather patterns, and know what temperatures and climatic conditions to expect. Use this information to plan your trip.

As you study your maps, determine where to obtain services—food, water, and gas. Anticipate when you'll need to replenish fuel and supplies, and purchase them whenever you have the chance, since gas stations and stores are usually few in the vicinity of remote parks.

Before you depart on a hiking journey, leave a detailed itinerary with a friend or family member. Be sure to indicate when you expect to return; call later if your plans change. Traveling without detailed maps, high-tech equipment, or packaged foods, the pioneers still managed to trek through the wild. Today we enjoy the benefit of all sorts of undreamed-of modern accoutrements, making journeys more comfortable than they were in days past. But the most important aids to backcountry travel remain as simple as they were two hundred years ago—common sense, advance planning and packing the right supplies. Individuals accustomed to spending their days in temperature-regulated homes and offices (far too many of us, truth be told) must take care to regulate their own body temperature. The prudent hiker prepares for extremes of hot and cold; a 100-degree day can become a 50-degree night. A 50-degree day can become a 15-degree night. It's important to be prepared—not simply for comfort, but for survival.

And one more reason for planning your way—most of the time it's a lot more fun. Just because you're sure of the way from Point A to Point B doesn't mean you can't take the scenic route or improvise.

If there are two routes to the trailhead—one direct and one more scenic—I usually opt for the most direct route to begin the hike and save the scenic route for the return journey after the hike. Get the most of your time off the trail, too, by planning an itinerary that includes a museum visit, cultural attraction, lakeside picnic area, a drive-up mountain summit with a commanding view, or a post-hike meal at that roadside diner you've always wanted to try.

Mapping Your Route to the Trailhead

You need an accurate and up-to-date map to get you to the trailhead. A good area map might be a county map, a city map, a U.S. Forest Service map, or a map you make yourself by using an online mapping program.

The American Automobile Association's county and regional maps are among my favorite varieties of paper maps. The AAA's maps excel at delineating parks and natural areas, are kept up-to-date, and are easy to read.

In the first years of online mapping programs, paper maps remained in high demand because of the relatively poor readability of online maps and the reputation (often deserved) of maps on the net being out of date. Today online maps are likely no more (or less) accurate than paper ones.

Such major players as Google, MapQuest, and Yahoo offer excellent mapmaking applications as well as excellent and fast-evolving personalization and customization features. Google Maps in particular is an excellent and easy-to-read map application. The clarity is good and the information (usually) is quite up-to-date. Most internet users, even the least technically inclined, appreciate the simple process of getting directions and mapping a route. And the satellite imagery and its various uses—wow!

MapQuest, too, is another top application and has been for many years. The routes are easy-to-read and the directions first-rate.

Take advantage of the technology but don't substitute it for common sense. Heed warning signs, factor in the environment and surroundings, pay attention to road and weather conditions. And yes, stop and ask for directions.

From the hiker's point of view, it's the online directions accompanying the map, more so than the map itself, that tend to be problematic, particularly if you're trying to locate a trailhead in a remote area. The left-right-left-north-west-north-style directions presented by the major online map providers are usually quite accurate when you're motoring from one street address to another—say from your home to a visitor center in a popular park. When traveling to a trailhead off the beaten path though, consider such directions a useful tool rather than put your complete faith in them.

Call me old-fashioned, but I like a trusted narrative to go with my online map. That's why I favor getting directions to a trailhead via a guide (print, online, or even by phone or in person) from a trusted source rather than only from an online mapping program. Often highly specific directions are needed to find trailheads because trails don't always start from such obvious places as park visitor centers and campgrounds, departing instead from unmarked highway turnouts and lonely dirt roads.

GPS maps are really the new standard for auto-navigation. Complaints about outdated GPS have lessened over the years and the length of time between road changes and updates in a GPS device is much shorter these days; soon they'll have two-way connectivity that will enable a receiver to get updates automatically.

Paper maps will always have their place, even if only as a back-up navigation strategy when the battery in your GPS dies or onboard navigation system crashes. A paper map, even if you spill some coffee on it, won't malfunction.

Notes on Backcountry Driving

Because there are so few amenities available in and around the more remote parks, you must bring not only your own supplies, but consider your vehicle a self-contained "survival module." Be certain that your vehicle is road-worthy and capable of withstanding whatever conditions you might face—a bumpy dirt road to the trailhead, high altitude, a rainstorm, etc. In case of emergency, your safety could literally depend on it.

I understand why the image of bouncing over a dusty road in a vintage auto has some romantic appeal; it symbolizes the highly cherished notion of the freedom of the open road. I've never let having an old car (albeit a reliable one) stop me from getting to the trailhead. Ever since my college days, I've driven across the desert, high into the mountains, and from sea to shining sea to trailheads in vehicles made in America, Germany, Sweden, and Japan with considerably more than 100,000 miles on their odometers.

Most hikers, though, will probably be more confident driving a well-maintained, comfortable, and reliable vehicle, one that provides a sense of and security—and a real measure of safety as well.

Naturalist Joseph Wood Krutch described venturing into nature as "rewarding travel in an unfrequented land." Such travel is rewarding for a number of reasons, not the least of which is the fact that many of our best hikes are across an "unfrequented land." We drive to remote trailheads on lonely roads that are part of the solitude that wildlands offer.

In an unexpected situation, though, such as a vehicle breakdown, that feeling of peaceful solitude can quickly become a fearful experience in a hostile environment. Therefore, driving a road-worthy vehicle is of utmost importance.

The perils of driving include extreme heat and glare (especially when driving east in the morning or west in the afternoon); winter cold, ice, and snow. Long, straight roads can become monotonous and sleep-inducing day or night. Dirt roads require special driving skills, and the unfamiliar territory demands navigational expertise. Weather conditions, including dust, wind and thunderstorms which can cause flash floods, are other difficulties faced by drivers.

Gear To Keep in Your Vehicle

- **Flashlight** Bring extra batteries.
- **Phone** Cellphone coverage is expanding rapidly but don't count on reaching out from every remote mountain locale.
- **Extra food and water**
- **Emergency supplies** Waterproof matches, fire-starting tablets, a well-stocked first-aid kit and a couple of blankets. Replenish as needed. One of the best ways to be prepared in a medical emergency is to have taken a Red Cross CPR class.

- **Toilet paper and tissues**
- **Sunscreen** Get the SPF rating that's right for you, and use it. Reapply frequently.
- **Lip balm** To protect from chapped lips, look for one containing a sunscreen for best protection.
- **Camera** Be sure battery is charged, have sufficient memory.
- **Insect repellant** Keeps the critters off you.
- **Notebook or journal and pen** Scribble your thoughts, and take notes about your hike.
- **Binoculars** For bird-identification, wildlife-watching, route-finding.
- **Medication** Prescriptions and over-the-counter remedies
- **A good book** The perfect companion during fair weather or foul, on the trail and off.

Consider Alternate Transport to the Trailhead

Getting there can be part of the fun. When you take a bus through a scenic area, you'll often find that the driver is an enthusiastic local who is proud of the region and eager to share an insider's insights and tell you what not to miss.

Public or private transport that serves multiple trailheads might enable you to take a one-way hike—where you're dropped off at one trailhead and picked up at another.

Local businesses, particularly hotels, gas stations, and outdoor stores offer parking/transport; in fact, often for a modest fee, you can pay someone to give you a lift to trailhead.

In some national parks, in an effort to preserve the environment, private vehicles are either banned or severely limited in some areas. Instead, free shuttle buses depart from large parking and staging areas and deliver hikers to trailheads. Other parks and popular hiking areas offer private shuttle services to trailheads. By all means take advantage of them.

One of my favorite private shuttle services serves Zion National Park; the outfitter offers an early morning van ride to the top of Zion Canyon. You then hike down (and splash through) the Virgin River, squeezing through the Zion Narrows and emerging in the heart of the national park.

In Grand Canyon National Park, I've enjoyed the option of taking a private shuttle that services the south and north rims of the Grand Canyon. Hikers can do a one-way hike: down the South Rim and up the North Rim and get a ride back to the South Rim.

I once took advantage of a van ride and jet-boat service to travel up Oregon's Rogue River. I then hiked from lodge to lodge (pretty cush, huh?) down the Rogue River National Recreation Trail. Contouring over bare canyon walls, the path offers dramatic views of the river and the rafters below and of high canyon walls towering 1,500 feet above the trail. Rogue River Trail is well worth hiking round trip, but with limited time, I appreciated the transit-assisted opportunity to hike it one-way instead of out-and-back.

One of the great pleasures of hiking in England is the availability of public transportation. In regions such as the Cotswolds and the Lake District, you can hike half a day or all day from point to point and catch a bus or taxi (Americans, don't laugh; taxis are easy to hail and not all that expensive) to take you to the beginning or pick you up at the end of a footpath. British rail service is excellent, too, and can be used to take you to or near a trailhead. Train from town to town, take a hike, and return.

For a change of pace, try leaving your car in the garage and using the alternative transport options near home. Metropolitan transit systems in Boston, Philadelphia, Seattle, and even Los Angeles are surprising in their scope and get you to some surprisingly remote parks and trails.

In terms of trails and transit to trailheads, San Francisco leads the way among American cities. A far-reaching bus system, along with a subway under San Francisco Bay and ferry service across the bay, enables hikers to access a spectacular network of trails.

Hiker Safety (Before You Go)

- Plan ahead (your pre- and post-hike plans, too)
- Be prepared
- Ready your vehicle

- Prevent problems before they occur
- Know your limits
- Dress your best
- Map your route
- Know strengths and weaknesses of your companions
- Check the weather
- Pack food and water
- Ask questions

Trailhead Safety

Returning to the trailhead after a joyful day on the trail to find a car window smashed and the laptop computer and down jacket that you left on the back seat missing, can really make a day hike memorable—but not for the reasons you want it to be. Trailhead safety—for both vehicles and visitors—can be increased with a little knowledge about who is likely to do what where—and what you can do to prevent it.

The biggest (and almost only) bummer about hiking in vacation destinations like Hawaii is the number of car break-ins at trailheads. With lots of visitors who like to hike, lots of rental cars, and lots of unpatrolled trailheads, there are beaucoup break-ins. I don't mean to pick on the Aloha State, because such trailhead break-ins occur in all fifty states. Break-ins are also a problem for New England hikers, who often cross state lines to take a hike; cars with out-of-state plates parked at rural trailheads are particular targets.

My friend Doug's old Volkswagen camper sustained one of the worst incidents of trailhead vandalism that I can remember. The VW was selectively stripped of knobs, hubcaps, a sun visor, a seat and much more—apparently all the parts the thief needed for *his* VW camper. Cost of the camper's replacement parts exceeded the value of the vehicle.

Surely some of the strangest occurrences of "vandalism" occur at the Mineral King trailhead in Sequoia National Park. Rangers and fellow hikers report that, for reasons unknown, the local marmots have developed a taste for rubber, and during spring and early summer they sometimes gnaw on vehicle belts and hoses. Hikers either pray the critters leave their cars alone or park further down Mineral King Valley where the marmots are less numerous and walk up to the trailhead. Rangers advise hikers to check their engines before departing.

Some statistics are emerging that suggest that after three decades of LOCK YOUR CAR AND TAKE YOUR VALUABLES WITH YOU signs and campaigns, hikers are finally heeding this safety advice and locking their cars and taking their valuables with them. The result? Fewer reported car break-ins.

Anecdotal evidence supports another reason for a trailhead crime decline: the widespread acceptance of hikers and hiking. Years ago more tension existed between hikers (usually urban-dwellers) and rural locals, who felt resentful that land was taken out of productive use for something as silly as a park or trail. The economic benefits of visiting hikers are now more fully appreciated by rural chambers of commerce and most locals; hikers are apt to be warmly welcomed these days with helpful information and improved trailheads.

Still, if you have any suspicions (gut instincts are worth heeding as well) about parking at a particular trailhead, call a local ranger station or hiking club and inquire if any vandalism has occurred at the site. If you have any concerns, park in town or somewhere else.

If, despite all precautions, your car is broken into or vandalized, report the incident to regional park authorities and/or the local law enforcement agency, and post an account of the incident online at an appropriate web site in order to alert fellow hikers.

Trailhead Parking Precautions

- Ask parkland managers about the safety—for people and property—of a particular trailhead.
- If a trailhead has a recent history of break-ins, plan to park elsewhere or arrange for a drop-off and pickup.
- Note the trailhead's appearance. Graffiti, broken auto

glass, piles of beer cans or suspicious characters loitering about are clues to park elsewhere.

- Leave valuables at home (best idea) or lock them in the trunk (second-best idea). Bring your wallet and keys with you rather than hiding them in your vehicle
- Hide a spare key under your car if you wish. Just remember that car thieves know all the easy places, so hide it in a greasy, grimy, difficult to reach spot.
- If you have a choice of trailheads, know that more formal trailheads (paved parking, a restroom, picnic area) tend to be safer than wide spots in the road, pullouts and dirt lots hidden from the highway.
- Don't leave a note on your windshield explaining who you are, where you're going and when you're planning to return. Talk about an open invitation for a break-in!

Along
The Way

12

On The Trail

"Commonly we stride through the out-of-doors too swiftly to see more than the most obvious and prominent things. For observing nature, the best pace is a snail's pace."
—Edwin Way Teale

"There is more to life than increasing its speed."
—Gandhi

GET TO know yourself as a hiker.

In this chapter, I'll share the hiking world's collected wisdom about how average hikers traveling at an average pace over average terrain in average climatic conditions will arrive at their destination in an average time.

Of course there's no such thing as an average hiker. Every hiker is unique. That's why you have to get to know yourself and discover your personal pace and capabilities. The best hikers are not necessarily the ones who hike the farthest in a day, but the ones who know themselves, who stay within their limits, who truly enjoy happy trails.

I've learned that getting to know yourself as a hiker means not only knowing your good qualities, but also looking at parts of yourself that might be far from perfect. Naturally, this kind of self-examination isn't easy—but it will make you a better hiker.

For example, I'm proud of my trail-reading ability and endurance, but a bit dismayed by the amount of urban-life impatience I bring with me on the trail. You'd think I would mellow out after all these years of hiking or that I would instantly de-stress and adapt to nature's rhythms the instant I reach the trailhead, but the fact is it still takes me a while on the trail to slow down mentally and to appreciate where I am in the moment, leaving city stresses behind.

As you get to know yourself as a hiker—your physical condition and limits, pace, moods, and mental outlook—you'll have a more satisfying experience on the trail.

Some (okay, many) hikers are goal-oriented and want to explore the entire length of the trail, climb every mountain, ford every stream, and take in every sight along the way.

Other hikers want to sleep in, start late, and believe that one of the great pleasures of hiking is taking it slow and easy, savoring a welcome break from over-scheduled lives.

Dawdling down the trail or sprinting to the summit are fine ways to go—as are a dozen different speeds in between. For safety's sake, at whatever your chosen pace, you need to be able to estimate your hiking speed and estimate how long it will take you to complete your hike. It's also helpful to understand how a trail's grade and conditions on the day of your hike affect your hiking time and how park authorities determine how to rate a hike's difficulty—easy, moderate, difficult.

Timing is Everything

"Walk while ye have the light with you, lest darkness come upon you: for he that walketh in darkness knoweth not whither he goeth."
—John 12:35

When does darkness fall?

No, this isn't a cosmic question; it's a highly practical one.

If it gets dark at 6 P.M., and you start what should be a three-hour hike at 1 P.M., you should be fine because you've left a two-hour cushion. If it gets dark at 5 P.M. and you started what turns out to be a ten-hour hike at 9 A.M., you might find yourself in serious trouble.

Hikers lose track of time just about as often as they lose the trail. Rangers say that beginning and intermediate hikers rarely lose the well-traveled, well-signed footpaths in state and national parks; however, they frequently underestimate the length of time required to travel a particular trail.

Day hikers who miscalculate their time on the trail are sometimes unable to return to the trailhead before dark. This miscalculation can mean spending the night in the great outdoors (usually without the proper gear). Provided it's not ultra cold and you have the Ten Essentials with you, this could simply result in spending one uncomfortable, never-to-be-forgotten night of your life sitting by the trail, eagerly awaiting dawn's first light.

Or, absent the right gear, in bad weather, an unexpected night on the trail could be a disaster.

For your safety, you need to learn to estimate how long a hike will take you to complete.

In the interest of full disclosure, The Trailmaster must confess that his very worst habit as a hiker is cutting things too close—that is to say, staying on the trail until the last rays of day. Curiosity, I suppose. I just have to see what's on the other side of the mountain. While I've never been caught out after dark, I have had to sprint back to the trailhead in the twilight more times than I care to remember or admit—sometimes while enduring the ire of a hiking companion

If you get an early start and by noon you're only halfway to your destination, re-evaluate your goal. Either you've underestimated the length of the trail, misjudged the difficulty of the terrain, or over-estimated your pace. Whatever the reason you end up on the trail far longer than you anticipate, it can be discouraging to say the least—and quite possibly dangerous to so miscalculate.

Another factor in timing a hike is your energy level. If you use up two-thirds of your energy getting to the hike's halfway point, what happens? Sometimes you can reach down inside yourself and come up with some reserve steam, but sometimes you just can't. Avoid putting yourself in the position of having to muster every ounce of strength just to get back to the trailhead.

Pacing Yourself

- Choose the pace that's best for you.
- Rest once an hour for five to ten minutes. To keep your momentum and to avoid stiffness, several shorter rest periods are better than one long one.
- Set a steady pace, one you can keep up all day.
- Wear a watch, not because you have an appointment with a waterfall and you have to be punctual, but because a watch gives you some idea of pace and helps you get back to the trailhead before dark.

No less an authority than the U.S. Army figures that a male soldier hikes about 100 steps a minute and a female soldier hikes about 120 steps a minute to maintain a three-mile-an hour pace. (Of course, average number of steps per minute and per mile have to do with size differences not gender differences. Men and women of the same size have about the same size stride.)

Leave it to the army to quantify everything for us. Let's remember that the military's stats are based primarily on hikers aged 18 to 22, who are likely in better physical condition than the population at large.

Miles per Hour, Minutes per Mile

"Mostly, two miles an hour is good going."
—Colin Fletcher

Some fitness experts divide walking into three speeds:

- **Strolling:** 20 minutes per mile, low-key exercise.
- **Brisk walking:** 15 minutes per mile, the pace of the vigorous exercise walker.
- **Aerobic walking:** 12 minutes per mile, for very advanced fitness walkers.

Exercise walking speed is much better defined than hiking

speed, which is influenced by many variables. Here are three speeds for the sake of discussion:

- Hiking on level or near-level ground: 2 to 3.5 mph
- Hiking uphill or at elevation: 2 mph
- Cross-country travel or steep climbs: 0.5 to 1.5 mph

Adding up the Miles

Beginning hikers in particular can get overly obsessed by mileage, sometimes equating a hiker's success with mileage covered. Those who run for exercise and pay close attention to their miles jogged per week often bring a goal-oriented, gotta-do-x-number-of-miles mindset to their hikes.

Of course a hike's "success" can be measured in many more ways than miles covered: the number of bird species counted, finding one rare wildflower, exploring that side trail to a hidden waterfall, reduced stress levels.

Your friend who's been hiking for years might consider ten miles a modest day hike. You might think five miles is an ample amount of ground to cover.

Judging a Hike's Difficulty

A trail's degree of difficulty—also called its difficulty level or difficulty rating—can greatly vary hiking time.

Park agencies and guidebook writers often assist hikers by rating the degree of challenge a trail presents to the average hiker.

Of course, the "average" hiker varies widely, as does the average hiker's skills, experience, and conditioning. No matter how skilled the trail-evaluator, "degree of difficulty" for a particular hike or trail is inevitably subjective.

A path's elevation gain and loss, exposure to elements, steepness and the natural obstacles a hiker encounters along the way (boulder field, six creek crossings, etc.) figure prominently in the hike difficulty equation, too. High or low temperatures and common climatic conditions also influence a hike's difficulty rating.

During a couple of decades or so of making difficulty

evaluations, I've rated hikes with a modified easy-moderate-difficult system. My day hike rating in brief is:

- **Easy** Less than 5 miles with an elevation gain of less than 700 to 800 feet. An easy day hike is suitable for beginners and children.
- **Moderate** 5 to 10 miles with less than a 2,000 foot elevation gain. You should be reasonably fit for these.
- **Difficult** Hikes over 10 miles, and those with more than a 2,000-foot elevation gain.

I often qualify the basic ratings; for example: easy—except for the steep side trail to Trillium Falls. Sometimes a hike's difficulty doesn't fit neatly into one category so I'll combine ratings, as in "moderately easy" or "moderately difficult." I've been known to add a personal touch to my ratings, too: easy—a walk in the park; difficult—a challenge to mountain goats.

During my long tenure as the *Los Angeles Times* hiking columnist, one editor, for reasons that I never fully understood, insisted that I substitute "strenuous" for difficult, so during his editorship of my column, I rated my hikes easy-moderate-strenuous.

Some trail-guide authors and publishers use graphics, such as a one-to-five-star method or a one-to-five hiking boots system to rate a hike's difficulty; others use a numeric hike-rating system from one (easiest) to ten (brutal).

The U.S. Forest Service (as well as some park agencies) uses a Level of Difficulty system that seems to rate the hiker as much as the hike:

- **Easiest** A trail requiring limited skill with little challenge to travel.
- **More difficult** A trail requiring some skill and challenge to travel.
- **Most difficult** A trail requiring a high degree of skill and challenge to travel. Such a hike may be at high altitude, be extremely rugged, or have a major elevation gain.

Some hiking-guidebook writers and park agencies dodge the whole "How difficult is this hike?" question entirely and instead state the time it will take to walk the trail, i.e. 2.75 hours. Guess-timating a hiking time for someone else usually irks hikers far more than giving a particular hike or a trail a rating and is often considerably more inaccurate.

Easy? Moderate? Difficult? It's difficult to be objective even after rating hundreds of hikes. I've done hikes when I was feeling very low-energy and (until I double-checked mileage and elevation gain with rangers) was ready to pronounce them more difficult than they really are. On the other hand, I've had high energy days, when I charged up 3,000 feet in 5.5 miles and nearly gave the hike a moderate rating until I looked at the elevation gain figures.

Making the Grade

"It is easier to go down a hill than up it,
but the view is much better at the top."
—Arnold Bennet

Grade is the amount of elevation change between two points on the trail over a given direction. This elevation change between points is expressed as a percentage (change in feet in elevation per 100 horizontal feet of trail, known to trail-builders and engineering types as "rise over run"). What you and I call uphill and downhill, trail-builders call positive grade and negative grade.

To determine the grade of a trail, divide the number of feet of ascent per mile by 5,280 feet per mile. Hikers who can work such problems in their heads while walking a trail have my admiration; the rest of us will probably need to pause here and use pencil and paper or calculate on a digital device.

Let's say you're hiking exactly one mile from the trailhead (elevation 1,200 feet) to the top of Inspiration Point (1,412 feet). Subtract the trailhead elevation from the destination to get the trail gain in feet. Next divide 212 feet by 5,280 feet in a mile. You get about 0.04 or a 4 percent grade—a very modest grade.

After a while you'll start calculating your hiking speed and grade automatically just like trail writers and park agencies do.

Try it again. Let's say you're bound for Eagle Roost, a 4-mile round trip hike with a 1,000 foot elevation gain. That's a gain of about 500 feet per mile, or a 10 percent grade. Most national park trails, as well as those trails of many other park agencies are designed to a maximum 10 percent grade, which presents a mildly aggressive but not too difficult pace.

Lots of trails in lots of places were built before this 10 percent grade standard was widely adopted, so if you find yourself breathless on a 15 percent or steeper grade don't be surprised.

Estimating Hiking Time

Those new to hiking and/or who want to be sure to stay out of trouble can use a very conservative formula. Figure your average hiking pace at two miles an hour and then add an hour for each 1,000 feet of elevation gain.

Returning to our hypothetical example of that 4-mile hike to Eagle Roost with the 1,000 foot gain. We figure two hours for the distance (2 miles an hour) plus another hour for the 1,000-foot elevation gain. Estimated hiking time is three hours.

Here's what you might read in a guidebook and how you can do the math:

Eagle Roost Trail
Pine Camp to Eagle Roost
4 miles round trip; 1,000 foot gain

Miles ÷ miles per hour = Hours for mileage
4÷2 = 2 hours

Elevation ÷ 1,000 = Hours for elevation
1,000 ÷ 1,000 = 1 hour

Hours for mileage 2
+ Hours for elevation 1
Estimated hiking time = 3 hours

During all my years of chronicling hikes, no reader has ever complained to me that a hike I described was too easy.

The worst and most frequent complaints about mileage come not, as you might expect, from tenderfooted newbies, but from fitter-than-average individuals who walk or jog regularly—usually on flat terrain and on even surfaces such as city streets or the track at the local high school. A typical complaint: "I run five miles a day, five days a week and I know what five miles is and believe you me, that hike you described was no five miles. It had to be seven miles at least, maybe eight."

Gently I respond by first noting how pleased I am that they are out there enjoying nature. I then point out how every hiking step, because of the uneven surface of the trail and its ups and downs, is just a little bit different from the last; a jogger on the track has a much more measured gait. That hike might have seemed like eight miles, but it measures only five. Really.

Tangible and Intangible Factors Affecting Hiking Speed

- **Trail tread** (detailed in "All About Trails" chapter) is another determining factor in hiker speed. Obviously a brisk pace is easier to maintain on a smooth and wide trail than on a rocky and root-covered one, when it's necessary to look down at your feet just to stay upright.
- **Switchbacks** Some trails have few or none, others have an adequate number for steady, hiker-friendly ascents and descents. Most hikers will be able to maintain a faster pace overall on a well-engineered pathway with plenty of switchbacks than on a straight-up-and-down route.
- **Hiker biorhythm** Not to get too New Age-y on you, but every hiker has a different biorhythm—you might be a "morning person" and your hiking partner a night owl. We all have different internal clocks and different energy levels.

I'm an early morning, crack-of-dawn kind of hiker—provided I've had a cup of coffee before I hit the trail. Bottom of my biorhythm is mid-afternoon, 2 P.M. to 3 P.M., when my usually frisky self slows to a banana slug-like pace. After that, I tend to get a second wind, so to speak, and resume a normal speed.

Knowing my own biorhythm, I try to accomplish most of a hike's steepest climbs and elevation gain in the morning. When I hike with companions, I try to get a feel for their internal clocks as well, and pace the hike accordingly.

Taking Care of the Trail

Deadfalls Consider moving that fallen tree off the trail so others may pass. If you can drag the deadfall off the trail without hurting yourself (no heroics, please) or ripping up the trail corridor, go for it. If the tree or tree limb is too heavy or positioned too awkwardly to move, choose a route around it that's sensitive to the environment and the safety of your fellow hikers.

Travel in single file Most footpaths are made one-hiker wide and should not be widened by hikers who tromp on either side of the tread. Doubling up on a single-track trail is neither a safe nor an eco-friendly way to go.

Never cut switchbacks Repeat: Never cut switchbacks. In fact, help trail maintenance crews by moving brush, rocks, or other impediments to travel across those shortcuts made by less eco-enlightened trail users.

Sensitive areas Staying on the trail is always a good idea, but it's absolutely essential for the protection of certain fragile types of terrain such as bogs and alpine meadows. Also be sure to stay on the trail while hiking through sensitive bird and wildlife habitat.

Muddy going We hikers have a lot to learn from six-year-old boys, especially when it comes to mud. Your basic little boy has a primal attraction to mud and, if left to his own devices, will hike right through the middle of a muddy trail. Funny enough, so should you. To best preserve the trail, hike through the mud rather than creating a new route that detours around mucky areas.

Washouts Overuse, poor design, and weathering contribute to trail erosion. Step carefully across or around washouts, searching out the most secure footing. Tell the local land managers about pathways that need repair.

13

Finding The Way

"If you don't know where you are,
you don't know who you are."
—Wallace Stegner

"My own most memorable hikes
can be classified as Shortcuts that Backfired."
—Edward Abbey

IN AN era when humans are ever more oriented to getting there, not being there, to highways not footpaths, to the built world not the natural one, the people who navigate by way of rivers, mountains and valleys are becoming rare birds indeed.

Count me as one modern who does his best to keep his sense of direction in this hurry-up world by staying centered and by getting located in relation to the surrounding natural geography. I don't always succeed, but I've found the effort well worthwhile.

In an attempt to encourage students to rediscover their place in nature, outdoors educators ask them to give directions to their homes using only natural landmarks in their descriptions. The students are to assume their visitor will arrive on foot. No street names or structures are permitted when giving the directions.

Poet Gary Snyder, who writes lovingly and wryly about the land and the way we live on it, asked his audience to try this exercise at a reading I attended. I've tried giving directions myself by way of natural features and it's quite a challenge. "I live at the base of the mountains, on the east side of a creek that flows to the Pacific. . . ."

I've met some hikers who have a great natural sense of

direction and many more who, while lacking an innate sense of direction, have developed one by practice. A good sense of direction begins with paying attention to the geography around you—on the trail and off.

You don't have to venture into a remote wilderness to lose your way. Hikers even get lost in Rhode Island, where trails experts have figured that no state footpath is farther than a mile from the nearest road.

No one expects to get lost—particularly when hiking the well-signed park and forest trails that most hikers choose to follow.

"After all," say novices, "our mountains aren't big and icy like the Rockies and we're only out for the day and. . . ."

Even experienced hikers can get lost. Getting lost is usually the result of taking a "shortcut" off an established trail. Danger is magnified if a hiker ventures out alone or fails to inform someone of an itinerary or return time.

An early twentieth-century U.S. Geological Survey report noted, "With some persons, the faculty of getting lost amounts to genius. They are able to accomplish it wherever they are." If those words strike home, remember that map-reading and navigating are skills. And like any other skills, performance improves with practice.

Hikers can take many common sense precautions to avoid getting lost in the first place. Know your physical condition and don't overtax yourself. Check your boots and clothing. Be prepared for bad weather. Inquire about trail conditions. Allow plenty of time for your hike and allow even more for your return to the trailhead.

Unless you repeat the same hike over and over again, in order to stay oriented on the trail—any trail—you really need to learn the basics of map reading and how to use a compass.

Trail Maps

I've supervised the making of more than a thousand trail maps, plain and fancy, simple and detailed. And I've reviewed thousands more as a backcountry traveler and an as an armchair traveler.

I have a deep appreciation for mapmakers in general and

trail mapmakers in particular. Like trail-building, trail-mapping is both an art and a science. A science certainly with its precise measurements and an art with its often colorful presentation.

My favorite maps for hiking really highlight trails. While this would seem like a no-brainer (of course a map for hiking highlights trails) it pains me to report that many trail maps poorly represent the trail, display it in an awkward scale and for any number of reasons are not as hiker-friendly as they could be. Irking The Trailmaster to no end are mapmakers who draw maps (and publishers who print them) with an orientation other than north at the top of the page. Some park maps are just that—maps of parks with pathways lost in a clutter of features or not clearly marked.

Tom Harrison has field-checked (read walked) thousands of miles of trail while producing detailed maps of California's scenic gems—Death Valley, Yosemite Valley, Lake Tahoe, the Santa Monica Mountains, Point Reyes, and many more terrific places to hike. The master cartographer offers a half-dozen tips for selecting a good hiking map:

- **Look for a map that is easy to read.** The type should be large enough to read comfortably, the little squiggly lines should be crisp and clear, the colors should be well-balanced.
- **Most maps have North at the top of the page, but some don't.** A map without a North arrow or a map with the north arrow pointed sideways can be disorienting to the hiker.
- **Make sure the map covers the area you want.** You may have to get more than one map for the complete route.
- **Get a set of maps that have an appropriate scale for your trip.** Small-scale maps show a large area but not a lot of detail. These are great for planning a multi-day trip or getting a general overview of an area. Large-scale maps show a small area but in greater detail—these are the best for day-to-day hiking.
- **Waterproof and tear-resistant plastic is becoming the standard material for maps**, and they hold up really well outdoors. If you need to write on them, use a ball-point pen, not a pencil. And keep them away from solvents like stove

fuel, insect repellant, and sunscreen. The ink sits on top of the plastic rather than being absorbed on paper so it is vulnerable to solvents.

- **If you use a GPS then look for a map that has a grid**—either a UTM grid or a latitude/longitude grid. Then set your GPS to the datum of the map. Most maps use 1927 NAD (North American Datum) and a few use WGS 84. Most GPS units have a factory default of WGS 84 so reset your unit according to your map.

U.S. Forest Service maps Many hikes take place in national forests: U.S. Forest Service maps are available at ranger stations and some outdoor retailers. They're general maps, showing roads, rivers, and trails and little else. The Forest Service keeps its maps fairly up-to-date, so they're useful for checking out-of-date topographic maps. USFS maps that show a portion of a national forest, such as a particular region or a wilderness area, are more useful than the maps that put a million-acre forest on one page.

Each road and trail in the national forest system has a route number. A route number might look like this: 2S21. Signs, inscribed with the route number, are placed at some trailheads and at the intersection of trails to supplement other directional signs. The route numbers on a Forest Service map usually correspond to the route numbers on the trail, but not always; be careful because the Forest Service periodically changes the numbers.

Trails on Forest Service maps are drawn in red and black. Red trails are usually maintained and in good shape. Black trails are infrequently maintained and their condition can range from okay to faint to impassable.

By the way, don't be so quick to throw away that out-of-date forest map. Some veteran hikers swear that budget-conscious Forest Service bureaucrats erase trails from the agency's maps with each new edition. If the trail isn't on the map, it doesn't exist; and if it doesn't exist, the Forest Service doesn't have to pay to maintain it.

I'm not saying I agree with these hiking trail conspiracy theorists, but I do treasure my collection of old Forest Service maps, some of which date back to the 1960s. And I've discovered more than a few hiking trails that disappeared from the map but may still be enjoyed on the ground.

National Park maps These are excellent getting-to, and getting-around-the-park maps. Because the cartography and map symbols are so classic, as well as so easy to read, picking one up feels like hanging out with an old and familiar friend.

No need to wait until you drive up to a national park entrance station to get a map. Go online and look up the National Park Service's Cartographic Resources Home Page. You can quickly review any national park map from Acadia National Park to Zion National Park and download them in a variety of formats.

Blow it up! Make your area map or trail map easier to read by blowing it up. Photocopy the map at 150 to 200 percent of original size and mark your way with a yellow highlighter.

For the many of us who need to wear glasses or contacts, are far-sighted or near-sighted, this is a great tip. I'm near-sighted myself, so while contact lenses or prescription sunglasses correct my distance vision to 20-20, when I wear them, I cannot then read the fine print on a map.

Many of you have the opposite problem—far-sightedness. You see well for distance, but need glasses for reading—particularly the fine print of a map.

So enlarge the map on the photocopier. Suddenly the map's six and eight point type gets twice as big and lots easier to read. You'll have an easier time staying on the trail with a map that you can actually read.

Topographic Maps Some hikers have a real aesthetic appreciation for topographic maps. Those blue rivers, green woods and labyrinthine contour lines are—well, artistic.

Topographic maps are valuable for any off-trail hiking or as a back-up in case of any route-finding challenges. Topos show terrain in great detail, including trails, elevations, waterways, brush cover, and improvements.

Topos come in two scales, the 15-minute quadrangle and the 7.5-minute quadrangle. The 15-minute series scale is approximately 1 inch to 1 mile and the contour interval (the gap between contour lines) represents an elevation of 80 feet. The 7.5-minute series maps have a scale of 2.5 inches to a mile with a contour interval of 40 feet. For the hiker, the 7.5-minute series is preferable.

Topos usually come in a sheet size of about 18 × 22 inches. If you're thinking about getting a set of topos to cover the whole country, you'll need a place to store 57,000 maps.

Fortunately, topos, like everything else, have gone high-tech and are now available for free, courtesy of the USGS. While printed maps still cost, you can download any of the agency's maps, which open in Adobe Acrobat as PDF files, with free and easy mouse clicks. Go to http://store.usgs.gov, find the "map locator" and click to connect to a Google maps interface of the U.S. You can search by place name and then select for the corresponding topo map.

Topos are valuable maps all right, but sometimes even seasoned hikers tend to put a little too much faith in a topo's depiction of terrain. Some of the most common misrepresentations are the omission of creek branches and seasonal watercourses, misplaced trails and trail junctions. While the feds make an effort to update topos, some maps go decades without meaningful improvement.

During the 1980s, with hopes of shrinking the federal budget deficit, government agencies such as the U.S. Geological Survey, never known for marketing savvy or an entrepreneurial bent, came under pressure to produce revenue. The USGS began to aggressively push its product lines, from aerial photos to maps of all kinds.

One happy result of Uncle Sam-turned-salesman is that topo maps are much easier to obtain these days. A hiker can go online and locate the topographic map for anywhere in the U.S. with a click of a mouse. The USGS offers GNIS (Geographic Names Information System), a complete listing of federally recognized geographic place names, accompanied by a powerful search program that allows the user to locate maps based upon these place names. Enter any place name and the name of the map title will be listed.

Let's say your friends recommend that you take a hike to Lonesome Lake in New Hampshire's White Mountains. You enter Lonesome Lake, New Hampshire, and *voilà*—the system suggests you buy the topo map named Franconia and tells you the latitude and longitude of all geographic features named "Lonesome Lake."

> Lonesome Lake
> 44deg08min/071deg42min
> Lonesome Lake Hut
> 44deg08min/071deg42min
> Lonesome Lake Trail
> 44deg08min/071deg41min

Review Area Maps Before You Hit the Road

Go over the map before you get into the car. Have a good driver-navigator chat. Certainly there is nothing more nerve-wracking or upsetting than the experience of a frustrated driver demanding directions from an unsure navigator. Not only is it frustrating, but potentially hazardous, especially when intensified by traffic, inclement weather, fatigue or confusing territory.

To avoid such disorienting and upsetting scenarios, spend time before departure planning and mapping out excursions. Write down directions, road names and numbers and pertinent landmarks to prevent on-the-road confusion.

While chances are most of the main access roads on your way to the hike are well-marked, lesser roads may not be signed at all. Therefore, pay close attention to mileage on the odometer when following directions to trailheads in backcountry locations.

Using a Map and Compass

Some moderns argue that learning to use a map and compass is a hopelessly old-fashioned outdoors skill, akin to fashioning a rabbit snare from twigs or tying a diamond hitch on a mule. If you have a good guidebook with step-by-step directions and stay on maintained, signed trails, what need do you have for a compass? Many hikers have walked the entire length of the Appalachian Trail without consulting a compass, so why bother with one in the local mountains?

It is true many a trail has been immortalized in a trail guide, and described with step-by-step directions and that very few hikers ever have to depend, really depend, on map-reading skills. Still, a familiarity with a map and compass can at least help you be aware of your direction of travel. (You'd be surprised how many hikers don't.) If you are on a trail, a quick map and compass consult can help you determine if you're going in the right direction. If you lose the trail, a map and compass can help you find it. If you are supposed to be hiking north on a trail to your destination and you find yourself on a trail leading west for miles and miles, a map and compass can help you decipher if you took off on the wrong trail.

One poor way to use a map is to employ it as a last resort measure after getting lost. Hikers often make the mistake of failing to consult a map at all as the miles disappear under their boots. Without stopping occasionally to match the map to the territory, hikers have no ready point of reference from which to fix their spot on the map.

These days the best backcountry navigators know how to use a map and compass, as well as a map and GPS receiver. You need map reading skills because a map, without the ability to put your finger on your position, does a hiker little good. At the same time, a GPS receiver is of little help unless you can take the coordinates and then locate them, and yourself, on a map.

Hikers can put the map and compass combo to two good uses:

1. Find out where you are
2. Determine where to go

The best way to learn map and compass skills is by taking a short field course. These courses are offered by hiking clubs, outdoor retailers, and community colleges. Once you learn a few basics, it's wise to practice them occasionally.

When I took my first compass class, I suspect I had the same two reactions that many other hikers have. First I was genuinely dismayed how utterly inadequate my map-finding skills were. Secondly, after mastering a few of the fundamentals, my overall confidence on the trail was bolstered.

Learning to use a map and compass is one of those things that's far easier to learn by doing than by reading about it. (Some orienteering how-to books begin with the history of latitude and longitude and make it difficult to get at the few basics that would be useful to the hiker.) I'm not going to attempt to give compass-reading lessons in the pages of this book, but I want to offer a brief overview of a few of the skills that you'll need to learn.

To find out where you are, you'll employ what's called the Triangulation Method. First you'll locate two landmarks—ideally about 90 degrees from each other relative to your position. Next you'll take a bearing for these landmarks, adjust for magnetic declination, then plot these two bearings on your map. Your position is the point where the two bearings intersect. Repeating the process with more landmarks and more bearings can improve accuracy.

To locate a lost trail, or when hiking cross-country, you'll need a precise way of determining the right direction to proceed. To accomplish this, plot your chosen route on the map to determine you compass heading. Next, you'll hold the compass at eye-level to take a bearing to determine which landmark you wish to reach. Hike toward that landmark until you reach it or it disappears from view. Keep repeating the map-compass bearing process until you get where you want to go.

GPS

Even if you're hiking in a pea soup fog, on a moonless night or in a white-out, a GPS receiver will plot your exact location anytime, anywhere. Key to the GPS are two dozen satellites orbiting the earth twice a day, beaming time and position data.

Receiving a satellite's signal, a GPS unit calculates the time gap between transmission and reception of this signal, thus establishing the distance from satellite to receiver. Next, using data from a minimum of three satellites, the GPS receiver, via triangulation and a lot of complicated math, delivers exact longitude and latitude and a precise position fix. By making contact with a fourth satellite, the GPS receiver will display exact altitude, too.

The units can be quite useful on the trail, particularly if the hiker gets some instruction in their use. Remember that a GPS unit, like a compass is just a navigation tool, not a skill, and certainly not a substitute for common sense and trail sense.

Just like a map and compass, the main purpose of a GPS is to keep you on course as you hike to your destination. A GPS can also help total altitude gain and loss, as well as where you've been and how far you've gone. A GPS can help you locate a favorite fishing spot or a historic site, and assist you to get to the trailhead with detailed driving directions.

You can download crucial waypoints to a GPS and use them to plan your route. Once on the trail, the route can be used to estimate distance and travel time. After completing a trail, the GPS helps create a record of the hike, useful for sharing with friends or to reference on a future outing on the same trail.

What users want from a GPS varies widely. Hikers need different GPS features than boaters and motorists. In fact, hikers should steer clear of GPS units designed for in-the-car or "street" use.

A good hiking GPS is compact enough to take on the trail, waterproof, rugged, and works with the kind of software hikers need for planning, following, and recording a travel route. A basic GPS unit can be turned on and, with a minimum of user input, deliver a precise position fix—a good part of what a hiker really needs.

A basic hiking GPS should be waterproof (rated Submersible) so it will work in the worst downpours. The unit should have long battery life because you don't want to carry a lot of extra batteries—particularly on a long hike.

The unit should have at least a twenty-route storage capability to allow you to retrieve nearby trails and choose from a variety of routes. Waypoints, the more the better, is another important feature. Bearing to the next waypoint is almost always included in the unit and absolutely essential to hikers.

Make sure it has an easy-to-read map screen, which allows you to ascertain your location in relation to particular reference points. Built-in maps are a big help of course. And if you're a hiker who likes using topos on the trail, the GPS system should support that and display the maps well.

Staying on the Trail

> If a body takes out to follow a made trail down over the hills, he'd best hold to that trail, for there are not too many ways to go. Most of the trouble a man finds in the mountains is when he tries shortcuts or leaves a known way.
>
> —Louis L'Amour

When you're on the trail, keep your eyes open. If you're hiking so fast that all you see is your boots, you're not attentive to passing terrain—its charms or its layout. STOP once in a while. Sniff wildflowers, splash your face in a spring. LISTEN. Maybe the trail is paralleling a stream. Listen to the sound of mountain water. On your left? On your right? Look up at that fire lookout on the nearby ridge. Are you heading toward it or away from it? LOOK AROUND. That's the best insurance against getting lost.

- **Watch for way-marks.** Parks are marked with basic trail mileage signs and in many other ways, including blazes, disks, posts and cairns. If you're hiking a woodsy trail signed every 150 feet or so by a blue disk and ten minutes pass without seeing one, you may have left the main trail.

- **Be aware of your surroundings.** Note passing landmarks and natural features. Stop now and then to compare your progress on the ground to the route on the map.
- **Think for yourself.** Just because you're in the middle or at the end of the line of hikers doesn't mean you can switch over to autopilot and stop paying attention to where you're going.
- **Eyes in the back of your head.** Look behind you frequently. Knowing where you come from always gives you a better feel for where you're going and prepares you for the return trip.
- **Put the trail into words.** Sharing what you see and what you expect to see when with your trail companion can confirm whether you're on the "same page" in regard to the hiking route. Two heads are better than one, four eyes better than two, when it comes to staying on the trail.
- **Here comes the sun.** Use the east-rising, west-setting sun and its respective position to the trail to help you in your orientation.

Locating a Lost Trail

How many ways can you lose the trail? Quite a few! Unsigned or poorly signed junctions, paths crowded or covered by brush, buried by rock-falls or mudslides, covered by fallen trees or a recent dusting of snow. . . . If you suspect you've lost the trail, stop immediately.

Ask yourself: "If I was the trail where would I go?"

Sure, it's a weird question, but if you know where you've come from and where you're going, you can often figure out how the path should take you there. Often a trail has a logic all its own and sometimes the hiker can dial into it. A trail traveling a blufftop high above the surf will rarely all of a sudden plunge down the cliffs to the sea. Chances are a path contouring gently around a mountain will not suddenly veer straight up a steep slope.

Four ways to locate a lost trail are:

- **Return to the last point you're certain was on the trail.** You'll likely find you missed a turn or switchback.
- **Look for way-marks.** Find the last sign, blaze, disk or mileage marker.
- **Look for help.** If you're hiking with a companion and one of you goes looking for the trail, stay in voice or whistle contact.
- **Don't get more lost.** Before you wander off in search of the trail, fix your current location in your mind so you don't get more lost. Memorize distinctive features—a twisted tree or unusual rock formation, for example.

Really Lost

So you're really lost? Stay calm. Don't worry about food. It takes weeks to starve to death. Besides, you have that trail mix in your daypack. You have a water bottle. And you have a jacket in case of rain. You're in no immediate danger, so don't run around in a circle.

LOOK AROUND some more. Is there a familiar landmark in sight? Have you been gaining elevation or losing it? Where has the sun been shining? On your right cheek? Your back? Retrace your steps, if you can. Look for other footprints. If you're totally disoriented, keep walking laterally. Don't go deeper into the brush or woods. Go up slope to get a good view, but don't trek aimlessly here and there.

The universal distress signal is three visible or audible signals—three shouts or whistles, three shiny objects placed on a bare summit. Of course, you will have already tried to summon help with your cellphone, which unfortunately won't get a signal in the mountains. Don't start a fire! You could start a major conflagration.

If it's near dark, get ready to spend the night. Don't try to find your way out in the dark. Don't worry. If you left your itinerary, your rescuers will begin looking for you in the morning. Try to stay warm by huddling against a tree or wrapping yourself in branches, pine needles, or leaves.

Relax and think of your next hike. Think of the most beautiful place you know—that lovely stream, that stony mountain, a place where the fish bite and the mosquitoes don't. . . .

You'll make it, don't worry.

Really Lost Hikers Should:

- S.T.O.P. (Stop, Think, Observe, Plan)
- Blow a whistle to signal you need assistance
- Stay put. Most likely, if you've informed friends and authorities of your itinerary, a rescue effort will be launched quickly on your behalf after you fail to show at the appointed time.
- Drink enough water.
- Put on your extra clothing. Avoid getting cold, and worse, hypothermic.
- If appropriate, build a fire for warmth and as a locator. Pay attention to environmental conditions and the flammability of your surroundings, and don't set the woods on fire with your blaze.

14

Cautions and Precautions

> It is safer to wander in God's woods than to travel on black highways or to stay at home.
> —John Muir

BEFORE tackling the world-famous West Coast Trail, I bought the book, *Blisters and Bliss: A Trekker's Guide to the West Coast Trail.*

"Blisters and Bliss" is an apt description indeed of the 47-mile trail along the coast of Vancouver Island that attracts hikers from five continents. Blisters are only one of the many hazards facing the hiker. More about that in a moment, but first let me report on the bliss I found hiking the West Coast Trail.

If your idea of hiker's heaven is a coastal wilderness, this is paradise indeed. The route is a mélange of forest trails, beach, and low-tide sidewalk of sandstone at water's edge. Bold headlands book-end large crescent beaches. Above the beaches are coastal slopes forested with Sitka spruce, western red cedar, and western hemlock.

Wildlife abounds: bear in the forest, bald eagles roosting on shoreline snags, plenty of pesky raccoons and mice. Sea otters and whales are often spotted offshore.

Hike highlights include the cable-car crossings of dramatic, cascading creeks, fabulous beach walks, a hike through a rock arch, magnificent Tsusiat Falls, and so much more.

I was well prepared for walking in the rain and didn't get any blisters—unlike a significant percentage of other hikers I met en route, who were hurting, even hobbled by them. Still, blisters are but one challenge to hikers on the trail to bliss.

Water hazards, for example, are many. Two major rivers and more than thirty creeks cascade from the coastal slopes into the ocean. Bridges and cable cars span many of the creeks; ferry service shuttles hikers across the Nitinat Narrows and Gordon River.

Pacific Rim National Park's "West Coast Trail Preparation Guide" has enough caveats to stop even the most experienced hikers in their tracks: "Do not attempt to cross Adrenaline Surge Channel. People have died there!" Or "Don't throw anything at a bear—it may provoke an attack."

The park map highlights evacuation sites. Park wardens recommend that each party carry a 45-foot length of rope for crossing creek mouths, or to facilitate rescue.

Difficulties facing hikers include mud and muck, high rivers, high tides, rogue waves, and fallen trees. More than 100 inches of rain a year falls on the trail. Even when it's not raining, everything—logs, rocks, sand, and trail—is usually wet. And remember this bit of trail trivia: poison oak was discovered by the prolific botanist David Douglas on Vancouver Island, Canada, in 1830.

While the West Coast Trail still enjoys (if that's the right word) a reputation as one of the continent's most grueling treks, trail upgrades and better prepared hikers have made it less arduous. It remains a challenge to the average hiker, but is no longer the province only of hardy mountaineers.

On the West Coast Trail, and on trails everywhere around the world, hikers face a variety of hazards. Blisters happen. Mountain meadows are lovely, but they are often inhabited by swarms of mosquitoes. You can have fun in the sun, but too much sun on unprotected skin is no fun at all. You take a hike to get away from it all, and most of the time you succeed; occasionally, though, even way out there, big-city problems such as vehicle break-ins occur.

Even with the best of precautions, you can't avoid hazards altogether on the trail, but you can learn to minimize them and to deal with them when they occur. In this chapter we'll explore how to handle some of the more common health and safety issues facing the hiker.

Hiker Safety

Alas, backcountry travelers are not always immune from urban attitudes, stresses, and crimes. Most people you meet in the great outdoors are as friendly and as well-intentioned as you are, but it's not unheard of to meet a creep on the trail.

While most of our parks and preserves are far safer than our urban environment, hikers—particularly women hikers—must stay alert. Your "street smarts" coupled with your trail sense are two keys to avoiding trouble.

Know that national park, national forest, state park, and regional park authorities are committed to protecting the public. Many of the "rangers" you see on patrol are peace officers—meaning they have the authority to write citations, make arrests, etc., just like their city law enforcement counterparts.

Many park users—both good citizens and miscreants—don't realize that such rangers have arrest powers. A couple of times I've watched rangers make arrests, which are handled by the book just like any trained police officer, though often with the addition of an interchange something like this one:

> DRUNK: *(belligerently)* So what if I did? What are you going to do—arrest me?
> RANGER: Yes, I am.
> DRUNK: But you're just a ranger. You can't do that.
> RANGER: *(pulling handcuffs from belt)* Yes, I can.

Call on land agency law enforcement personnel if you feel at all uncomfortable about anyone/anything; they're dedicated to not only protecting the land, but public safety as well.

Safety Tips for Hikers

- Tell a trusted friend or relative where you're going. If the itinerary is at all complicated, write it down, have your friend write it down. At the very least, include a phone number for the park or place you're visiting, the trail you're taking, and expected return time. Along with making contact in person or by phone, e-mail your itinerary as well.
- While telling someone your plans is better than telling no one, telling someone familiar with hiking is better than dear, sweet, but trail-clueless Auntie Em.
- If you're traveling a remote trail or taking an unusual route, or simply want to cover all the safety bases, leave your itinerary and an emergency contact number with the supervising ranger station.
- Sign in and out at the trailhead register. If you get in trouble, emergency workers will know where to start looking.
- Use caution when sharing plans with strangers. By all means small-talk about hiking or anything else, but perfect strangers don't need to know where you're spending the night or your exact plans.
- Beware of anyone who acts hostile, drunk or drugged. Don't respond to taunts or provocation of any kind.
- Hiking with one or more companions reduces the potential for harassment.
- Dress conservatively (the hiker's layered look is definitely in that category) to discourage unwelcome attention.
- Hike trails away from roads accessible to four-wheel drive vehicles; unfortunately, a very small minority of the four-wheelin' crowd sometimes hassles hikers.
- Have an emergency plan. Know where the nearest ranger station and hospital emergency room is located in relation to the trail you're hiking.
- Pay attention to your instincts and abandon your plan if it feels wrong. More than once I have terminated a hike when the activities of the characters nearby felt suspicious.

All About Blisters

Blisters are one of the annoying realities of, well, wearing shoes. Most of us have gotten a blister or two at some point from ill-fitting or not-yet-broken-in boots or shoes, damp feet, or too-thin socks. Since hikers place heavy-duty demands on their feet, they need to be especially vigilant against anything that rubs the wrong way.

Blisters are the painful result of constant friction between your foot and boot. As your foot rubs against the inside of the boot, the point of contact on your foot becomes red and irritated (this is often referred to as a "hot spot"), and sure enough, a pocket of fluid—a blister—then develops under the top layer of skin.

Blister prevention

- Wear thick socks made for hikers. Or double up with thin socks on the inside and thicker ones on the outside. The theory behind wearing two pairs is that the first pair keeps your feet protected from any chafing between the second pair and your boots.
- At the first sign of a hot spot, tape the sore area with sport tape or a bandage to protect it from further chafing. Band-Aid makes "Blister Block" strips for this very purpose.
- Rub petroleum jelly on blister-prone areas. This can reduce friction enormously.
- Never start out in damp boots or socks. In addition to keeping your feet cold and clammy, damp footwear will ruthlessly chafe your poor old feet.
- Keep an extra pair of socks in your pack. If your feet get wet during the day, change into the spare pair.

Treating a blister

If the blister breaks, dab the area with antibiotic ointment. When you get home, wash it well and re-apply ointment. Then cover with a bandage. For the next several days, be sure to wear a different pair of shoes than the ones you wore on the trail.

If the blister doesn't break, leave it be until you get home. Once off the trail, wash the area thoroughly, then pierce the blister with a sterile needle, drain the fluid, and follow the above directions.

During the hike, however, a bandage is unlikely to last more than ten steps before rubbing off altogether. The following treatments are better on-the-trail fixes for blistered feet:

"Second Skin" by Spenco is one of the latest and greatest blister treatments around. It is a little like wearing a cold, wet, slimy bandage—which sounds disgusting, unless you have a blister, of course. To use, cut a piece of the Second Skin large enough to generously cover the affected area, and then seal it up with the dry and un-slimy "knit" tape provided in the box.

"Molefoam" by Dr. Scholl's is another great blister-treatment innovation. Though it doesn't ease the pain of a blister quite like Second Skin, it certainly keeps the blister from developing any further. To use, cut a donut-shaped piece of foam so that the hole is larger (but not by much) that the actual blister. Peel off the foam backing and press it firmly to the area surrounding the blister. The theory behind this treatment is that the raised foam will protect the blister from any contact with the sock or boot.

Big Things That Bite

North American animals that kill humans are few in number and, with some exceptions, roam remote territory. Not so long ago, humans were commonly prey for animals. Nowadays, though, when a human is mauled by an animal it is headline news.

Quite understandably, many hikers want nothing to do with some animals—snakes, bears, and mountain lions. When traveling the territory, it's important to learn about the habits and habitat of creatures that bite; use common sense and follow the time-proven rules posted at parks and at trailheads.

Many of the largest predators have very limited ranges. Don't let the fear of certain animals stop you from a wonderful walk in the woods.

Bears and mountain lions are two of the big animals that

some hikers would prefer not to encounter—or at least watch only from a safe distance. The wise hiker has a healthy respect—even a little fear—of big animals that bite. Nevertheless, don't stay away from the trail because of fear of wild animals. Do, however, learn about their habits and habitat, use common sense, and heed the time-proven rules posted at park and forest offices and at trailheads. Most parks that are habitat for mammals and reptiles potentially hazardous to human health have web sites or links to web sites that detail how to recognize such animals as well as the creature's likely behavior—and a human's best behavior in response.

Little Things that Bite

Late spring and summer are excellent times of the year for hiking. The air is mild, streams are flowing, birds are chirping and, unfortunately, bugs are biting. Blood-sucking insects are out in full force when the weather is warm—and they sure know how to spoil a good time.

In North America, hikers' most prevalent buggy foes are mosquitoes, black flies, and ticks. The good thing is that bites from these insects are very rarely life-threatening and at least somewhat preventable.

Best Ways to Avoid Bites

- Wear long pants and a long-sleeved shirt with elasticized, buttoned, or Velcro-tabbed cuffs. With the exception of gigantic biting flies, bugs can't reach you through your clothing. If the weather is really warm, wearing pants and long sleeves may not sound like a great idea, but some of the newer, more breathable hiking fabrics may change your mind, however. Check out the latest in lightweight, long-sleeved clothing—garb that can help keep you dry, cool, and bug-free.
- Tuck in your shirt! Bugs can easily fly or crawl up your back if you aren't careful.
- Wear bug repellant that contains DEET. Regardless of any

misgivings you may have about slathering chemicals on your skin, there is no denying that DEET keeps bugs away. Re-apply on exposed skin throughout the day as directed.

- Stay on the trail. Bushwhacking through heavily forested areas or grassy fields will increase your chances of picking up ticks.
- Don't take long rests near swamps or marshes. Mosquitoes love standing water, and will assault any human visitors who linger nearby.
- As silly as it might look, mosquito netting can actually be a real blessing in buggy conditions. Netted hats, pants and shirts can be found at hiking or travel stores and online.

Ticks

Ticks are small arachnids (like spiders) that feed on the blood of mammals, birds, and even reptiles. They frequently attach to human hosts in warm areas where they will likely go undisturbed—behind the ears or knees, armpits, and in the scalp. If left undetected, ticks will feed up to five days before moving on to another host.

Ticks are usually most prominent in moist, wooded areas with lots of leaf litter and dense underbrush, or in overgrown grassy areas. Ticks often wait for passing animals under leaves or the tips of grass blades.

Not only are they ugly and insidiously vampire-like, ticks are liable to carry nasty diseases. In North America, the most common tick-borne illness is Lyme disease, a bacterial infection that can be very serious if left untreated.

Preventing tick problems Some places are more likely to harbor ticks than others. Thick, wooded areas, for example, are often laden with these nasty bugs.

- Before you head home from a hike, check your fellow hikers (and have them check you!) for ticks. Brush off your clothes before you climb into the car.

- Did you bring your dog with you? He or she needs to undergo a thorough inspection as well. As you probably know, dogs spend a lot more time "hiking" in the surrounding shrubbery and running through grassy fields than sticking to the trail.
- In a post-hike shower, scan your body one more time—your hair, behind your ears, your lower legs, etc.
- Make sure to wash your hiking clothes soon after you get home.

Removing a tick Removing a tick can be tricky. While it's tempting to pull it out quickly, be careful—it's easy to leave the tick's head behind.

Pay attention to what happens afterwards! I once ignored a tick bite on my abdomen until my wife alarmingly pointed out what appeared to be a rapidly growing red bulls-eye on my stomach. A quick trip to my doctor, a prescription for antibiotics, and a little time-off the trail tamed my encounter with the tick.

If the tick's head does stay in the skin, you can remove it yourself or with the help of a friend.

First: With your thumb and forefinger, pinch the skin around the embedded tick head.

Second: Carefully scrape the area containing the head and mouth with a sterilized razor blade. If the head is in too deep, use a sterilized needle to break the skin and gently pull it out.

Third: Clean area with rubbing alcohol or other antiseptic.

Dos and Don'ts for Getting Rid of Ticks

Do—

- Dab rubbing alcohol on the skin around the tick and on the tick itself. It sterilizes the area and some experts argue that it causes the tick to loosen its grip, making it easier to pull out.
- Firmly grab the tick with a pair of sharp-pointed tweezers right where the head meets your skin.
- Slowly pull the tick straight out.

- If Lyme disease is a problem in your area, save the tick in a plastic bag or jar for later testing.

Don't—

- Smother the tick with petroleum jelly or butter. Some people believe that this will suffocate the tick and cause it to pull out on its own. To my knowledge, this method does little more than create a greasy mess.
- Use the heat from a match or cigarette to remove the tick. Like the petroleum jelly idea, it was once thought that ticks will pull themselves out to escape the intense heat. Instead, it is more likely that they will burrow even deeper into the skin.
- Try to pull on the tick with your fingers.
- Twist the tick as you pull it out. This may increase the chance of leaving the head behind.

Lyme disease Hikers in the Northeast, Mid-Atlantic and the Northern Midwest are more likely to contract Lyme disease (a tick-borne illness) than hikers in other parts of the country. In fact, the disease was named for Lyme, Connecticut, in the 1970s.

So, how do you know if you have it?

Symptoms of Lyme disease generally show up within four weeks of being bitten. One nearly universal symptom is the development of a circular rash at the tick site that looks a little like a bullseye—red with a pale center.

A smaller number of Lyme disease sufferers also exhibit flu-like symptoms, including headaches, fatigue, swollen lymph nodes, chills, and fever. Lyme disease is a bacterial infection, and can be successfully treated with a regimen of amoxicillin, doxycycline, or other antibiotic drugs.

Mosquitoes

Mosquitoes are the most universally well-known—and deeply hated—insects around. Both historians and biologists believe that they've plagued human civilization since its inception.

Like ticks, mosquitoes feed on the blood of animal hosts. But unlike ticks, only the females bite. They lay eggs in standing water, in anything from large swamps to tiny puddles, which makes it nearly impossible to avoid them on a summertime hike.

Not only do mosquitoes leave behind irritating, itchy bumps after feeding, they sometimes carry—and spread—deadly diseases like the West Nile virus, malaria, and the occasionally fatal Dengue fever.

It is extremely unlikely that hikers in northern climes will contract these diseases, no matter how often they are bitten. However, a handful of West Nile virus and Dengue fever cases are reported every year in the United State. Despite the low risk, it is important to take appropriate precautions.

Black Flies

Black flies are small, annoying, and almost everywhere. They feed on the blood of humans and other mammals, and occasionally birds. Like mosquitoes, only the females bite. But unlike mosquitoes, black flies can breed in moving water.

The good news is there are no known diseases carried by North American black flies. The pain and itch of a bite is about as bad as it gets.

DEET is Hard to Beat

DEET, or N,N-diethyl-m-toluamide, was developed by the USDA in the mid-1940s for American soldiers, and its effectiveness against biting insects was striking. It became commercially available in the 1950s, and has been used ever since in most over-the-counter insect repellants.

Like other insect repellant agents, DEET overpowers the scent that mosquitoes normally pick up from humans. What is different about DEET, however, is that it lasts much longer than repellants that contain citronella, eucalyptus, lavender, menthol, soybean oil, and other natural ingredients known for their anti-bug properties. I completely understand how uncomfortable some otherwise green-oriented, natural-living hikers might be with the idea of applying a chemical with the potency of DEET on themselves or their children. By all means give those natural soaps, sprays, and lotions a try; those fresh herbal scents may just fool the little buggers into avoiding you—for a limited time, anyway.

The *New England Journal of Medicine* published a study that listed the results of a study that compared "first bite" times of eleven commercial insect repellants. Study participants coated their arm with one of these substances and inserted it into a cage containing ten mosquitoes. Researchers noted the time it took until the first mosquito bit with each repellant.

Sure enough, the products that contain high concentrations of DEET fended off mosquitoes far longer than DEET-free or low-DEET repellants. The time to the first bite with OFF! Deep Woods (with a 23.8 percent concentration of DEET) was the longest, 301.5 minutes, whereas OFF! Skintastic (with 6.65 percent concentration of DEET) lasted 112.4 minutes, and Skin-So-Soft Bug Guard (with a 0.1 concentration of Citronella) lasted a mere 10.3 minutes.

DEET is powerful stuff, however. It can damage some plastics, spandex, leather, and rayon. Parents need to exercise caution when applying DEET products to children. The St. Louis Children's Hospital offers these guidelines:

- Children under the age of 12 should not be allowed to apply DEET themselves.
- Apply DEET only one time per day and wash off daily.
- DEET should not be used in a product that combines the repellent with a sunscreen. Sunscreens often are applied repeatedly because they wash off and DEET is not water-soluble. Repeated application of DEET may increase its potential toxic effects.
- Apply DEET before applying sunscreen.
- Up to 30 percent DEET is safe if used properly, with the duration of need determining the appropriate percentage, e.g. use a lower percentage if you're going out for a short period of time.
- 10 percent DEET will provide up to two hours of protection.

Some Things about Stings

Bees, yellowjackets, and wasps can be major problems as well, but they are unlikely to seek out hikers. Leave them alone, and they'll likely leave you alone.

Most of us experience slight swelling, itching, and redness from a bee sting. But there are many people who have severe allergic reactions that can include:

- extreme swelling in areas other than the sting site
- tightness in the chest
- dizziness or sharp drop in blood pressure
- unconsciousness or cardiac arrest

Most adults who have allergic reactions are aware of their allergy already. If you are one of these people, bring along an epinephrine kit wherever you go, especially on extended trips in the out-of-doors. If you are unsure whether you have bee sting allergies, please consult with your doctor.

Some hikers who aren't allergic, but do react with swelling and itching, carry Benadryl and administer it on the trail.

Tips for staying sting-free Don't wear bright clothing or scented lotions or perfumes (yes, I've been on hikes with women whom you could smell a hundred yards away). Bright colors and sweet smells attract bees and can fool them into thinking you're a delicious smelling flower.

Never swat at stinging insects. Waving your hands in front of your face may shoo away a mosquito, but it will likely provoke bees, wasps, and yellowjackets. As hard as it may be, let them linger awhile, and eventually they'll take off.

Removing a stinger To remove a stinger, don't pull it straight out. A bee stinger has tiny barbs that cling to your skin, making it difficult to remove. Rather, scrape the stinger and surrounding area with a credit card or fingernail to gently work it out of the skin.

Oddly enough, a bee stinger continues to pump venom into

the body for up to twenty minutes after the bee has stung. So it is wise to be expedient when removing the stinger.

While bees sting only once, wasps and yellowjackets may sting repeatedly. Calmly remove wasp and yellowjacket stingers in the same manner you would those of a bee.

Poison Ivy and Poison Oak

Some 90 percent of the population is susceptible to poison ivy, poison oak, and poison sumac. Some people appear to be immune because they don't get a rash after repeated exposures; sometimes, though, the apparently immune are affected by repeated heavy contacts.

Poison ivy was discovered early in American history. Captain John Smith named it in the early 1600s. Poison oak was discovered on Vancouver Island by famed early nineteenth-century botanist David Douglas. Fortunately for his revered place in floral history, he is remembered for the Douglas fir, not the "Poison Douglas oak."

Poison ivy often grows as a vine, creeping over the ground or climbing tree trunks. It can also be a self-supporting bush.

Poison ivy's middle leaflet has a much longer stalk that its two side ones. The leaves vary in size from about one quarter-inch to more than two inches in length. The infamous leaflets three are red in the spring, changing to a shiny green. Autumn leaves are red, yellow, and orange hues. The plant displays small greenish flowers and clusters of poisonous berry-like white drupes.

Poison oak grows abundantly throughout Western mountains up to an elevation of 5,000 feet. It's a sneaky devil. It may lurk under other shrubs or take the form of a vine and climb up an oak tree. The leaves are one to four inches long and glossy, as if waxed.

Urushiol (you-ROO-shee-ol), an oil similar to carbolic acid, is the "poison" in poison ivy and oak, and it's incredibly potent. Only one nanogram (billionth of a gram) is needed to cause a rash. Five hundred people could get a rash from the amount on the head of a pin. Just one-quarter of an ounce could cause a rash to erupt on every person on earth.

Urushiol is fast-acting, too; within 15 minutes of contact, it binds to skin proteins. If you wash it off with soap and water before the 15-minute mark, you have a shot of preventing a reaction. However, once the antigen is fixed, it can't be washed off.

Rhus plants (poison oak, poison ivy, and sumac) are by far the most common cause of what health professionals call allergic contact dermatitis in North America. A blistery, itching rash usually develops about 24 to 36 hours (though sometimes it doesn't manifest for several days) after a person makes contact with the plants. The usual course of reaction lasts 12 to 15 days.

All parts of the plant at all times of the year contain poisonous sap that can severely blister skin and mucous membranes. Its sap is most toxic during spring and summer. In fall, poison oak is particularly conspicuous; its leaves turn to flaming crimson or orange. However, its color change is more a response to heat and dryness than season; its "fall color" can occur anytime. Leaves on some plants can be turning yellow or red while plants in most spots are putting out green leaves. In winter, poison oak is naked, its stalks blending into the dull hue of the forest.

Contrary to popular belief, you can't catch it from someone else's rash, nor from oozing blisters, but petting an animal or handling a piece of clothing that carries it can make you a victim.

Rubbing or scratching the rash won't spread it to other parts of the body. Breaking blisters won't spread the rash, but can increase the possibility of infection and lead to scarring.

There are many effective remedies. Perhaps most common is the regular application of calamine lotion or cortisone cream. If you're particularly sensitive to poison oak, always wash down thoroughly immediately after a hike with cold water and a basic soap such as laundry detergent. Launder your hiking clothing separately as soon as possible. A dip in the ocean can help; a few tablespoons of baking soda added to a tub of lukewarm water calms the itchies as well. Organic types will probably want to pick some mugwort, an effective panacea. Its fresh juice applied directly to the pained area relieves itching.

Sun Protection

Skimping on sun protection just isn't worth it. Just ask anyone who's recently felt the sting of a bad sunburn, and they'll tell you one thing: OUCH! Not only does a sunburn feel terrible, it increases your risk for melanoma and other types of skin cancer. Given the vast array of sun protection possibilities on the market today, there's no excuse for not covering up, or slathering on sunscreen when heading outside.

No matter what the weather—sun, fog, haze, or snow—you'll need to take some precaution against sun damage. Wearing good, waterproof sunscreen or a wide-brimmed hat is your best bet, and the combination of the two is even better.

Picking out the right sunscreen can be confusing. Do you want something water-proof or water-resistant? Non-comedogenic? Something that offers UVA protection? UVB protection? Both? What does SPF mean, anyway?

Basically, UVA and UVB describe two different wavelengths of ultraviolet light. While UVB causes the most immediate and visible burn damage, both UVB and UVA rays are found in sunlight and can cause major damage to human skin. It is widely recognized that overexposure to UVA and UVB rays can dramatically increase your risk for skin cancer.

SPF stands for Sun Protection Factor and refers only to UVB protection. It tells you how much time you can spend in the sun before your particular skin type will burn. An SPF-20 sunscreen, for instance, should provide twenty times your natural skin protection against UVB damage. So if you ordinarily begin to turn pink after eight minutes in the sun, the application of SPF-20 sunscreen will theoretically give you 160 blissful, burn-free minutes in the sunshine.

But these numbers aren't always so accurate. While you can find sunscreens that boast an SPF of 45 or higher, most experts agree that there is little to indicate any real difference between an SPF-45 from SPF-30. And while a high SPF sunscreen can offer great UVB protection, it doesn't necessarily protect against UVA damage—the main culprit in the premature aging of the skin.

There are, however, sunscreens that claim to provide "broad-spectrum" (UVA and UVB) protection. These are your best bets. *Consumer Reports* magazine found that a few sunscreens provided the promised amount of UVB protection, and offered complete (or near complete) UVA protection. Rite AID Sunblock (SPF-30) and Walgreens Ultra Sunblock (SPF-30) proved to offer the best bang for the buck. Both rated "excellent" and are easy on the wallet. If you want to spring for a brand name, Banana Boat Sport Sunscreen and Coppertone Sport Sunblock rated "excellent" as well.

Studies vary in their evaluations of water-resistant and waterproof sunscreen protection. I recommend that you opt for the waterproof, and if you tend to sweat a lot while hiking, reapply sunscreen every couple of hours to be safe.

Hay Fever

Some 35 million Americans suffer from seasonal allergies, otherwise known as hay fever.

Unfortunately, hikers are not immune to the uncomfortable symptoms—the itchy eyes, runny nose, sneezing fits, and utter exhaustion—that accompany a sensitivity to pollen. Hay fever tends to be worse in the spring, but can hit anytime, anyplace, particularly when unfamiliar weeds and grasses are in bloom.

My wife, for example, experienced one of her worst-ever attacks on an idyllic, flower-bedecked trail near Telluride, Colorado. Thankfully, Cheri had an allergy medicine in her daypack and, after taking it, we were able to complete a hike far from home. Another time, we had to visit the local chemist in a tiny shop in the English countryside when she endured what the locals call "pollen nose."

Allergy-prone hikers have a couple of strategies to deal with the discomfort: avoidance and treatment.

Avoidance

- Hike early in the morning when pollen counts are low.
- Learn to identify which pollens trigger your allergies and avoid particular blooming plants.

- Substitute one hike for another. For example, avoid allergy-prompting mountain meadows by hiking near a lakeshore or seashore.

Treatment of symptoms

- Consider trying one of the new low-side-effect allergy treatments.
- Consider taking a natural or an herbal approach.
- Some allergy-prone individuals undergo desensitization treatment with varying degrees of success.

Hiker Hygiene—Ten Tips for Healthy Hiking

- Sometimes chemical toilets, even relatively clean ones, reek to high heaven, but use porta-potties whenever possible.
- Avoid leaving behind a urine smell for other hikers to whiff by peeing well away from picnic areas, campsites and the trail itself.
- Don't pee into the wind. Guys may write their names in the dust.
- Properly dispose of human waste. Dig a cat-hole six inches deep with your heel—better yet with a plastic trowel. Choose a disposal site out of sight of the trail, trail camps or vista points and at least 200 feet away from water.
- Dispose of toilet paper by sealing it in a plastic bag and packing it out.
- Wash your hands. Wash after going to the bathroom and before preparing or eating meals.
- Treat *all* backcountry drinking water.
- Don't share water bottles, bandanas, etc.
- Towel dry. After getting wet, you can drip dry or use a bandana, but a better way to dry is to take along one of those small but extremely absorbent "hike/camp" towels that you can purchase at an outdoor retailer.
- For women only: Hiking, like other challenging physical activities, can alter your menstrual cycle. Bring necessary sanitary supplies and pack out any waste in plastic bags.

Hiker Myths—or Advice to Forget

- **Fast-moving water is the safest stream water to drink.** Nope. Turbulent water keeps that nasty *Giardia* in suspension while slow water at least lets it settle to the bottom.
- **Warm someone with hypothermia by slipping naked into a sleeping bag with the victim.** Better not. The sudden heat can warm the blood too fast, straining the heart and propelling the victim into shock.
- **Moss grows only on the north side of trees.** In near-perfect conditions, moss (and lichens) do tend to thrive on the northeast sides of trees and rocks. Don't count on moss for finding your way, however, because it also grows almost anywhere that's wet and out of direct sunlight.
- **Treat a snake bite by making cuts around the wound and sucking out the venom.** Such treatment can spread the venom and cause infection, and it has long been medically out of vogue. Get the victim to the hospital!
- **Pee around the campsite perimeter to mark your territory and scare away wild animals.** Sorry, it's not an effective technique and apparently not at all scary to the animals.
- **Lost? Hike downstream to civilization.** Following a river might help you find your way out of the woods, but don't count on it. In the High Sierra, streams dead-end at glacial lakes; in Florida, streams flow into swamps and bogs. In many mountain ranges, the lost hiker would do better to follow a ridge.
- **Menstruating women shouldn't hike in bear country.** Bear experts say there's no evidence bears are drawn to women at "that time of the month".
- **Start a fire by rubbing two sticks together.** Theoretically possible, but most people will fall over exhausted before getting even a wisp of smoke. Ever watch the fire-deprived contestants on the TV show, "Survivor"? They don't have much success getting sparks, must less fire. Think matches and a fire-starter kit—flint and steel if you want to play frontiersman.

Hiker Ethics

Leave No Trace Principles of Outdoor Ethics

1. Travel and Camp on Durable Surfaces
2. Dispose of Waste Properly
3. Leave What You Find
4. Minimize Campfire Impacts
5. Respect Wildlife
6. Be Considerate of Other Visitors

—Courtesy of The Leave No Trace Center for Outdoor Ethics

15

Seasons

"In beauty may I walk
All day long may I walk
Through the returning
seasons, may I walk."
– Navajo Prayer

SOME High Sierra visitors insist there's little good about a day that begins with frost at dawn, gets hot enough by noon to peel your nose, and becomes downright chilly with afternoon shadows. I say autumn days are among the most magical of the year.

I like to hike the John Muir Trail in fall. During July and August the dazzling 212-mile trail along the Sierra crest vibrates under the passage of hikers, horses, and pack animals, but October brings miles of solitary walking.

I love leaf-peeping, Sierra-style. Red-leaved dogwoods glow against the redwood bark of the Sierra sequoia. Along meadow rims, golden aspen flicker like fire in the wind.

But really, it's not the leaves but the light that gives autumn its color in the Sierra Nevada. The sunlight is strong, the shade deep and black, a profound difference between light and shadow. Early sunsets over the summits are amazing, as the gravity-defying liquid shade flows uphill. The sun glows red, then rose, then indigo, coloring the minarets until there's no light left in the sky. Then the great daystar is replaced by a thousand constellations. Fall nights are long, but that gives you more time to gaze at the stars.

I like to hike in the "shoulder" seasons—just a little too early or a little too late for most visitors. And I like to hike some favorite places (the ones that aren't snowbound in winter, of course) in all four seasons and observe changes in nature along the trail.

Whether you choose to hike in-season, out-of-season, early in the season or late in the season, you need to know what you're getting into. Checking the weather forecast, dressing in layers, and being prepared are key to hiking safely through the seasons.

I love living in a part of America that offers four-season hiking. That doesn't mean every trail near my home is accessible year-around—far from it—but it does mean that at least some trails are open during each season.

Many regions in America, from Florida to the Southwestern Sunbelt, that receive little or no snow, also rightfully claim four-season hiking. Some states, such as Washington, with both snow-covered and snow-free locales, dry and very rainy areas, have regions of two-season, three-season, and four-season hiking.

Some avid hikers are bound and determined to hike all year whether conditions permit it or not. Several proud Connecticut hikers insisted to me that their state is the only one in New England where four-season hiking is possible. By New England standards, Connecticut's winters are relatively mild, these gonzo hikers pointed out. Southeastern Connecticut is spared the worst of winter's wrath, sometimes staying snow-free for much of the winter; it's usually among the first areas in New England to burst into spring.

Hmmm . . . Well, three seasons are pretty terrific for hiking: a muddy, but magnificent spring, a hot, humid summer, a New England autumn with all its leafy splendor.

While I encourage you to extend the hiking season—to hit the trail earlier in the spring and stay on the trail in autumn—I don't mean to suggest that you should push your luck. After a discussion about the splendors of hiking in spring and autumn, I detail some of the precautions necessary when hiking in cold weather, hot weather, and on rainy days anytime during the year.

Hiking in the Springtime

Spring is the exact same length as other seasons. But wherever you live, and wherever you hike, spring is the one season that everyone agrees is too short. Just when you notice the days are longer and the flowers are in bloom, it's summer.

April showers bring May flowers.

True enough at very particular latitudes and altitudes. In the low desert, however, for example, January showers bring February flowers. And in the Rockies, June showers can bring July flowers.

If an advertiser claimed, "April showers bring May flowers," the government would require a lengthy disclaimer.

I'm indebted to rangers at the Sequoia National Park Visitor Center for pointing out to me that certain parts of the country—most particularly the regions around Sequoia, Kings Canyon, and Yosemite national parks—have nine months of spring: January through September. These parks offer a way of resolving the "National Spring Deficit," the rangers joke.

More accurately, Sequoia National Park has 13,000 feet of spring, interpretive rangers explain. Elevations in this park range from just over 1,000 feet to the 14,494-foot top of Mt. Whitney. For every 1,000-foot increase in elevation, there is a corresponding temperature drop of 3° F.

So what does a change of elevation really mean? And how does it get us more spring?

In Sequoia National Park, and in other fabulous hiking areas around North America, if you're willing to gain elevation, you can partake of the joys of spring for far longer than the traditionally defined three-month period between the vernal equinox and the summer solstice. In certain mountain ranges, a wide range of temperatures and elevations create a variety of habitats and climates, both macro and micro.

In the case of the High Sierra, the first flowering plants can appear as early as January in the lowest foothills that rise from California's flat Central Valley. At Sequoia National Park's middle elevations (4,000 to 7,000 feet), where the mighty sequoias thrive, spring flowers begin to bedeck the meadows in April. On higher slopes, hikers will notice the more obvious signs of spring—tender grasses and wildflowers—in June and July. In the very highest alpine ecosystems, spring comes very late—August, even September. Spring and summer are greatly compressed at such high elevation. Spring comes and goes in a matter of weeks.

In Sequoia National Park, you can drive to a 7,500-foot trailhead, gaining more than 6,000 feet and losing nearly 20° F in temperature. You can then hit the trail for the 14,494-foot top of Mt. Whitney, losing another 20° F or so as you climb to the top of the highest peak in the continental U.S. Hikers pass a lot of "Spring" as they make one of America's most classic climbs.

Flowering plants are not the only life forms following spring uphill. Bears emerge from hibernation, foraging at ever higher altitudes to sniff out their vegetal preferences. Birds and bees and many more creatures thrive in spring, whenever and wherever they find the season.

So, if you want to prolong spring, hike higher and higher into the high country. Pause along the trail to admire the wide variety of flowering plants that adorn different elevations.

Hiking in the Rain and During the Rainy Season

Rain, rain, go away,
Come again some other day.

That chant from childhood never works very well does it? At least not for me.

Besides, some of my most memorable hikes have been rained on. I've taken my friends and family for hikes in the rain. Hiking in the rain gives us a chance to enjoy a kind of hiking that's experiential—not goal oriented.

I've been on expensive European hiking vacations when it rained and you know what? Yes, that's right, the guest hikers had a wonderful time. The group camaraderie and bonding increases exponentially with the shared experience of hiking in the rain.

I'd rather be rained-on than rained-out.

You could stay indoors and watch the rain come down and re-schedule your hike for a clear day. But sometimes you can't re-schedule. Or you could take a hike.

Part of being a hiker is embracing all kinds of weather. Certainly the drier you are, the happier your trails will be.

It rains when the weathercaster calls for clear skies. It rains on the coast on supposedly good "beach days." It rains in the middle of a record drought. It rains in the desert where it's not supposed to rain.

Rainwear, therefore, is essential. Carry it at all times.

Hikers who wear prescription glasses will probably wish to avoid the surreal visions caused by water-smeared lenses. A rain jacket hood will keep your head dry but not your glasses. A baseball cap will help deflect rain, but eventually gets soaked, and a plastic visor (don't quibble about aesthetics) works well. A rain hat with a wide brim is your best bet for keeping rain off your glasses.

Contact lenses certainly offer hikers the best rainy-day view of the world, but not everyone can wear them. Some hikers who wear glasses on a daily basis are able to wear contacts on a limited basis, such as on a day hike.

Rainy Day Hiking Tips

- **Unzip your pits.** Assuming your rain gear has armpit zippers, regulate your temperature by zipping and unzipping your pit zips.
- **Keep your map dry.** Carry a waterproof map or put your paper map in a plastic sleeve to keep it dry.
- **Keep everything else dry.** Ah, the wonder of self-sealing plastic bags. Use them to keep dry the more vital of your pack's contents—maps, camera, food, and more.
- **Enough is enough.** It's fine to hike in the rain up to a point. If you get wet and cold, though, get back to the trailhead and hike again another day.
- **Don't be surprised.** Experienced hikers aren't surprised by sudden wet conditions. Sometimes when hiking to the coast

you can all of a sudden experience fog so dense you might as well be walking in the rain. It's common to labor up a high and dry mountain pass, crest the range and find wet and rainy conditions on the other side of the mountain.

- **Keep snacks at the ready.** Keep food and snacks in a handy place on your person so you don't have to stop and retrieve them from the depths of your pack. If the rain is intermittent, use the dry spells to eat and drink and never mind your normally scheduled break or meal times.
- **Snack at will.** When the rain stops, take a break and start eating, even if it isn't your regular break time or meal times. Keep trail snacks handy so that you can refuel on the go.
- **Keep your clothing dry.** Carry a change of dry clothes in waterproof stuff sacks.
- **Watch out for post-rainstorm drip.** Rain-soaked undergrowth can drench the passing hiker. If hiking in a forest, beware of trees drizzling down on you, sometimes for hours after the storm passes. Remove your rainwear when it's dry-going on the trail not the instant the rain stops.

Thunder and Lightning

One strike and you're out, maybe out permanently, so you want to take some precautions against getting struck by lightning.

Lightning strikes hurl 30,000 amps of electrical current at the earth. To put such a force in perspective, that amperage is two thousand times greater than the 15 amps that circulates through our homes. Imagine, if 15 amps can kill us, what 30,000 can do.

The odds are comforting to the hiker, though. Odds of being struck are only 1-in-600,000. Most of the 300 or so Americans killed by lightning each year perish in cities, not in the backcountry.

Some people seem to be lightning attractors, however. Shenandoah National Park ranger Roy Sullivan was struck seven times (in the sense that he wasn't killed by these strikes, seven was a lucky number). Nature writer Gretel Erhlich was struck twice by lightning and wrote *A Match to the Heart,* a moving narrative about her experience and its life-altering effects. The lightning strike propelled the author to journey from one natural world to another, and to undertake a spiritual inquiry, as well.

"Quick as lightning" is an accurate description. Lightning strikes in a fraction of a second. The many branched streamers of electrical current (of which only two will strike the earth) charge out of the clouds. About 100 meters from the ground, the negatively charged "leaders" of electrical current meet positively charged "streamer" currents rising from the closest (often the highest) grounded object. A significant charge (return strike) shoots from the ground back up to the cloud.

Calculate how far away lightning is from you by counting the seconds between seeing the strike and hearing the sound of the resultant thunder. Each five-second interval equals about one mile.

Most lightning strikes occur directly below one of those scary-looking cumulonimbus clouds, but there are exceptions, including the proverbial "bolt out of the blue," a sudden, horizontally traveling bolt of lightning that can strike from as far away as ten miles.

Lower Lightning Risk

- Carefully time hikes to high-risk regions in coordination with evolving weather patterns
- Finish your hike before thunderstorms start.
- If you hear thunder, seek the safest terrain in the immediate area—a low area with short trees or shrubs.
- Avoid tall or isolated trees.
- Assume the recommended "lightning position."

If you're out on the trail and no shelter is readily available, scamper off high, exposed peaks and ridges and away from tall, isolated objects. Look for a low spot. If in an expansive woodland, take shelter under the shortest of the trees.

If you can hear thunder, you're the target of a lightning strike. If your hair stands on end and your skin tingles, you are in a mighty high electrical field and at a high and immediate risk of being struck by lightning.

Assuming you can't dash to a building or a hard-topped vehicle, you need to find the safest ground possible to wait out the lightning storm. As quick as you can, get off high, exposed terrain and find the lowest spot—or at least a lower spot—with the most low-growing trees and shrubs. Avoid fences, poles, and isolated trees.

Recent data suggests that the old mountaineer's advice about how to avoid lightning—"Up high by noon, down low by two" is still fairly accurate. According to the National Lightning Safety Institute, most lightning-caused injuries take place during the summer months between 11 A.M. and 9 P.M.

If a storm is developing, plan to get to your destination and back to a low-lightning-risk spot by noon. If you're hiking above the treeline and hear thunder, descend immediately.

When you've reached the best lightning-safe spot you can immediately find, assume the "lightning position." Squat or sit, balling up so you are as low as possible, in order to become the smallest target possible. Don't lie down; you want to minimize your contact with the ground.

Stay 50 feet or so away from hiking companions. Drop or move away from metal objects such as frame packs or hiking poles.

If one of your fellow hikers is struck by lightning and isn't breathing, immediately begin CPR. (It's just an enduring myth of the mountains that a lightning victim retains an electrical charge and is unsafe to handle.) Conscious victims with lightning-caused injuries usually survive, but should have a comprehensive medical evaluation as soon as possible.

Flash Floods

When a thunderstorm breaks over the mountains and desert, rain falls fast and furious. These rains—calling them torrential is not overstating their severity—quickly spill into gullies, arroyos, and canyons, dislodging and carrying along boulders, trees, and massive amounts of mud. Animals—and occasionally people—can be trapped or surprised by a flash flood cascading down what was a dry passageway just a short time earlier.

Flash floods are a danger in the canyon country of the American Southwest, and in many other regions of the world.

Flash Flood Precautions

- Keep an eye on the sky. Watch for storm cloud patterns. Listen for thunder.
- If a storm is approaching, avoid slot canyons and other narrow canyons and gulches.
- Check weather reports frequently, particularly on the morning of your hike.
- Backpackers should camp on high ground, but avoid the crests of ridges or peaks.

Your classic cumulonimbus, or threatening cloud, is not a subtle presence in the skies over the Colorado Plateau. When it's right over you, it appears dark and ominous and often assumes the shape of an anvil. While it's easy for the hiker to make a thunderstorm ID when one of those nasty looking clouds looms overhead, the same storm cloud may look white and bright when observed from farther away. Since flash floods can roil down a canyon as a result of a storm unleashing a deluge on a mountain located many miles away, a thunderstorm need not occur directly overhead to pose a danger to hikers.

Flash floods, at least in the American Southwest where they are most notorious, can occur from isolated thunderstorms at any time, but there is a distinct "Flash Flood Season" that extends from early summer to early autumn.

Hiking in the Mud and During Mud Season

It's kind of a northern New England thing, but the rest of you listen up because, even if mud season isn't a defined season where you live and hike, you're apt to encounter muddy conditions from time to time.

Vermonters take a kind of perverse pride in mud season, which extends from about mid-March to Memorial Day, give or take a few weeks. Vermont's "Fifth Season"—and mud season anywhere—can be the beginning of hiking season, provided the just-can't-wait-for-better-conditions hiker chooses the right trail on the right day. (Of course, if it's too darn muddy, stay off the trail; when hikers slosh across saturated soils, they damage trails and adjacent flora.)

Some Canadians trump New Englanders by claiming six seasons: spring, summer, fall, mud season, winter, and mud season again. During a year of maximum mud, the two mud seasons add up to six months, America's neighbors to the north claim.

You get mud when water can't soak into the soil quickly enough to be absorbed. Water runs off sandy soils but not so over other soil types. When water lingers on the surface of soil, you get mud. Snowmelt, often combined with spring rains, produces the volume of water necessary to make mud.

Theories abound explaining why one mud season might be worse than another: Could severity be related to how deep the frost permeates the ground? How quickly the ground defrosts in spring? The amount of snow on the ground when it starts to melt?

Vermont is more firm about closing hiking trails during mud season than other states. Mud season hikers of years past, along with foot-traffic-accelerated erosion in all seasons, has worn portions of Vermont's Long Trail down to bedrock. Some of the Green Mountain State's most famed trails, such as the ones leading up to Camel's Hump, are closed to hiking until the end of mud season.

Along with muck, mud season seems to bring more than its share of psychic misery. But don't succumb to this mud season of the soul, take a hike!

Some hikers can find beauty in any season—even mud season. It can be literally and figuratively dazzling for the hiker when a cold night's temperatures temporarily re-freezes puddles and create a mirrored surface, or when water-saturated mud refreezes, adding a frosting of ice crystals that sparkle in the morning light.

Mud Season Hiking Guidelines

- If a footpath is so muddy that you must hike atop the plant life or alongside it, retreat to the trailhead and select another hike in another area.

- Observe posted trail closures. Never hike on a trail closed due to wet conditions.
- Least muddy trails are apt to be found in lower-elevation hardwood forests with southern exposure. Sunny, south-facing slopes are among the first to dry out in spring.
- Hike through the mud on a trail not around it.
- Avoid high elevation conifer forests, alpine areas, and other fragile ecosystems.
- Remember that mud season is not just a spring thing; it can occur in late autumn with lots of rain or in winter with an unusual warm spell and sudden thaw.

Hiking in the Summer and in Hot Weather

Hot and bothered after a mid-day hike? Well, it's no wonder.

Recent studies have shown that optimum temperature for long-distance walks or hikes is 50° F to 55° F. Above this range a hiker's performance degrades as much as two percent for every five-degree increase in temperature. Air quality, wind (or lack of same) and the amount and kind of reflective heat are also environmental factors that affect a hiker's performance.

As temperatures rise, hikers must adjust their routine. Too much sun, too much hiking and too little fluid intake can make even a strong hiker an accident waiting to happen. Heat cramps, heat exhaustion and heat stroke can result.

California hikers, who tend to be a bit blasé about hiking in the heat, were shocked by the death of a 22-year-old hiker who died of heat stroke in the Santa Monica Mountains near Los Angeles. The healthy young man perished not five miles from air-conditioned restaurants, shopping malls, and suburbs full of swimming pools.

He and his companions started their hike near the hottest part of a day when the temperature climbed to 88° F. There was little shade en route on a strenuous hike with a hefty elevation gain.

We can learn at least two major lessons from this kind of tragedy: (1) heat illnesses and deaths are preventable by taking the right precautions, and (2) a hike near suburbia can be just as deadly as a trek across Death Valley.

The main environmental factors contributing heat-related illnesses are temperatures above 90° F., humidity above 80 percent and sunlight exposure (partial to full).

"People can lose up to 2 percent of their body weight in water before even knowing they are dehydrated," states Dr. Bob Girondola, professor of exercise science at the University of Southern California. Therefore, the often quoted, regularly ignored advice, "Drink before you're thirsty."

Of course, "Wait 'til it cools off" is always the best advice for the hiker contemplating a hike in the heat. But some hikers like it hot and, if you're determined to hit the trail in the heat, you must take the right precautions.

Tips to Beat the Heat

- **Time your hike for the cool of the day**—early morning is best, late evening second best. Avoid midday when the sun's rays are directly overhead, and late afternoon when the earth has absorbed the sun's rays but the heat hasn't dissipated at all.
- **Wear a hat.** A baseball cap will do, but only if you wear it with the bill in the front (not quite the hip-hop look, but effective). A better bet is an expedition-type hat that has protective flaps to cover the neck. Another style is the wide-brimmed bucket hat; again, don't worry about looking geeky on the trail. A hat is crucial to help you keep cool in hot weather.
- **Apply sunblock** (minimum SPF-15) on all exposed skin. Read the product directions: some varieties of sunblock need to be put on some time before exposure in order to be effective.
- **Wear loose fitting, light-colored, lightweight clothing.**
- **Carry—and drink—lots of water.** You need to consume 6 to 8 ounces for every 20 minutes of exercise on a hot day.

Heat exhaustion can occur when the body is stressed by hot weather and depleted of fluids and salts. Symptoms of heat exhaustion include pale skin, dizziness, agitation, nausea, headache, and rapid heartbeat.

Drinking lots of water or a mix of water and an electrolyte replacement drink will help ward off the condition as will moving from the sun to the shade. Eating a salty snack and taking a good rest will also help combat heat exhaustion.

More dangerous, heat stroke occurs when temperatures increase to the point where the body is unable to cool itself and brain function is affected. Symptoms of heat stroke include rapid pulse and breathing, irrational behavior, hot, dry skin, and unconsciousness.

Treat this condition by cooling down the victim with cool (not cold) water and cold compresses. Immediate evacuation and medical help is required.

Hiking in Autumn

Autumn has its critics and its fans. Some say there's little use for a day that begins with frost, becomes hot enough to sunburn your nose by noon, and has you shivering by sunset. Wiser heads, those attached to hikers no doubt, believe autumn is the best of all seasons. The high country air is crisp, but still inviting, the woodlands offer great opportunities for wildlife watching. Southern regions and the high desert cool enough for pleasant hiking.

Some of my most enjoyable hikes have been autumn adventures. In addition to the obvious lure of colorful fall foliage displays, hitting the trail in autumn offers an insect-free environment, sparkling clear-day views, and an excellent opportunity to view woodland wildlife during the "leaf-out" season.

I've found solitude in this season on trails around Europe and across America. Even the wildlands around such major tourist destinations as Aspen and Cape Cod have little trail traffic in the fall.

Planning for an Autumn Hike

Fall weather often brings highly changeable hiking conditions. You could face an unseasonable heat wave or an ice storm, an Indian summer or early winter.

Check the weather forecast for the day you're hiking and, if you can, check again with local authorities on the morning you start up the trail.

Autumn days are shorter. Remember that sunsets come earlier at this time of the year, so be sure to return to the trailhead before dark. Because of the shorter days, try to get a very early start. If you're on the trail bright and early, behold the many birds, usually most active and in best songster form during the first few hours of daylight.

Layer, now more than ever. Layering, as an outdoor dress methodology, is important in every season, particularly in autumn. With layers, the hiker can prepare for early morning and late afternoon chills and bright and sunny conditions at midday. Wear three or four layers and shed them as the temperature rises.

The autumn hiker should also remember rainwear. Pack it, even if the weathercaster is predicting a week of clear days. Fall sunlight can be intense; remember sunscreen and sunglasses.

Autumn is the season to don those convertible pants, the ones with zip-off legs that convert to shorts. A hat will keep your head warm in the morning, cool in the afternoon.

Autumn's Special Pleasures

- **Leaf-peeping** New England is ablaze with red, amber, and gold. Other regions boast brilliant, but less-renowned fall foliage.
- **Wildlife-watching** Late in the fall, with the deciduous trees now bare, birds, deer, and many more creatures are easier to spot.
- **Bug-free trails** No insects to plague hikers! After the first cold snap or frost, most of the little biters and stingers are dead or hibernating.
- **Solitude** Park trails are almost always uncrowded and it's possible you could have a whole mountain, small or large, to yourself.
- **Travel deals** Take a trip and take a hike. From airplane tickets to lodging at mountain resorts, travel is cheap in the fall. Be spontaneous to take advantage of last-minute deals.

Hiking in Winter and Cold Weather

> "Take long walks in stormy weather or through deep snow in the fields and woods, if you would keep your spirits up. Deal with brute nature. Be cold and hungry and weary."
> —Henry David Thoreau

For some American hikers, the end of hiking season comes on Columbus Day, for others on Halloween. Still others regard Thanksgiving as the end of the traditional hiking season.

I say wait a while before you hang up your hiking boots. Plenty of good hiking awaits you in the woods and mountains before the snow sticks.

Apparently many hikers who live in lands of little or no snow have deep empathy for their snowbound brethren because they, too, drastically curtail their hiking in mid to late autumn. Other hikers who could enjoy cold, but snow-free, winter hiking don't. Such reluctance could be the guilt caused by partaking of the pleasures of the trail while hikers in colder climes are housebound, but more likely their reluctance is really resistance to the notion of venturing out into the cold.

Cold-weather hiking has its rewards for the hiker who makes extra preparations and takes extra precautions. One reward for hiking in the colder months is more solitude on the trail. A deciduous woodland of leafless trees sure looks different in December than it does in its fully leafed-out splendor in July. The cold air is invigorating and vistas inspiring in the clear mountain air.

Dressing for a Cold Hike

Get all the synthetic-fabric clothing you have out of the closet and get ready to do some serious layering. If it's really cold, begin with polyester long-johns, top and bottom—a poly T-shirt if it's not quite so cold. Continue with a fleece jacket or vest and fleece pants. Top that with an outer layer of wind–rain jacket and pants and you'll be ready for just about anything.

Don't forget some kind of neck covering like a scarf or hood. Remember to wear a hat and a pair of gloves or mittens.

Weatherproof boots and warm socks are essential. Each year bootmakers make footwear more water resistant and more breathable, but a hiker's socks still get wet and sweaty. To keep your feet warm and happy, bring extra socks and change them out during the day. Gaiters help keep mud and moisture out of your boots.

Food and Fluids

Fueling the body in cold weather is a challenging task because stopping to prepare or consume a meal means that at-rest body temperature drops, often leading to stiff fingers and numb toes. Rather than stopping for a sit-down lunch, refuel "in flight," so to speak, munching along the trail. Choose "high octane" high-carbohydrate, high-fat snacks and stash them in your jacket pockets and pack pouches for easy access. Chocolate bars, energy bars, dried fruits, and nuts are ideal snacks for this purpose.

When hiking in cold weather, you'll burn more calories in order to stay warm; however, if you're well dressed for the cold, you really won't be burning too many more calories than normal to maintain your body's core temperature.

Even in cold weather, even though you're not feeling particularly thirsty, drink plenty of water—two liters per person per day. Pack a thermos of hot tea or soup.

Dehydration increases the effects of the cold on the hiker, further exerting the heart and muscles, and contributing to fatigue.

If the temperature is below 32° F., wrap your water bottles in insulated sleeves to keep them from freezing. You can also slip them inside your jacket to keep warm.

Adding a sports drink or sugary mix such as an electrolyte mix or Kool-Aid to your water will lower the freezing temperature. However, if you put too much sugar into the water, you'll increase diuresis (in other words, you'll pee out more fluid than you gain)—not good when you're trying to stay hydrated.

Safety

Start with the weather forecast from radio, TV, and the internet, but remember most of the reports are oriented to population centers. Often the park or remote wildland where you wish to hike is off the radar—literally and figuratively—of the weather service and may have a distinct microclimate that's different from the nearest city. Call the local authorities or land manager to get more specific weather information about the terrain you plan to trek.

Hike at a steady pace, fast enough to generate some body heat, but slow enough so that you don't start sweating a great deal. Find a pace you can sustain and stick with it, so you don't wear yourself down and you don't have to stop very often to rest.

Those short autumn–winter days mean that the day hike you planned could unexpectedly turn into a night hike. Take along a flashlight or headlamp (and spare batteries) in the event your return to the trailhead takes longer than expected.

Autumn is a great season for wildlife-watching, a chance to view land birds and waterfowl, deer, moose, and many more creatures. It's also hunting season in many regions of the country. To avoid being mistaken for any animal that a human needs a license to kill, wear at least one article of bright orange clothing if you intend to walk in the woods during hunting season.

Cold Weather Hiking Tips

- Get the latest weather report and adjust and scale your trip with regard to any approaching storms. Keep an eye on the sky and be flexible with your hiking goals and itinerary.
- Dress in layers (synthetic garb, of course) and prepare for a wide range of temperatures.
- Pack waterproof outer layers of clothing.
- Wear a hat, scarf or hood, gloves or mittens.
- Practice with walks near home to determine how you and your apparel fare in cold weather.
- Drink plenty of fluids.

- Eat regularly, with lots of high-energy snacks.
- Wear heavy socks and weatherproof boots.
- Bring along a hand warmer.
- Use trekking poles to keep balance on slippery slopes.

Hypothermia

Hypothermia is the sudden cooling of the body's core temperature and the body's subsequent inability to respond by generating enough heat to make up for its loss. Many hikers have a tendency to think of hypothermia as a problem only for such hardy outdoors-folks as scientists on Arctic expeditions and snow campers, but the potentially fatal condition can result from a variety of mishaps or mistakes.

Hypothermia, rightly associated with cold temperatures and inclement weather, can also affect hikers in more moderate temperatures and conditions. Wet clothing, a plunge into an icy river, sitting atop snow and exposure of sweat-soaked person to a cold wind are some of the ways hypothermia can strike hikers.

Hypothermia is a difficult challenge to treat, but in most cases, easy enough to prevent with some commonsense precautions and preparations. Staying dry, wearing warm, weatherproof clothing that keeps some of its insulating qualities even when wet, wearing a hat (nearly half our heat loss is through our heads) and gloves, and drinking plenty of liquids are ways to ward off hypothermia.

Often it's not backpackers but (too) casual day hikers who are most at risk. For example, that five-mile ascent to the top of Bald Mountain looked like it was going to be a breeze until a sudden storm swoops in with a cold rain. You forgot your rain gear and are soon soaked to the skin.

You're really piling up the miles on a long day hike and decide to extend your outing a couple of miles. In mid-later afternoon, just short of Beaver Meadow, you slip off a log while crossing Wild Rose Brook, and plunge into the rushing, snowmelt-swollen waters, soaking you and all your gear. You're a long, long way from the trailhead, the sun seems to be rapidly dropping behind the mountains, and it's getting cold fast.

Backpackers, with their portable camps on their backs, and often clad in better and more weatherproof apparel, can simply stop, set up camp and take the necessary steps to get warm. Not so day hikers, who must hike back out to camp, lodge, parking area, or wherever they started the hike.

Many hikers try to get away with carrying the minimum on a day hike—sometimes just a water bottle and lunch—and don't even bother with the Ten Essentials. To guard against sudden weather changes, rainwear and extra layers of clothing are a must. Just pack this gear and clothing, even if the weather forecast is for a beautiful day, even if you don't feel like carrying it, even if such precautions seem excessive to you.

Having it, but not needing it, is a good feeling. When you're well prepared, you'll feel blessed in good weather, secure in bad weather.

At the first serious complaint of cold (hey, we all tend to kvetch at the trailhead, *Oh my God, it's freezing!*), add a layer of clothing to the complainant and hike a bit more to see if s/he warms up. If not, return to the trailhead. If you or your day hike buddy is wet and cold and lacks a change of clothing, end the hike and head back to the trailhead via the shortest route.

Symptoms of mild hypothermia include shivering, complaints of being cold, difficulty performing simple motor skills, apathetic behavior, apparent disinterest in taking care of personal needs, and body temperature falls to 96° F. Symptoms of more severe hypothermia include stumbling or falling, slurred speech, irrational behavior, decreased pulse and respiration, a possible slip into unconsciousness, and the body temperature drops below 96° F.

Never push a hiker with any of the symptoms of hypothermia to "push through it." Strong hikers are often the ones who become subject to hypothermia because they tend to have a no pain-no-gain mentality, ignore symptoms and continue hiking.

Who among us hasn't shivered and displayed some impressive goose bumps in chilly weather? Shivering per se doesn't necessarily mean a hiker is developing hypothermia; shivering is part of the body's normal heat-generating response to a cold environment. Look out, though, for prolonged shivering and the other warning signs of hypothermia. Remember that in all stages of hypothermia, the victim might be in total denial of his condition.

Move the person with mild hypothermia into a warm environment as soon as possible. Remove wet clothing and replace it with dry garb—or wrap them in blankets or a sleeping bag. If conscious, give the person warm (not hot) liquids and food.

More severe hypothermia means the person can no longer warm himself. Getting the victim to a hospital should be the highest priority. If this is not possible, standard first-aid is the application of warmth (warm water bottles, hand-warmers, etc.) under the armpits, to the head and neck, and to the groin area. Treat and move the victim very gently.

Once the victim's temperature rises back to normal, she must hike back to the trailhead or be evacuated. Don't even think about resuming the hike.

Prevent Hypothermia

- Double-check the weather forecast. Learn about any predicted storms or cold fronts moving into the area where you'll be hiking.
- Dress warmly in layers. Be sure to pack a rain jacket.
- Pack an extra set of clothes, particularly if your hike includes creek crossings.
- Wear a hat and carry some gloves.
- Stay dry.
- Drink plenty of fluids.
- Eat high-energy foods and snacks.

16

Terrain

"The wild requires that we learn the terrain, nod to all the plants and animals and birds, ford the streams and cross the ridges, and tell a good story when we get back home."
—Gary Snyder

FROM a muddy overlook in the middle of the Hawaiian island of Molokai, in the middle of nowhere, I marveled at Waikolu (Three Waters) Falls thundering in the distance, gazed out at precipitous cliffs and over what looked like an impenetrable rain forest.

"How can anyone get over terrain like that?" I wondered out loud.

"You just have to know the land and how to hike it," answered Mike, my guide, who patrols Kawinkou Preserve for its steward, The Nature Conservancy.

The first part of the trail through the preserve is on a narrow wooden boardwalk that leads through Pepeopae Bog, believed to be 10,000 years old. Violets and orchids brighten the primordial ooze.

Then the boardwalk runs out and the fun began. My guide issued me a pair of rubber boots—the same make and model he's wearing—and strode into the bog with what seems to be an effortless gliding motion. I followed and in ten paces came out of my left boot, which seemed super-glued to the muck. Ten more paces and my right boot stayed behind. While Mike skimmed over the surface of the bog, I sank like a stone.

"After a couple of miles, you'll pick up the right technique," my guide advised. "You know, more than 200 plants grow here and nowhere else in the world. They probably wouldn't have survived if just anybody could hike here."

Clearly, different kinds of terrain call for different kinds of preparation and different hiking techniques. You might not ever hike through a bog that looks like a setting for Jurassic Park, but you're likely to encounter a variety of other kinds of terrain, each with its own challenges to the hiker. To prepare yourself for where the trail takes you, learn to safely cross streams, keep your footing on rocks and slippery slopes, and remember the safety precautions necessary for a hike at high altitude.

Hiking Uphill and Down

"To climb steep hills requires a slow pace at first."
—William Shakespeare

Hiking uphill takes energy, lots of it. Hiking two miles an hour up a 10-percent grade requires as much energy as hiking four miles an hour on level trail.

Use your arms to help your legs. When climbing steeply, as you step upwards, press down on your forward thigh with your hands. The use of trekking poles can give you a boost uphill, too.

Take some of the pain out of the gain by mastering the rest step (see below). It doesn't look like much and, frankly, it looks a little silly, but it does work.

Hiking up means slowing down. Slow and steady will get you up that steep trail to the summit.

Slow-down on downhill trails, too. A moderate pace will help prevent injuries on steep descents. Use small steps on steep descents and keep your knees loose. And the same trekking poles that gave you a boost uphill also add stability going downhill.

Going down too steeply? Don't be embarrassed to sit on your butt and (carefully) slide down the hill. Better to wear out the seat of your pants than blow out a knee or risk a fall.

Master the Rest Step

To ease the strain of hiking up steep terrain, learn the rest step. This special step is a very useful technique when you're tired; it assists weary legs and helps you to slow and regulate your breathing.

As you step forward and down with your foot, pause a second or two while your weight remains on your trailing leg. During the pause (a kind of stop-motion) your hip will take on some of your weight and relieve your lower leg muscles, Next transfer the weight to the front leg, step forward and pause again.

While the rest step isn't exactly a rest, those short pauses between steps adjust your pace to a more comfortable one and sure beats the alternative—climbing twenty steps, gasping, resting, then climbing, gasping, and resting again. Because it helps prevent muscle strain, the rest step is a particularly good technique to employ at the start of hiking season when your muscles aren't quite in top form.

Some hikers do a great job of coordinating their breathing with the rest step, which can bring on a kind of meditative state, a Zen-like consciousness.

The Fall of Man

"If you get up one more time than you fall, you will make it through."
—Chinese Proverb

Hikers fall. Some rarely. Some frequently. Softly. Seriously. Falling is by far the most common hiker accident. Fortunately, most falls result in no more than scrapes and bruises, though serious injury and even death can result from falls.

If you hike long enough on a variety of terrain, sooner or later you're going to fall. Canadian park rangers tell hikers bound for Vancouver Island's supremely slippery West Coast Trail that they should expect to fall. Wear gloves to protect your hands, they advise hikers.

Considering the remarkable number of obstacles nature puts

in the path of bipedal mammals to trip them up, it's a wonder humans evolved to walk on two feet instead of sticking with the far more secure four-footed locomotion.

Every experienced hiker can rattle off a long list of the types of terrain that seem to conspire to cause us to face-plant or fall on our butts, do the splits or split our heads: muddy paths, scree, earth slumps, algae-covered rocks, roots, logs (wet or dry), rounded boulders, sandy slopes, bogs, and deadfalls. The trail itself can add more hazards: iron stakes, washouts, slippery footbridges, drainage culverts, wooden steps partially buried in mud.

Hikers can also fall prey to other trail users. Hikers get tangled in each other's boots or bump each other off the trail. Be sure to move off the trail during rest stops so you don't crowd another hiker into slipping off the footpath. Mountain bikers colliding with hikers get into some terrible accidents—and usually it's the hiker who takes the hardest fall.

Fall-back Positions

Best advice for backpackers is to fall backwards onto the backpack. (This advice has some application for day hikers who happen to be wearing a well-designed, well-cushioned daypack.) Landing on the pack cushions the impact. Such a fall often momentarily traps the backpacker on his back ("turtling," in hiker jargon), an indignity to be sure, but usually not a serious situation. If you're the hiker doing the turtling, get back to your feet before your trail buddy snaps a silly picture of you,

If you know you're going down, sometimes you have a split-second choice of which body part to land on. The derrière is often a good choice.

Some fall experts (you have to ask yourself how they became experts—by falling?) opine that there's a chance a hikers can get more hurt by Herculean efforts to stay on the feet and prevent a fall. So the idea here is to go with it—fall, but fall down as safely as possible. Drawing your hands and arms into your chest as you fall helps reduce the chance of injury to your arms and helps protect vital organs.

Hiking over Rocks

Constant vigilance is the key to hiking over rocks. Whether picking your way over a shoreline that resembles piles of broken bowling balls or traversing a wide expanse of scree high on the shoulder of a mighty mountain, rock work is hard work, each step different from the last.

"Rock!"

In the time-honored tradition of the mountaineer, yell, "Rock!" if you dislodge one and send it hurtling down the mountainside.

Wet rock per se doesn't reduce your traction all that much, as long as the angle of the rock is low and your boots have a good sole. However, rock (wet or dry) coated with gravel or slime can easily up-end a hiker.

Scree, an accumulation of loose, sliding stones found above the timberline, can be a challenge to hikers used to firm dirt trails. Ascending scree is two-steps-up–one-step-back kind of hiking. (Sometimes scree-walking is two-steps-up– three steps back!)

One way to climb scree is by kicking steps into it with the toes of your boots. Scree is shallow, so it's easier kicking into solid ground than you might imagine but a tedious way to ascend nevertheless. A better bet is to ascend a scree slope by switchbacking your way upward, gaining elevation a little at a time.

Descending scree is a bit like surfing the curl. Catch that wave of small rocks and ride it, knees bent, skidding down on your boot heels.

Another high-mountain challenge for the hiker is talus, rock rubble that ranges in size from boot-sized rocks to SUV-sized boulders. Bigger rocks mean bigger steps, which mean increased demands on your knees, particularly on descents. Ascending this kind of a boulder field requires strength and stamina but is easier than descending.

Hiking downhill on talus requires some nerve and coordination. Those new to the sport tend to hop from one rock to the other, one rock at a time. Talus-experienced trekkers learn to look several steps ahead and, knees bent, dance their way in a side-to-side motion down the slope.

Hiking Across Streams: Crossing to Safety

While most good trails have good crossings (i.e. shallow fords or footbridges), some do not. Wilderness trails sometimes present challenging stream crossings. Rapid snowmelt or a sudden rainstorm can make a tame stream treacherous. Heed the following river-crossing tips:

- River reconnaissance is well worthwhile. A trail might not cross a waterway at the very best place. Survey the scene up and downstream.
- If possible, cross a mountain stream early in the morning when the flow is lowest. (Snow melts slower during the night than during the day.)
- Cross at the widest (usually the most shallow) part of the stream. Look for a flat water section below a wide bend.
- Cross at an angle (downstream is usually best) because heading straight across exposes you to the full force of the current.
- Given a selection, choose a sandy bottom over slippery rocks for your way across.
- Use a hiking stick as a third means of support (third and fourth leg if you're using two trekking poles). If you hike without one, search for a suitable makeshift stick along the stream bank.
- Loosen your shoulder straps and unfasten your pack's waist band. You must be able to wriggle out of your pack if you take a tumble; your pack could trap you in—or under—water.
- Step slowly and cautiously. Securely plant your front foot before moving the trailing one.
- Discretion is indeed the better part of valor. If a stream looks too dangerous to cross, it probably is. Retreat and come back another day.
- Whitewater kills; even fairly shallow fast-moving water can knock you down and hold you under.

- Keep your boots on to protect your feet and maximize your footing. Bare feet are okay for crossing wimpy watercourses with sand bottoms.
- If you're hiking a trail with lots of stream crossings, employ alternative footwear such as a sturdy pair of sneakers or a pair of amphibious sports sandals.

Hiking on Snow and Ice

Hikers who surmount high mountain passes in the summer, begin hiking in the spring before all the snow is melted, or continue hiking into the snow-dusted late autumn months may encounter the white stuff. The following discussion is not a correspondence course in crampons or a detailed discussion of winter mountaineering, but only a few tips for dealing with snow and ice.

I strongly suggest that hikers take a winter travel lesson (from a climbing or mountaineering school, the Sierra Club or hiking clubs). Look for a one-day introductory class that teaches such basic snow hiking skills as crampon use, self arrest, the plunge step, and using an ice axe.

Sometimes on early season (spring in colder climes) hikes, the hiker must negotiate snowbanks that blanket or partially obscure the trail. Unless it's too deep or too steep to cross safely, just walk over it. If, for the same reasons, the snowbank looks nonnegotiable, hike around its periphery.

If you're the first hiker—or one of the first hikers—to cross a snowbank, be a good trail citizen by blazing a path across the snow that as nearly as possible follows the route of the path that's hidden underneath. The way the path goes might be obvious or you might need to take an educated guess. When the snow does melt, your pathway through the snow will be right on top of the dirt trail and you won't have created an unsightly, slope-eroding new one.

Hiking at High Altitude

"Never measure the height of a mountain
until you have reached the top."
—Dag Hammarskjöld

From tenderfoot to world-class mountaineer, every hiker can feel the effects of altitude sickness. A strong hiker can be subjected to a trip-ending bout of nausea while a less-experienced and less-fit hiker might make it up the mountain with little or no effects from high altitude. Even Everest conqueror Sir Edmund Hilary experienced altitude sickness when, years after climbing into the record books as the first to reach the 29,028-foot summit of the world's highest peak, he hiked at far lower elevation.

Contrary to what seems like common sense, youth and fitness seem to offer no particular advantage to a hiker's susceptibility to altitude sickness. A fit hiker will perform better than a couch potato on the trail, of course, but fitness—or lack of same—is not a predictor of one's sensitivity to altitude sickness.

Every person's response to oxygen deprivation is different. Few feel the effects below a mile high—5,000 to 6,000 feet or so. Headaches and stomachaches are common symptoms of altitude sickness at higher elevations. Many hikers are willing to push through these discomforts in order to experience alpine beauties and/or reach the top of a mountain.

If you're in good shape when you hit the trail at high elevation, you'll certainly breathe easier. A fit hiker loses about 2 percent of aerobic capacity for each 1,000 feet in elevation gain over 4,000 feet, while someone who's been sedentary down in the flatlands loses double that.

That old bit of mountaineering advice, "Climb High, Sleep Low," has only limited application for the day hiker. Spending a night—and ideally a day and a night or more—at a high elevation camp or lodge before embarking on an alpine sojourn, will help you acclimatize.

Maintaining a moderate rate of ascent—1,000 feet per day above 7,500 feet—is an ideal, but usually impractical, way to acclimate.

Among the worst acclimatization offenders are American West Coast dwellers from San Diego to Seattle, who drive directly from their sea-level homes to very high trailheads. Getting out of the car and beginning a hike at 9,200 feet . . . well, so much for any altitude adjustment plan.

Dehydration contributes to altitude sickness and worsens it as the condition progresses. Limit or eliminate coffee, tea or caffeinated beverages because all are diuretics and accelerate fluid loss by prompting increased urination. (The well-hydrated hiker's urine is clear or fairly clear.)

Avoid adult beverages, too, because alcohol is a diuretic. Unfortunately, the symptoms of a hangover are similar to those of altitude sickness, which can be confusing to someone attempting to make a diagnosis, particularly if that someone is the one with fuzzy judgment resulting from a double whammy of altitude sickness and a hangover.

A dose of acetazolamide (more commonly known as Diamox), available only by prescription, has been found to assist in the adaptation to high altitude and alleviate some of the effects of altitude sickness. Diamox is not an immediate fix for acute mountain sickness; rather, it helps speed up the process which in turn helps to relieve symptoms.

The drug has been used by hikers and climbers for more than thirty years and many swear by it, though it does have side effects. Diamox is a diuretic so if you take it you'll have to drink even more fluids than usual. Those who are allergic to sulfa derivatives need to be aware that Diamox is in the sulfa family, which produces various other side effects in some people. Consult your physician before use.

Altitude Sickness Indicators

- Shortness of breath
- Appetite loss
- Low energy, fatigue
- Headache
- Nausea
- Poor sleep, insomnia

In mountainous regions with less oxygen, the hiker's blood thickens making oxygen dispersal to the muscles far less effective than at sea level.

Drink, drink, drink. And drink some more, more than you think you need. While a liter or two of water may get you through a day of hiking along a coastal trail, doubling that intake might be necessary for a day at high altitude.

Of course when we're hiking hard at elevation, we hikers tend to breathe through our mouths, which dries us out even more.

Even very experienced lowland hikers should not expect to cover as much ground in a day at high elevation as they do at lower elevation. Pace yourself with one of two tried-and-true methods:

- **A slow hiking pace** Start out slower than you think you can go. Keep it slow and steady. You might think your muscles are capable of a faster pace, and they probably are, but your body needs time to adjust to decreased oxygen levels.
- **Make frequent stops** Keep a moderately slow, but not very slow, pace and stop frequently.

For some hikers, the symptoms start at about 9,000 feet with a headache that won't go away and stomach distress. Many hikers show the signs of altitude sickness the night before when they can't get a "good sleep" or can't sleep at all.

Aspirin can help alleviate a hiker's headache. This particular pain-reliever has the added benefit of helping to thin the blood.

You're unlikely to notice much in the way of effects of altitude at 3,000 feet but already, even at that modest elevation, the body is making adjustments—primarily increasing the rate of respiration. As altitude increases, so does respiration rate.

At sea level, an individual's capacity for exercise is limited by the heart's ability to supply oxygen to the muscles; at high altitude, an individual's capacity for exercise is limited by the amount of oxygen that can be gathered by the lungs.

Those hikers planning an extended high-altitude expedition, say to the Himalayas, will be pleased to know that the average hiker can get about 80 percent acclimated to high-altitude within ten days.

Reduce the odds of getting altitude sickness by drinking lots of water, eating well (even though you might not have much of an appetite) and ascending gradually.

When Altitude Sickness Strikes

What goes up must come down is one law of physics that applies to hikers. Descending the mountain is the obvious response to an ascent that makes you sick.

An early morning headache that won't go away and a queasiness in your stomach are more annoyances than serious health threats, and nature's way of reminding you that you need to get acclimated.

- Stop the ascent and descend
- Keep drinking fluids
- Rest
- Aspirin

Strong hikers often suffer the most from the effects of altitude sickness because they tend to ignore their symptoms and "hike through the pain," particularly if what they consider to be wimpier companions are not similarly stricken. Apparently, an increase in altitude does not bring hikers an increase in humility and a willingness to admit that on some days the mountain just wins.

Ignoring the symptoms of altitude sickness (accurately called acute mountain sickness by the emergency medicine community) can put you in danger. Once a hiker moves from the initial symptoms of headache and nausea to the second set of symptoms—slurred speech, staggering around—it gets really ugly. At this point, a "designated hiker" must escort the sufferer down the mountain right away.

Left untreated, acute mountain sickness can result in a pulmonary or cerebral edema—that is to say, blood plasma gets in the lungs or brain. Add to the above symptoms of altitude sickness a rapid pulse, raspy breathing, and increased confusion, even unconsciousness. The victim must be moved immediately to a lower elevation or s/he will die.

High-Altitude Sunlight

Those deep blue skies over the mountains, so inspiring to hikers and to our landscape photography, mean thinner air, which in turn means intense sunlight bearing down upon us. By some accounts, the fair-skinned hiker who starts to sunburn in 30 minutes at sea level can begin burning in just six minutes at high elevation.

Oftentimes high-altitude hiking takes place in environmental conditions that include low temperatures or a brisk breeze. When hikers are cool, not hot, they sometimes forget to apply sunscreen. Do remember, because you can get sunburned very badly very quickly at high elevation. After applying sunscreen to your face and neck, remember to dab the back of your hands, too. To avoid painfully chapped lips from the very-dry high altitude air, use a lip balm or ointment.

A hiker's high-altitude headache can worsen as the result of the glare of sunlight on the eyes. Ice and snow compound the glare, reflecting the rays right back up at the hiker.

17

Wildlife

"There are some who can live without wild things and
some who cannot. Like winds and sunsets, wild things were
taken for granted until progress began to do away with them.
Now we face the question of whether a still higher
'standard of living' is worth its cost in things
natural, wild and free."
—Aldo Leopold

ONE OF my earliest nature-writing assignments was to write voice-over narration for a series of (very low budget) wildlife films. Together with the director-cinematographer, I reviewed hours and hours of raw footage of elephant seals, condors, snakes, and snow geese and learned how challenging it is to create an entertaining half-hour film that communicates the essence of a particular animal.

While the filmmaker had captured some gems—a baby condor's first flight, bull elephant seals fighting for dominance—he also came back from the field with endless shots of animal posteriors, as well as creatures eating and just standing around.

In the midst of writing narration for a grizzly bear documentary, trying desperately to craft a half-hour storyline from twenty-five hours of film, I wrote the worst line of my career: "Here comes the big mother now."

My all-too brief experience in the nature-film biz helped me appreciate the extraordinary patience required of those who make wildlife films and the great lengths people will go to observe and record animals in their wild kingdom. I learned how difficult it is to capture those "magic moments" when a creature does something we all-too-anthropocentric humans find entertaining.

Making nature documentaries was fun, but I'd rather watch wildlife in the wild instead. Some of my most memorable moments on the trail have been hikes during which I marveled at creatures great and small. That moose in Cape Breton, Nova Scotia, that 'gator in Everglades National Park, that tortoise in the Mojave Desert—all cherished memories indeed from terrific hikes.

A memorable wildlife sighting can make a good hike great. Learn where the wild things are by consulting a regional guidebook or asking staff at park visitor centers. A little research will tell you that the buffalo roam in South Dakota not South Carolina. Bighorn sheep gambol through the Rockies, not the Berkshires.

Adult wildlife-watchers tend to gravitate toward the larger creatures—a moose with a sky-scraping rack of antlers, for example—while children delight in watching pint-sized critters. Kids will while away half an hour playing peek-a-boo with a pocket gopher popping its head above ground.

I've led children on hikes who were hugely fascinated by watching a banana slug move across a trail. Much to my impatience, the kids wouldn't budge until the slug crawled sluggishly away.

Some would-be wildlife-watchers hit the trail with such high expectations that they're invariably disappointed. Expecting to see a rare species—whether it's a mountain yellow-legged frog or a moufflon (a Greek mountain goat)—is not a good way to start a hike or enjoy wildlife-watching.

All too often hikers setting out to observe wildlife—often narrowly defined as medium- to large-sized mammals—are disappointed if they see "only" raccoons, a wood rat, or a covey of quail. A better attitude to take on the trail is a sense of wonder—be surprised, be delighted by any creatures you see!

Most wildlife checklists obtained from park offices are big on birds, and there are reasons for this. Your basic birdwatcher is a compulsive note-taker who always records sightings, and often reports species seen to the park naturalist. Whether flying or roosting, birds are often easy to spot—at least easier than most quadruped-type animals.

Birds—with the exception of owls—are active during the day while many animals are nocturnal. Unless you're a night owl and equipped with infrared night vision goggles, wildlife-watching at night is unlikely to be fruitful.

Nocturnal animals such as rabbits and skunks, however, are often spotted during the daytime. Best chance for glimpsing nocturnal animals—and many diurnal species as well—is to hit the trail by dawn or still be on the trail at dusk. Obviously the optimal times for wildlife-watching may not coincide with the best time for you to take a hike.

Marvel at how many animals remain unseen, hidden from view of the passing hiker: resting in trees, sleeping underground, feeding in the tall grass, nesting in the undergrowth. We see signs of them in the form of tracks, scat and chewed branches.

Often we hear animals without seeing them—the call of the wild, indeed. We hear their rustlings in the brush—which our imaginations often magnify and lead us to believe come from animals far bigger than the ones really producing the sounds.

Official Watchable Wildlife Viewing Areas

Repeated surveys have shown that wildlife-associated recreation is hugely popular with Americans, who love observing and photographing wildflowers, wildlife, and scenery.

The National Watchable Wildlife Program is a coalition of government agencies and private conservation groups working together to promote wildlife-watching. The underlying premise for the program is the belief that if the public is provided with ample and engaging opportunities to view wildlife, citizens will become better informed about plant and animal species conservation.

A binocular logo designates official wildlife-viewing areas. Strategically placed signs with the logo direct motorists from highways and secondary roads to the sites, which often feature leg-stretcher type trails that lead from parking lots to viewing outposts. Some wildlife-viewing areas feature longer hikes.

Hiking on the Edge Can be a Good Practice

Good wildlife-watching is often found on the edges of habitats. Ecologists say many of the most interesting and dynamic habitats are on the edges: places where the forest meets a meadow, where the land meets the sea, where the city meets the country.

Here plants and animals confront conditions that give rise to increased variety. Studies of bird populations reveal that species are more abundant in places where the chaparral meets the pine forest than in chaparral-only or forest-only environments. Various plants and animals that might be rare in one community or the other may flourish on the edge between them.

Areas of transition between ecological communities are called ecotones: their existence depends on two differing environments, yet also create a world unto themselves. In his classic text, *Elements of Ecology,* George Clarke states, "As a rule, the ecotone contains more species and often a denser population than either of the neighboring communities, and this is generally known as The Principle of Edges."

Wildlife-Watching Tips

- Do it at dawn and dusk. Animals are particularly active at these times.
- Hike slowly, hike quietly. Loud talking—even snapping a twig or dislodging a stone—alerts wildlife to your presence.
- Keep your distance. Approach wildlife in a roundabout way. Never purposely scatter birds to get them to take flight or give chase to an animal.
- Use the right tools. Binoculars or a spotting scope help deliver close-up views. A telephoto lens—400mm or so—on your camera will capture what you see.
- When duck hunting (with a camera, of course), go where the ducks are. Some sites have greater wildlife-spotting potential than others: springs, ponds, perches, ledges and meadows.

- Hide out behind boulders, bushes and tree trunks. Assume as small a profile as possible.
- Consult park wildlife checklists and field guides to determine which animals are likely to be spotted where.
- Stay on maintained trails. Not only is sticking to the trail an environmentally sound practice, it can actually help you see more wildlife as well. Animals often take the easiest and most direct path through the woods—just like hikers.
- Look for signs: tracks, scat, bedding sites, burrows, mounds, cavities.
- Patience, please. Don't expect to spot a moose around the first bend along the trail to Moose Bog.
- Don't feed wildlife. Nature provides adequately without supplemental feeding from human handouts. Such foodstuffs can hurt an animal's digestive system, even kill it.
- Wear natural-colored clothing and lotions and deodorant without fragrances.

Bird-watching

"I hope you love birds, too. It is economical.
It saves going to heaven."
—Emily Dickinson

How to explain our fascination with the world's winged creatures? There are bird species aplenty in every ecosystem—resident songsters, waterfowl, migrants from near and far.

Much to the fascination of birders, there are more than 8,000 species. Each winter several billion birds fly south from the temperate zone

Watching birds fills us with wonder. We wonder how birds navigate by the stars. We wonder how fledglings learn their songs from parents and neighbors.

The names of groups of birds are intriguing, even joyous: a host of sparrows, a covey of quail, a flight of doves, an exultation of larks.

Birding is one of the most complementary activities to hiking. (Some enthusiastic birdwatchers might think hiking is complementary to birding, while others regard hiking as a necessary evil to reach the best birding spots.)

Basic birding equipment is simple: a field guide, a good pair of binoculars, a notebook.

Birders use a notebook to record observations about birds: where and when observed, appearance, movements and behaviors, call or song.

A good field guide highlights a bird in a drawing or photograph and gives a description (in capsule form or highly detailed). A bird's habitat and range, a bird's voice—its call or song—along with the time of the year it's likely to be sighted in a particular area, are all keys to identifying a bird species

Many parks and nature centers offer free or low-cost checklists of birds. A particular species will be easier to identify if you familiarize yourself with the species recorded in an area and review a regional bird guide and checklist.

Bird-watching Tips

- Identify the bird by observing its size compared to other birds, its body shape and its wings, tail, feet and bill, and its distinct colors or markings.
- Note the bird's location—in or near water, in a tree or in flight.
- Listen for the bird's song or call.
- Watch the bird's behavior. Is is perching, pecking, swimming, singing?
- Examine what birds leave behind: footprints, feathers, droppings and nests to expand your knowledge.
- Try to be unobtrusive when watching birds so they're not aware of your presence. Keep your distance, move slowly and quietly.
- Stay on established trails and resist the urge to trample fragile vegetation in order to get a closer look.
- Never touch eggs and young birds or get too close to a nest. You could frighten parent birds away from the nest and scare them into abandoning it.

Sharing
The Way

18

Companions and Going Solo

"Good company in a journey makes the way seem shorter."
—Izaak Walton

WHAT do you want to gain from a day on the trail? Happiness found? Friendship deepened? Curiosity satisfied? Calories burned?

Happiness is a particularly difficult benefit to evaluate; if we agree that humans are social animals and that happiness is a quality that must be shared, it would appear that the hiker in good company might be happier than the one who hits the trail time and again alone. Alternatively, if a hiker's strongest motivation is to discover what's on the other side of the mountain, such a discovery can be just as satisfying—perhaps more so—alone, as in a group.

I enjoy hiking alone and with companions. During the many years I wrote a weekly hiking column for the *Los Angeles Times,* I was required to hike—and write about—fifty-two trails per year. Since most of my friends have what they tell me are "real jobs," I took the great majority of my "work" hikes alone.

Occasionally I feel lonely on a solo adventure, but most of the time I'm happy keeping my own company. When I'm hiking alone, I particularly enjoy meeting rangers and passersby on the trail. As the nature writer Joseph Smeaton Chase put it: "You meet out-of-the-way people in out-of-the-way places."

I also enjoy hiking in company. I love hiking with my family, guiding groups of kids, hitting the trail with friends. When our family hosts out-of-town friends and relatives, I like to show them the wonders of our local trails.

Hiking alone or with company is strictly a matter of personal preference. Each way has much to recommend it.

Some newcomers begin hiking with a group until they gain a measure of confidence and then choose to go solo.

Other newbies start walking solo then discover they enjoy sharing the way with a particular trail buddy, a group of hiking companions, or a whole hiking club. Many hikers like to alternate between hiking with friends and family and hiking solo.

Hikers have a broad range of abilities, interests and enthusiasms. The company they choose to keep on the trail reflects that diversity.

Hiking with Others

"Even when walking in a party of no more than three
I can always be certain of learning from those I am with.
There will be good qualities that I can select for imitation and bad
ones that will teach me what requires correction in myself."
—Confucius

If you're accountable to someone other than yourself, you're more apt to walk the walk. When you're facing an early-morning start, weather that's hot and humid or cold and rainy, general malaise or low spirits, having someone you can depend on—or who depends on you—makes a difference.

Making an appointment with someone to take a hike, keeps you accountable for actually doing the hike. All too often in our busy lives we give up what's not critical to our work or family responsibilities, and cancel something like a hike because it has no immediate benefit or practical purpose that we can see. (I understand this attitude—and have struggled with it myself. However, I hope this whole book refutes the notion that there's nothing more to hiking than putting one foot in front of another.)

I'm convinced men and women are wired differently. Women can talk on the trail *and* observe the scenery, while enjoying every moment of the hike. Women multitask, even on a hike.

Contrary to the teasing we get, men can walk and talk at the same time, though men also like to hike along in what I call companionable silence—together, yet a little separate, wordlessly enjoying the presence of another while simultaneously appreciating being alone with one's own thoughts, too. Men without women have been known to go primal on the trail, enjoying the simple pleasures of sweating, scratching, and burping . . .

Finding a hiking companion means finding the right companion; look first to your spouse, another family member, or a friend. One presumes you have ready access to these individuals and have something in common with them. Time on the trail can enhance your relationships. Hiking offers a great opportunity to spend time with someone you care about.

Consider going with a companion on a walkabout. While the Australian aboriginal concept of walkabout is often viewed as a lone individual traveling through the bush for self-discovery, in fact, walkabouts are traditionally completed in pairs, each walker discussing an issue or challenge with a partner.

The accepted rules for a walkabout include:

- Conversation is completely confidential, and may not be repeated to anyone else.
- Each partner has the same amount of time to discuss their dilemmas.
- The pace should be unhurried.
- Silence is the occasional third partner on a walkabout.

Choose your companion carefully. Not every city friend is a good trail buddy. For truly happy trails, a good hiking companion should share similar fitness goals, pace, and nature appreciation orientation.

Join a Hiking Club—or Start One

With a hiking group, you get the same fresh air and exercise as you do hiking solo with the additional opportunity to visit with your friends or make new ones.

Many Sierra Club chapters have ambitious outings schedules. Beginners are welcome to join the club's easier jaunts, though it's a good idea to check first with the hike leader about an upcoming hike's difficulty or newbie suitability. Don't go to socialize if the "High Peaks" section is planning a 20-mile day hike.

Larger Sierra Club chapters not only sponsor hikes of various levels of difficulty in a variety of terrains, but boast subchapters that appeal to different interest groups. The Club's Angeles Chapter of Southern California, for example, has hiking groups that include older singles, younger singles, gays and lesbians, desert peaks enthusiasts, dog owners, four-wheel drive explorers, families with younger children, and many more subgroups with special outdoor interests.

Walking clubs are numerous and easier to find than hiking clubs. Call them or go on a walk. Check for walking/hiking club flyers posted at sporting goods stores, sports shoe stores, recreation centers, community centers, health clubs, and online.

Chances are some walkers in a given group are also hikers—or would like to become hikers. Another way to search for hiking groups is to call a few parks (with hiking trails) in your area and ask park staff if any organized groups lead walks.

Walking clubs vary in quality and orientation, ranging from mall walkers who do the same circuit over and over and never venture out of the shopping center to members of a particular religious faith, who find walking together deepens both fellowship and spirituality. Some clubs emphasize neighborhood jaunts and walks in the park, while others include challenging hikes in their schedules.

Look for a hiking group that has what you're seeking— weekday hikes or a women-only membership, for example. If you don't find what you're looking for, the best "hiking club" for you may turn out to be you and couple of friends.

Consider starting your own group. A hiking club can be very simple: a once or twice a month get-together with friends on the trail. Each member can take a turn choosing a trail, varying the difficulty of the hike in order to keep fellow hikers engaged.

Organizing a Hiking Club

- Gather hikers and would-be hikers together and decide on the group's reason for being and hiking together: Why a hiking club? Who can be a member? How many or how few members? What exactly will the group offer members?
- Get organized. Delegate tasks: member outreach, communications, scheduling, hike leading.
- Take a hike!

Along with offering a special kind of bonding that takes place only on a trail, hiking groups build camaraderie in other ways: breakfast before the hike, a shared meal afterwards, picnics and carpools to the trailheads. Experience suggests that the most successful clubs are the ones with a minimum of (non-hiking) meetings and a maximum of outings.

A few hiking clubs offer classes in hiking skills, but most teach hiking technique in far more informal ways—friendly members assisting newcomers one step at a time.

Clubs communicate to members through paper or e-mail newsletters or the old-fashioned phone tree. Some clubs have incentive programs and offer awards that hikers earn by reaching the summits of certain peaks, logging a certain number of miles or achieving other goals.

Some hiking clubs develop an ID and logo, stitch a patch on their daypacks, and enjoy wearing club baseball caps and T-shirts. Other clubs "adopt a trail," support trail maintenance projects, help disadvantaged children to learn to hike or raise funds for a park or nature center. Often the bonds formed while hiking together are very powerful and members become close friends who help each other off the trail in times of sickness or personal crisis.

Hiking Solo

"The man who goes alone can start today; but
he who travels with another must wait till that other is ready."
—Henry David Thoreau

Too many so-called hiking authorities have wrongly turned a positive suggestion, "For maximum safety, hike with a companion," into a negative absolute, "Never hike alone."

While there is no question that it's safer hiking with a group than solo, "How much safer?" is a legitimate question to ask.

Is the risk of hiking solo so great that each and every hiker should wait until s/he has company in order to hit the trail?

Absolutely not. Go take a hike. Alone. The risks, while often overstated, are real, and the precautions needed are crucial, but such risks and the requirement for additional precautions are not reasons to decide you can't hit the trail solo.

Having two or three in your party is a definite advantage if something goes wrong; someone can go for help. Four eyes are better than two; a hiking partner may notice a danger that you overlook. You might remember essential gear your hiking buddy forgot. This safety-in-numbers theory holds for hiking as it does for most forms of outdoor recreation from camping to kayaking, rock climbing to mountain biking.

Hiking with a group—or at least with a trail-seasoned friend—is a good idea for first-time hikers. Most inexperienced hikers are uncomfortable going solo.

Sometimes, after a few hikes, a craving for solitude develops—by which time you should be able to take care of yourself on the trail. There's a lot to be said for solitary hiking, as the writings of Thoreau, Whitman, and Muir would seem to indicate.

I can speak with some authority on the subject of hiking solo since I'm often alone on the trail. I enjoy hiking with my male friends, with my spouse and my children or "on business" with a ranger or a trail advocate showing me a new trail. Solo hiking, however must encompass about 80 percent of my hiking experiences.

Intrigued as I am by the natural world and grateful for the escape from everyday life, I've rarely been lonely on the trail. Not only do I value my time alone on the trail, I find that I often return with a deeper appreciation for the people in my life.

A significant number of hikers have a craving for solitude, which can only be accomplished by solo hiking. These hikers need time alone in the woods or on a mountain to recharge their spirits and be happy.

Some people need solitude occasionally, some regularly, and find the best opportunity for getting it is by taking a hike. Hiking solo serves to nurture a special relationship with yourself and with the natural world, and perhaps even provide a time to contemplate your spiritual path.

Tips for the Solo Hiker

- Know your limits. No one is going to monitor you but you. Don't exceed your personal speed limit or overreach your capabilities.
- Leave your itinerary with a trusted friend or relative. Even better, be personally accountable by reporting your whereabouts to someone at an appointed time.
- Adhere to your stated plans for both your hiking route and schedule.
- Go out of your way to contact park staff or land management personnel. Visit visitor centers. Check-in at ranger stations. Sign-in at trailhead registers.
- Add to your first-aid kit. It should contain more supplies to care for yourself—over a longer length of time, since there is a greater likelihood no one will be around to help you or go for help.
- Carry a whistle and mirror to signal for help and assist rescuers in locating you.
- Stay alert. Even a minor mishap like a slip and fall or twisting an ankle can be a serious incident for a solo hiker.

Canine Companions

Many dogs love to take a hike and love the "quality time" with their owners. Hiking with a dog on a woodsy trail beats walking the dog around the block any day. For many hikers, a dog is man's best trail friend—particularly for those who hike solo.

A dog is an energetic hiking companion and, with a superior sense of smell and relatively low proximity to the ground, may notice things about the natural world that would otherwise escape your attention.

Take sufficient time to prepare a canine companion and you'll discover that a well-equipped owner and well-trained dog will be the best of trail buddies, each enhancing the other's experience.

First, make a candid assessment of your dog's energy level and condition. Not every good dog is a good hiker. If your pooch is a canine couch potato, an "indoor" dog or a chubby chowhound that's scarfed a few too many table scraps, he might not thrill to the call of the wild. Hint: pooches that pant like crazy on walks around the neighborhood are going to have a difficult time of it on the trail.

Many dogs love to hike, though, and, with some conditioning outings, will improve over time. If you have any doubts, ask the vet if your dog is sufficiently physically fit for hiking. Ask your vet to suggest a canine conditioning program. Also ask if your four-legged friend might have any limitations that might restrict his hiking abilities. Have the vet check your dog for hip, back, and joint problems.

Which brings me to the dog-hiking business I encountered in the Santa Monica Mountains on the west side of Los Angeles. Dog-walking services have been around major (and many minor) metropolitan areas for decades. But this business takes dogs on a hike.

"The owners want the best for their dogs, and that's hiking," one of the professional dog-hikers told me. "Most of the owners wish they could hike, but they have stressful jobs. It makes them feel better, knowing that even if they can't hike, the dogs are out there on the trail having a great time."

Walkin' The Dog

- Make sure your dog has up-to-date vaccinations and current identification tags.
- Only hike where dogs are allowed.
- Help your dog out with some flea and tick repellant.
- Bring water and a collapsible bowl. Dogs can get dehydrated and overheated, just like humans.
- Heed leash laws
- Don't allow your dog to chase squirrels, deer or other wildlife.
- Clean up after your dog. If your dog brings it into the park, you need to hike it out. Use zippered plastic bags for disposal of waste. If you are far from the trailhead, bury dog poop in a "cat-hole," well off the trail.
- You and your dog must yield to all other trail users, including cyclists and equestrians. Leash up and allow other trail users to pass.
- After the hike, check your dog for ticks and foxtails.

19

Children

"It's a good thing to learn more about nature in order to share this knowledge with children; it's even better if the adult and child learn about nature together. And it's a lot more fun."
—Richard Louv

THESE DAYS our kids are way over-scheduled, and subjected to far more organized activities and more homework than were most of their parents. Play is indoors with video games, virtual reality experiences and going online. Overbearing, overprotective "helicopter" parents hover over their children, and encourage them to stay inside instead of sending them to play outside. These parents (and many schools that confine children indoors) are taking all the fun out of childhood and keeping kids from the natural world.

It's time for those of us who believe that getting outdoors and into nature should be an essential part of childhood to articulate an alternative vision. It's time to get kids to spend less time on MySpace and more time in open space.

Lately, all we hear about when the conversation turns to school is technology, technology, technology. How many times have you heard a candidate for the local school board or a candidate for state or national office say something like : "For Americans to compete in the twenty-first century, our schools need the latest in technology. We need to wire our classrooms."

I completely disagree. Kids don't need to be wired; they need to be walked. Walked in the mud and the rain and the heat and the cold. Walked in the forest and mountains, by the lakeshore and seashore. Walked until they're dirty and sweaty and tired. Walked until videophilia (our obsession with electronic screens) recedes and biophilia (our natural impulse to love the natural world) resumes.

Richard Louv, in his landmark book, *Last Child in the Woods,* writes movingly about how most kids have become completely out of tune with nature and how we adults allowed, perhaps unwittingly encouraged, it to happen. He refers to this as "Nature Deficit Disorder." Unfortunately, we all suffer from it in one degree or another in our speeded-up, high-tech indoor lifestyles.

Research suggests Americans of all ages, particularly children, are replacing outdoor activities with indoor ones. A study sponsored by The Nature Conservancy identified "videophilia" as a cause of obesity, poor social skills, various attention disorders, and poor academic performance. Rampant videophilia is replacing outdoor activities.

At the same time, other recent research has demonstrated that time spent in nature improves the health of children, increases their ability to concentrate, and boosts their self-esteem, emotional well-being and leadership skills. Clearly we have a real responsibility to get our children into nature. The question many hikers have is as simple as one a five-year-old might ask: "How?"

A few years ago, I wrote a book about hiking for kids. It's a very upbeat book, with an emphasis on the fun kids can have in nature. My toughest editor turned out to be my then-10-year-old son. When Daniel read my first draft he was critical of my approach: "How come you keep telling kids hiking is fun. Kids know that, don't they?" Then he added, "Duh-uh?"

My young editor even got on me about offering basic hiking advice: "Kids know to stay on the trail and not cut switchbacks. Duh-uh!"

"Daniel, if I don't write about the fun of going hiking and I don't give kids tips on how to hike, what am I supposed to write about?"

"Just tell their teachers and their parents and the rangers to take them on a hike."

Can't argue with that logic. "Duh-uh," as the kids would say.

Attention Parents

How long ago was it that you conquered snowy summits, explored remote canyons and partied hearty with the Sierra Club Singles after a 15-mile hike?

Seems like a century ago, huh?

When you have children, it can seem like the simplest hike is more difficult to organize than a Himalayan expedition.

But don't hang up your hiking boots. Tell your kids to take a hike—with you, of course. Children learn first-hand about nature and get valuable lessons in sharing and cooperation.

If you could use a little motivation to get on the trail, join a family outings group. Many parks and nature centers lead interpretive hikes that are open to both children and parents. I highly recommend the Sierra Club's Little Hikers, which welcomes families with children (newborn to pre-teen). Four- to ten-year-olds most enjoy the hikes, chosen for their level terrain as much as for their natural beauty.

Family hiking enriches family life; be sure to adapt your trail adventures as your children grow—faster than you think!

Bringing Baby

In my experience, babies, fed and comfortable, are great trail companions. Portable, easily amused, prone to napping in the fresh air, they're delightful, and delighted. This early introduction to nature and bonding with parents in the great outdoors combine for a meaningful hiking experience, a wonderful blend of nature and nurture.

- Choose a child-carrier that has good head support for the baby, and with a design that's secure but not ultra-constricting to the child. Like any backpack, a child-carrier should fit well and feel comfortable on the parent's back.

- Dress your baby warmly. Remember, the baby is lots less active than you and needs to be warmer.
- Bring all the usual baby stuff. Remember all the in-town baby essentials such as food, bottles, a toy, diapers, and wipes. Take a plastic bag to carry out soiled diapers and towelettes so they can be disposed of properly.
- Stop frequently to check—or have your hiking companion check—the baby's status. Make sure your baby is warm, but not overheated, and protected from the sun.
- Avoid hiking at high altitude. Babies, particularly those who live with flatlander parents, do not adjust well to increased ear pressures and other strains of high altitude.
- Take it slow and easy. Don't try to ford fast-moving rivers or descend steep grades with that bundle of joy on your back. And watch out for low-hanging branches!
- Use a jogger stroller. When baby outgrows the carrier, try an all-terrain stroller instead. These high-tech strollers, with their strong frames and lightweight construction, mountain bike-like tires, and good brakes, are highly maneuverable on flat and rolling terrain, on dirt roads, and on selected single-track trails. We used this type of stroller for years and it gave us much more mobility than we ever imagined. It definitely allows the whole family to enjoy more time in the outdoors—and allows a four-year-old to go lots farther than four-year-old legs can travel.

A Few Tips for Parents

I'm very pleased that my children have learned to enjoy hiking—though some would point out they had little choice! Nevertheless, I learned early on what a privilege it is to share the joy of time on the trail with the little ones.

Some of the most important lessons I've learned while hiking with my kids came to me when I stepped out of my role as parent and gave them a chance to lead me on their path. Along the way, they've taught me that they're well-attuned to nature's rhythms.

Parent to parent, let me caution you: the last thing children want to hear is too much information: Relax! You don't need to be a substitute science teacher and identify every plant and animal along the way. Just keep them safe and have some fun.

Ten Trail-Tested Tips for Hiking with Children

Keep your children in sight at all times. That may seem obvious, but you'd be surprised how fast kids can get off the trail.

Repeat and repeat again all instructions ranging from snack breaks to porta-potty locations.

Choose a hike with fairly modest elevation gains. Children prefer intimate settings, such as a little creek or a clump of boulders to those vast scenic panoramas favored by adults.

Feed the troops. Begin with a nourishing breakfast. Carry plenty of quick-energy snack foods and offer them frequently. (By the time kids tell you're they're hungry, they're often already cranky and out of energy and enthusiasm.)

Supplement the Ten Essentials. Bring extra snacks, whistles (in case you and your child become separated), a book or toy for the drive to and from the trailhead.

Check your child's temperature. While you'd think that kids would tell you if they're too cold or too hot, they usually don't. Dress them in layers and be sure to add or subtract clothing in response to changing weather conditions.

Teach respect for nature. Enjoy but don't disturb flowers, plants and animals. Environmental education is easy and fun on the trail, so be sure to pack a good trail guide or nature guidebook and visit park interpretive centers.

When children travel in groups, the kids motivate each other to go farther and faster. And there's less whining.

Play games. If young spirits sag, try playing games to regain good humor and maintain that all-important forward progress up the trail. With younger children, "play dog" by throwing an imaginary stick to the next tree en route and have them fetch it. "One-two-three-jump" is another popular game. With a parent holding each hand the child hikes along one-two-three steps, then jumps as parents raise arms and swing the hopefully-no-longer reluctant little hiker into the air. "I Spy" is another favorite trail game: "I spy with my little eye something that is—(fill in the blank).

Take it easy. It's much better for everyone to stop frequently and travel slowly than to try to make the kids go faster and then have to carry them. If parents know what kids can and can't do, everyone has a great time on the trail.

The Hiker's Way—for Kids

Parents of kids 12 and under: have your kids read this or read it to them/with them through page 260.

In America—and in other countries—hiking is the most popular form of outdoor recreation.

Surprised?

Well you wouldn't be if you if you knew how many people started hiking as kids and enjoyed the experience so much they kept on hiking as teens, as young adults and as grown-ups.

Hiking is taking a walk on a trail in nature. Walking sidewalks to school is not hiking, and neither is walking around the mall. But walking in the forest or mountains is hiking. So is walking a path in the desert or along the seashore. Every hike is a walk but not every walk is a hike.

Hiking takes you to many beautiful places you can only get to on foot and is a great way to spend time with your friends. Trails lead to waterfalls, meadows full of wildflowers, the tops of mountains, swimming holes, picnic areas and campgrounds.

You can hike with a school group, Scout troop, friends, family, and with park rangers and guides. It feels good to be out in the fresh air, getting some exercise and enjoying the wonders of nature.

A hike can be a half hour, a half day, or many days long. Some people hike the same trails near home over and over again. Others explore new trails in faraway mountains. Backpackers are hikers who carry enough gear to camp overnight.

What's there to learn about hiking? You just put one foot in front of the other, right? It's so simple.

Well, not that simple.

Here are some tips to get started.

Gearing Up

To get started hiking, you don't need a whole lot of high-tech equipment. The basics are a daypack, some good hiking boots, and outdoors clothing.

A daypack is a soft pack that attaches to your shoulders and usually includes a hip band or waist belt for support. It's okay to begin hiking with a school backpack (as long as you don't bring your books and homework, ha!), but if you want to be a real hiker, you need a daypack made to carry the things a hiker needs: the Ten Essentials, extra clothing, food, water, and a camera.

A good daypack has a padded belt, padded shoulder straps, plenty of pockets and compartments, strong buckles and straps and covered zippers. Before you buy a pack, put a little weight in it and walk around the store. Be sure the pack fits and is comfortable.

When packing a daypack, remember: (1) Pack stuff you'll most likely use on the hike in the places easiest to reach and (2) pack the heaviest items at the bottom of the pack, the lightest ones toward the top.

Some hikers, especially those who hike a lot in warm weather, prefer packs with a built-in hydration (water-carrying) system.

Ten Essentials

What must you always take on a hike? A Ten Essentials list was first shared among hikers in the 1930s and is still used today

- **Map** One that shows all the trails.
- **Compass** Goes hand-in-hand with the map. Bring a GPS unit, too.
- **Water** Bring plenty and drink before you're thirsty
- **Extra food** Bring more than you think you might eat. Your hunger or day's plans might surprise you, and you'll want to be prepared.

- **Extra clothes** Pack rainwear and be ready for sudden changes in weather.
- **First-aid kit** And bring blister-treatment stuff, too.
- **Pocket knife** Very handy. Keep it clean and sharp.
- **Sun protection** Sunglasses and sunscreen.
- **Flashlight/headlamp** You never know when you might have to hike after dark.
- **Matches and firestarter** Waterproof matches and something to get the flames going if you have to light an emergency fire.

Along with the Ten Essentials, consider packing these items:
- **Hat** keeps body heat in, solar heat out.
- **Camera** (in a protective case)
- **Insect repellant** Keep those bugs away!
- **Trekking pole(s)** Gives you third and fourth "legs" on the trail.
- **Bandana** Soak in water and wrap around neck to keep your cool on trail. Plus a hundred more uses.

Hiking Boots

Kids like the lightweight kind of hiking boots that are more like sneakers with a heavier sole. Make sure they fit your feet with plenty of toe room for downhill hiking, and are wide enough for comfort. If the boots are a good fit, you'll start out and stay blister-free.

Many hikers can wear new, lightweight hiking boots straight out of the box and onto the trail. If they feel a little stiff, though, break them in before you hit the trail.

Socks made especially for hiking prevent blisters, stay drier and are much better than cotton ones. Take an extra pair. If you get your feet wet, you'll be happy to have dry socks to wear.

Clothing

The best way to pick clothing for a hike is to understand what hikers call layering. Layering is just what it sounds like: if it's cold, rather than wearing one heavy sweater, wear two or three thin layers. That way, if you get warm, you can remove any or all of the layers of clothing.

A good choice when layering is a fleece jacket, which looks great and keeps you warm. It doesn't weigh much, so that when you take it off and stuff it in your pack, it's easy to carry.

Long pants are best in cold weather and some hikers like them in warm weather, too, because they protect against scratches and sunburn. Many kids like to wear what they call zip-off pants. These are long pants that have zippers above the knee so you can zip off the bottom half, changing them into shorts.

Favorite Trail Foods

It's okay to pack a basic lunch with sandwich, fruit, and a cookie. Experienced hikers like to pack a variety of healthy and high-powered trail foods that can be eaten throughout the day.

- **Dried fruit** Easy to pack, won't spoil, very tasty.
- **Jerky** Plenty of protein and a Cave Man experience: the chance to gnaw away at dried meat in the middle of the wilderness.
- **Cheese and crackers** Hard cheeses pack much better than the softer ones.
- **Ants on a log** Fill celery stalks with peanut butter and sprinkle with raisins.
- **Bars** Energy bars, granola bars, protein bars, sports bars, whatever you want to call them. Keep a few in your pack. If you don't eat them that day, they can keep for the next hike.
- **Chocolate** Tastes great at home, even better on the trail. Chocolate melts in the heat and turns into a gooey mess, but many kids think that it tastes better that way.
- **Trail mix** GORP "Good Old Raisins and Peanuts," or trail mix, has been a part of hiking for a way long time. But if trail mix only had raisins and peanuts it wouldn't be nearly as popular as it is. Hikers have added all kinds of stuff to it over the years and everyone has their own favorite mix.

Making your own trail mix at home is a cinch and allows you to throw together foods and flavors you really love: granola, M&Ms, carob chips, dried fruit (cranberries, apple, apricot, peach, mango, pineapple), banana chips, flaked coconut, shelled sunflower seeds.

All About Trails

A good trail is like a good guide, pointing things out and picking the very best route from place to place. The best hiking trails don't go from point A to Point B in the fastest way, but take the scenic route. A good trail switchbacks (zigzags) up and down a mountainside rather than head straight up it.

More than a hundred years ago, people began building trails, lots of them, just for hiking. Trails don't just happen, they're designed and built. What a hiker sees on a trail is often created by a trail designer.

Most hikers don't think about who keeps the trails repaired, but in most cases it's the trail users themselves who do the work. Consider volunteering to work on a trail where you like to hike. It's hard digging and clearing brush but it feels really good knowing that you're keeping the trails open and doing something for your fellow hikers. There's a big National Trails Day in June, when hikers from all over America work on the trails.

Trails and hikes are rated by their level of difficulty—usually Easy, Moderate or Difficult. For example, an easy hike might be less than 5 miles with an elevation gain of less than 700 feet or so. A moderate hike might be 5 to 10 miles with less than a 2,000-foot elevation gain. A difficult hike might be more than 10 miles long with an elevation gain of more than 2,000 feet.

Hikers can choose among many different kinds of trails. Nature trails are short trails that help you learn about plants and the nearby environment. An out-and-back trail is one you use both coming and going. Many hikers like loop trails because you circle around and see something different with every step along the way.

Often the best trails are hikers-only paths (no other users permitted) and single-track (wide enough for only one person) trails. Multi-use trails permit more than one group at a time (horseback riders, mountain bikers, hikers).

On the Trail

It's important to know how fast you hike (your pace) so you can choose a trail that's a good length for you. Find a pace that you can keep up for a long time. You need to know your limits, but you should also challenge yourself.

Adults hike 2 to 3 miles an hour. Kids hike about 1 to 2 miles an hour. Your speed will vary depending on the difficulty of the trail. Adults are often surprised how far kids can go in one day and kids surprise themselves, too!

Be weather-wise. Dress for whatever weather you're hiking in—and expect it to change.

Know where you're hiking. Get a basic idea of where you started the hike from and where you're going. Learn how to read a map and keep oriented.

Work as a team. Offer comfort to your friends or younger family members if they're slow, tired or don't feel well. Use kindness and encourage them with positive words. Help them out by carrying some of their things in your pack, or by offering water or a little snack. Think about how you would want to be treated if you felt the same way—and then do it.

There's no whining in hiking. You know how awful it is to be around someone who whines. If you feel like whining, do something else instead! Have a snack, drink some water, slow down, speed up, take a look at the view, pretend you're an animal—anything, but don't whine.

Always stay with your group. And to keep from getting lost (and to protect the environment) stay on the trail. Do that by paying attention to signs, mileage markers, disks, posts and piles of stones known as cairns or ducks.

Notice the landmarks you pass such as unusual trees or rock formations. Stop now and then to compare your progress on the trail to the route on the map. Look behind you to see what the land looks like from the other direction. Knowing where you came from always gives you a better feel for where you're going and prepares you for the return trip.

Always think for yourself. Even if you're in the middle or at the end of a line of hikers, pay attention to where you're going.

Fun On and Off the Trail

Just being out in nature with your friends can be fun, but some things make a good hike great. Like water. Swim, splash, or just cool your feet in a lake or stream. Ahhhh.

For some hikers, the best thing about being out in nature is seeing animals and interesting plants and trees. Ask park rangers to point out places where you're likely to spot wildlife.

Maybe you'll get summit fever, which sounds like something that makes you sick, but is actually a good thing for a hiker to catch: it means that you must hike to the top of the mountain and nothing will stop you!

Some hikers feel so good about reaching a mountaintop and signing the summit register (often a notebook in a can), they decide to become "peak-baggers" and hike to the top of many more mountains. Peak-baggers "collect" peaks (all the peaks higher than 3,000 feet in a mountain range, for example) and keep records of their climbs.

Another fun thing to do is to take lots of pictures of your hike to share back home and online. Take pictures of the trailhead or trail signs to remind you of the hike.

Along with pics of your smiling buddies, get real by getting close-ups of dirty, sweaty, tired faces. Get close-ups on nature, too: one big flower up-close is usually a better image than a lot of flowers in a faraway meadow.

Hiking the Scout Way

Older children/early adolescents with a growing interest in hiking might surprise you with their abilities and what they can accomplish. The Scouts expect a lot from the boys, usually in twelve- to fourteen-years-old age group, who want to earn the hiking merit badge—a must for any boy wanting to become an

Eagle Scout. The Scout's guidelines are an excellent departure point for developing a hiking program for your own child. (Of course if you have a boy in that age group and a good Scouting program in your area, give the local troop a try.)

Girls should not feel left out here. Girl Scouts offer several hiking-related programs, and merit badges to earn, including orienteering, outdoors survival, backpacking and geocaching. And any girl who is a true outdoors enthusiast can design her own program for the Silver and Gold awards. Contact your local Girl Scout Council for more information.

Scout Hiking Merit Badge Requirements

1. Show that you know first-aid for injuries or illnesses that could occur while hiking, including hypothermia, heat-stroke, heat exhaustion, frostbite, dehydration, sunburn, sprained ankle, insect stings, tick bites, snakebite, blisters, hyperventilation, and altitude sickness.
2. Explain and, where possible, show the points of good hiking practices including the principles of Leave No Trace, hiking safety in the daytime and at night, courtesy to others, choice of footwear, and proper care of feet and footwear.
3. Explain how hiking is an aerobic activity. Develop a plan for conditioning yourself for 10-mile hikes, and describe how you will increase your fitness for longer hikes.
4. Make a written plan for a 10-mile hike. Include map routes, a clothing and equipment list, and a list of items for a trail lunch.
5. Take five hikes, each on a different day, and each of 10 continuous miles. Prepare a hike plan for each hike.
6. Take a hike of 20 continuous miles in one day following a hike plan you have prepared.
7. After each of the hikes (or during each hike if on one continuous "trek") in requirements 5 and 6, write a short report of your experience. Give dates and descriptions of routes covered, the weather, and any interesting things you saw. Share this report with your merit badge counselor.

Ten Tips for Hiking with Teens

Attitude. Be aware that teens are prone to BAS (Bad Attitude Syndrome). More than any other age group, they're apt to be lazy, sullen, grouchy, or downright mean on the trail.

Have fun. Teens are human, too (really), and there's nothing like a hike to diminish BAS. In their own way, and in their own time, this age group does find joy in hiking.

Let 'em wear cool clothes. Provided teens dress in layers with the proper kinds of apparel, let them have input about colors and styles.

Involve them in the trip planning. Let them have some input about the hike's distance and destination and about where to stop for a dinner on the drive home.

Drama counts. Choose hiking activities with some excitement. A swimming hole is a more appealing destination than a historic grist mill.

Two is not necessarily better than one. Forget parent-teen quality time if you subscribe to the "They'll entertain each other" theory (effective with younger children) and let your teen bring another on your family hike.

Challenge them. Adults are often more surprised than the teens themselves at the mountains they can climb and the distance they can cover in a day.

Leave the electronics behind. Under no circumstances permit them to bring any audio/video/cellular device on the trail.

Give 'em space. A little separation at carefully selected times and places is okay. Let them hike a little ahead of the adults—provided there's a well understood agreement to meet at a particular time or place.

Correct is cool. Encourage them to wear their hiking backpacks correctly (which they probably don't do with their school backpacks). Insist they adjust the shoulder straps and fasten the hip band.

What Adults Can Learn from Kids

"Walk as children of light," advised St. Paul, the Apostle.

Children enrich any hike with their own special thoughts, feelings, and sensory impressions. They bring innocence, wide-eyed wonder and enthusiasm that knows no bounds on a walk. Their small steps are accompanied by great leaps in imagination.

When my daughter was a little tyke, one of her favorite books was *The Listening Walk* by Paul Showers. A little girl likes to take what she calls "listening walks" with her dad and notes the *thh-hhhh* of a sprinkler, the *bomp-bomp-bomp* of a dribbling basketball, the *creet-creet-creet* of the crickets in the grass. "I hear all sorts of sounds on a Listening Walk," she says. "I listen to sounds I never listened to before."

Another favorite children's book, *Funny Walks* by Judy Hindley, opens with a question rarely considered by adults but perhaps often pondered by children: "Isn't it funny how people walk?"

One of the senses better developed in children than in adults is the sense of the ridiculous. What is a child to make of a walker with a scowl and a head bent down or one with a "thinking face" and hands in pockets? And isn't it odd how animals walk when you take the time to stop and watch?

From infants through teenagers, I've observed no single "right" or "wrong" age to take children on a hike. On a practical basis, each style of childhood offers both pluses and minuses for hiking families; on a spiritual basis, the pluses prevail by far.

Practically speaking, infants are highly portable, but they require packing all this "baby stuff" to go along with them. Often they sleep a lot, but they cry a lot, too. Toddlers toddle—but only sometimes in the desired direction. Grade-schoolers take a vigorous interest in hikes—but it might not be the same vigorous interest as their parents. Teens can hike long distances, keenly appreciate both cultural sites and the natural world—but they often don't want to take such hikes with their parents!

I've discovered that my children have helped me become a better hiker—more adaptive, more sensory, more patient. On hikes near home or faraway, children are great conversation starters with strangers—particularly those with children of their own. Young hikers remind us that many of the world's most compelling sights are all around, just waiting to be discovered.

20

Sharing the Experience

"I know you, I walked with you once upon a dream."
—from Disney's *Sleeping Beauty*

"Take only photographs, leave only footprints."
—Sierra Club

THE NEXT best thing to walking a trail is talking about it. I love talking trail—whether it's recalling a marvelous hike or planning a new adventure.

Walk the walk *and* talk the talk: share trail accounts and meaningful moments with a circle of friends and the community at large. Encourage fellow hikers to hit the trail and to do so more often. Remind them of the many benefits of the green way.

While just about any way you share your enthusiasm for hiking is a good way, some ways are particularly effective at communicating the hiking experience.

Photos preserve memories of favorite hikes and to show your friends the pleasures of a particular trail so that they may be encouraged to follow in your footsteps. I've looked at thousands of photos of people hiking, and taken a whole lot of them myself, and let be tell you it's pretty difficult to make hiking look even halfway as fun and inspiring as a day on the trail.

The challenge of getting great hiking photos is due in part to the nature of an outdoor activity some bureaucrats label "passive recreation." Hiking per se, like walking, is not all that visually compelling. The natural world and the characters who encounter it can combine for terrific hiking photos, but only if some care and thought goes into their composition.

(Of course plenty of things are harder to photograph well than hiking—eating for example; no one looks good eating.)

Preserving memories is one part of the hiking experience and looking forward to the next hike is another. Often the two go hand-in-hand. Hiking, like so many of life's endeavors, is a process of examining where you've been to better determine where you're going.

Remembering Your Hike

"A good snapshot stops a moment from running away."
—Eudora Welty

A picture, as the saying goes, is worth a thousand words. A photograph speaks at least that, if not more. Many a hiker can be found peering behind a lens, in hopes of capturing a tangible impression of a journey that will linger long in the mind. Images you capture can become treasures that help describe to others the people, places, trails, details, and emotions of your hiking adventure.

There's no better way to hold on to the great memories of a hike in a unique place than to photograph it well. Many hikers take along cameras: point and shoot and hope for the best. But many of us are disappointed with the results of our efforts, realizing once we review the images that we didn't quite capture the place in the way we experienced it.

By remembering a few tips and with a little practice, you can get some good hiking photos with a basic digital camera. Even better is a more advanced, but nevertheless compact model with a feature that lets you manually override the automatic exposure. (Every year the automatic exposures get better and better, but they still don't "think" as well as an experienced outdoors photographer.) Digital camera-makers are producing ever more durable and weatherproof models.

Share your photos via mail or e-mail with your companions,

with folks you met on the trail, or anyone else you think might enjoy a glimpse into your hike. The cost is negligible, the good will immeasurable. Good photos are always welcome for nature center publications, outings club newsletters, outdoors e-zines, small newspapers and web sites. Your photos can help hikers plan a trip or, in some cases, aid preservation efforts on behalf of a particular park or pathway. You might find yourself a welcome guest speaker if you put your photos together with a narrative in a power point presentation.

Obviously studying photography as a hobby or art form will help you with your photos. Take a photography class at a local adult education center or community college. After you learn the basics, you might want to take a nature photography class or a seminar–field trip offered by a professional outdoors photographer.

Sharp focus, good composition, proper lighting are important, but in addition there are several other important criteria that will help you tell the story of your hike and help communicate the experience. Below are some hike-specific photo tips to help produce the results you want: increasing the visual appeal of a hike and sharing the experience with your friends.

The best images tell the story of a hike in an up-close and personal way, convey in an instant the charm, beauty and distinctive pleasures of experiencing a particular place on foot. The best photos subtly evoke emotion and beckon the viewer to action.

Emotion	**Desired Viewer Response**
What a great idea it is to take a hike!	"I'd like to do that!"
What a great place that is!	"I want to go there!"
Those people are having fun!	"I could have fun, too."
These people had a great hike.	"I'd like to do that hike."

Hiking along Photographs of people hiking alone or in groups tend not to be too compelling unless there are other elements to add scale, drama, perspective and color.

Smiling groups The typical image of the smiling group standing in a nondescript location—while nice for a memento—is not terribly fascinating. Think instead of an animated couple chatting or holding hands, a few women admiring something, kids wandering off and doing something silly, a couple of guys chuckling or a small group interacting with locals.

Large groups vs. small ones Long lines of hikers are particularly uninteresting because they often look like ants on the trail or you get the reaction: "I don't want to go there—it's too crowded." Depending on the setting, the magic number of hikers can range from four to eight. Look for a perspective, such as hikers on switchbacks, that uses numbers to your advantage.

Go for interesting characters—not just everyone who's young and fit. Someone with creases, wearing an old hat, someone grizzled, charming, weatherworn, exotic, etc. Shoot to get this reaction from the viewer: "I would love to meet someone like that!"

Pre-hike and post hike Relaxing in a woodsy campground, dining al fresco, sitting in porch swing at a graceful B&B, a quirky-looking innkeeper, a couple in a Jacuzzi with their hiking boots and walking sticks nearby; think of telling a story of the whole hiking experience.

Local culture Record not only the trail but the whole environment, including the nearby architecture and artifacts that reflect the spirit of a place: cottages, unique vehicles, boats, tools, signs, etc. Capture a time gone by with farm implements, an old settlers cabin, an abandoned barn. Look for individuals wearing distinctive clothing, who represent a distinct region, perhaps even a different time—people who definitely don't resemble your next-door neighbors.

Perspective shots Think of pulling the viewer into the photo—with narrow dirt roads, a fence line, a line of trees, a path leading into the woods, along a shoreline, a line of walkers shot from above (or below) These shots have great impact and emotional pull.

Color Think in terms of the vibrancy of a place. What are the distinctive colors and hues that enhance it? The cool greens and blues of Ireland . . . the emerald greens of the Pacific Northwest rain forest, the hot golden sands of New Mexico, the vibrant flower fields of Provence. Think not only of the color palette of a specific place; also consider the contrasting and complementary colors that will set it off and reflect its character.

Tips for Better Pics

Don't center your subject in the frame. Allow the terrain, the trail and the surroundings to help tell the story.

In a flash. For photography in the forest, overexpose by a stop or two and use a flash.

Don't fight the light—use it. Silhouettes add an offbeat dimension to the usual buddies-on-the-trail shots. By all means, take good advantage of bad weather and shoot in rain and fog.

A sign to remember. Include a sign in your coverage: a trail sign, wilderness, mileage. Signs are useful as little inserts in a publication or online posting to help you remember a great day on the trail.

Details please. One or two flowers are often more compelling than a long shot of a flower-dotted meadow.

Up-close and personal. Get some emotion. Sure a winsome grin is nice, but how about showing some fatigue, grime, sweat, tears?

Make friends with Mr. Time Release. Use your camera's delayed shutter release to good effect: Put yourself in the picture. I've strapped my camera to a tree with a shoelace, balanced it on rocks.

Don't be shy about asking someone to photograph you. I know hikers who made it to the top of Whitney and didn't ask a fellow peak-bagger to take a photo. And I know another hiker, who went on a trip-of-a-lifetime hiking vacation in Italy, returning with hundreds of images, and not a single one of herself.

Logbooks and Laptops, Journals Online and Off

"We do not remember days; we remember moments."
—Cesare Pavese

When you first tell the story, you'll recall the special moments of the trail: the lightning-split tree, burned but unbowed; the sword ferns that seemed to point the way to a babbling brook; the turkey vulture circling overhead that your friend joked has a taste for fallen hikers.

In the first telling, you'll recall many details, later retellings some of the details. As the weeks and months and years pass, the details will fade.

A memorable hike, like a memorable story, has a beginning, middle and an end. This built-in dramatic structure, this "epic" journey from trailhead to trail's end can help the novice wordsmith fashion a memorable narrative.

Those elemental "conflicts" that are part of the hiker's way can add drama—and humor—to a hiker's storytelling: Hiker vs. Nature, Hiker vs. Hiker (hopefully, this is only a friendly rivalry), Hiker vs. Himself, or Hiker vs. Herself. Whether recounting a serious true-life adventure or exaggerating and having some fun, be sure to put plenty of your personality in your story.

Most likely, you'll share your stories and opinions about hiking via e-mails, by sending text and photos to particular web sites or by posting comments about a particular park, pathway or issue online. In this respect, using a laptop to record your post-hike musings or keyboarding on your phone is a big help.

Still, writing in a journal has a certain slow-paced quality, and suggests a contemplative craftsmanship that seems to go with hiking, even in the modern age. There are whole books written on how to keep a nature journal, but the most important lesson to remember is to do it! Write what you remember so you never forget.

Sketching in a sketchbook is another time-honored wonderful way to record your impressions of a hike. Draw what you like or need to keep the scene fresh in your mind. If you're in an area where it's permissible to pick flowers, grab a few and press them in your journal.

Social and Emerging Media

Spread the good word by sharing your experiences on the trail in a variety of low-tech and high-tech ways. I asked Andrew Dean Nystrom, who manages to balance his appreciation for the natural world with a successful career in the new media world, how best to do this.

Nystrom has authored or co-authored two dozen travel

guidebooks on destinations worldwide, including *Top Trails Yellowstone & Grand Teton National Parks,* winner of a National Outdoor Book Award for Best Adventure Guidebook. The enthusiastic hiker and new media pro offers a half-dozen tips on how to share hiking adventures with friends and the online hiking community at large:

- During your trip-planning phase, start a blog (via a free hosting service like http://blogger.com or http://wordpress.com), or a free Twitter "microblogging" account (http://twitter.com); documenting your planning process online may connect you with folks willing to help plans your adventures.
- Consider using a Global Positioning System (GPS)-enabled digital camera, if you'd like to create visual maps on the fly and share location-specific imagery.
- For longer outings, pack twice the digital memory, extra backup rechargeable batteries, perhaps even a solar-powered charger.
- Post-hike, batch upload and tag photos and videos on Yahoo's Flickr (http://flickr.com) or Google's Panoramio (http://panoramio.com) with common keywords so more folks will see them. If you're new to online photo sharing or are shooting print film, check with your preferred photo developing service: most all of them now offer user-friendly digital photo sharing services.
- If you prefer low to high-tech, check out the "dead simple blog by email" service Posterous (http://posterous.com)—follow the simple directions to start your free multimedia blog, with one click.
- Don't lose sight of the real, tangible forest for the virtual trees. Take a break from snapping photos and recording video often to remember what being out-of-doors is all about: disconnecting from our frantic modern world. If you don't pay close attention, how will you caption your photos?!

Promoting Trails and the Hiking Experience

If you want the media to pay attention to a new trail or a guided hike opportunity, try to keep in mind that you're telling a tale (providing a storyline) and making a sale—getting the public to check out a new and improved whatever. Don't be reluctant to ask a professional publicist or marketing expert for help. You wouldn't hesitate to call a plumber for a broken pipe; don't hesitate to get help with a publicity campaign before it goes down the drain.

I've seen so many good hiking tours, trails events and conservation causes go unnoticed because the organizers didn't have the time or skill to put together a compelling press release, much less an effective media and marketing strategy. As a result, the public doesn't learn of a new pathway, one that may have required thousands of hours of volunteer time, and many thousands of dollars.

Remember you're telling your story to the media and to the public not just to fellow hikers or park volunteers. Stay away from policy-wonk words like public sector, mitigation, stakeholder, multi-agency, viewshed, and EIR.

I've written up a thousand hikes, hundreds of nature centers, greenways, open space districts, and parks administered by every possible government agency. I always take the time to distinguish one trail from another, one park from another, one nature museum from another. A trail/hiking-promoter must distinguish each park, trail, and interpretive activity from any other.

You can get lots of good ideas about Marketing 101 from books or from mining the experience of a seasoned pro. Keep building those great trails, keep leading nature hikes for kids, and keep in mind that this good work of sharing The Hiker's Way must be publicized.

EPILOGUE

"NOBODY expresses their gratitude about anything or ever thanks me," you say. Likely as not, you're probably right. Try to remember the last time anyone thanked you for anything. It was probably a "Thanks-and-have-a-nice-day" at the checkout counter from a supermarket cashier or a "Thanks for your order" from a fast-food franchise. Such gratitude!

Now try to remember the last time anyone thanked you for anything important. It's a dispiriting cycle: we rarely get thanks, and we rarely give it.

My suggestion: On one walk (better yet a hike) a week use a few minutes of your time to exercise your gratitude while you stretch your limbs. List everything in your life that you are thankful for, and everything that you enjoy. Contemplate this list on your hike.

We can be thankful for possessions and money and yet for the freedom to walk the whole earth, and for the great benefits of our creative spirit, our life and health, we consider ourselves under no obligation to express any gratitude.

By expressing our gratitude, we can hike from feeling stressed to feeling blessed. So hike with gratitude.

And keep on hiking. If you make hiking part of your life, you'll find that your whole being—body and soul—will reach wider horizons, greater possibilities.

Hike. Contemplate what makes you happy and what would make you happier still. Hike. Think about what you can do to expand your life and someone else's. Hike to remember. Hike to forget. Hike for recovery. Hike for discovery. Hike. Enjoy the beauty of providence. Hike.

In a life that takes us almost anywhere, we can hike almost anywhere. Hiking means continuing to hike: Today, tomorrow and for the rest of your life.

Trail Terms

alignment: The layout of the trail in horizontal and vertical planes. The bends, curves, and ups and downs of the trail. The more the alignment varies, the more challenging the trail.

bed: The excavated surface on which a trail tread lies.

brushing: To clear the trail corridor of plants, trees, and branches, which could impede the progress of trail users.

brushing-in: To pile logs, branches, rocks, or other debris at the start a closed trail to prevent it from being used.

center line: An imaginary line marking the center of the trail. During construction, the center line is usually marked by placing a row of flags or stakes.

crowned trail: A trail bed built up from the surrounding area and sloped for drainage (usually by excavating trenches parallel to the trail).

flagging: Thin ribbon used for marking during the location, design, construction, or maintenance of a trail project.

grade: The amount of elevation change between two points over a given distance expressed as a percentage (feet change in elevation for every 100 horizontal feet, commonly known as "rise over run"). A trail that rises 8 vertical feet in 100 horizontal feet has an 8 percent grade. Grade is different than angle; angle is measured with a straight vertical as 90 degrees and a straight horizontal as 0 degrees. A grade of 100 percent would have an angle of 45 degrees.

grub (grubbing): To dig or clear roots and tree stumps near or on the ground surface of the trail tread.

gutter: A trough or dip used for drainage purposes that runs along the edge of a trail.

maintainer: A volunteer who maintains a section of trail as part of a trail-maintenance program of a trail organization.

maintenance: Work that is carried out to keep a trail in its originally constructed serviceable condition. Usually limited to minor repair or improvements that do not significantly change the trail location, width, surface, or structures. Involves four tasks: cleaning drainage, clearing windfalls, brushing, and marking.

pruning: The removal of normal vegetative growth that intrudes beyond the defined trail clearing limits.

read(ing): To study the terrain and obstacles to determine a course or possible locations for a trail through the area.

reconnaissance (recon): Scouting out alternative trail locations prior to the final trail route location being selected.

rehabilitation (rehab): All work to bring an existing trail up to its classification standard, including necessary relocation of minor portions of the trail.

rut: Sunken groove in the tread, perpendicular to the direction of travel, usually less than two feet in depth.

trailbed: The finished surface on which base course or surfacing may be constructed. For trails without surfacing, the trailbed is the tread.

tread: The actual surface portion of a trail upon which users travel excluding backslope, ditch, and shoulder. Common tread surfaces are native material, gravel, soil cement, asphalt, concrete, or shredded recycled tires.

waterbar: A drainage structure (for turning water) composed of an outsloped segment of tread leading to a barrier placed at a 45° angle to the trail; usually made of logs, stones, or rubber belting material. Water flowing down the trail will be diverted by the outslope or, as a last resort, by the barrier. Grade dips are preferred on multi-use trails instead of waterbars.

waterfall: Steep descent of water from a height.

Books that Inspire

SOME OF our favorite stories are accounts of great walks. And some of our favorite walks seem to inspire great stories.

Narratives of Great Hikes

Journey Home, A Walk Across England, by John Hillaby. Holt, Rinehart & Winston, 1984.

A Tramp Across the Continent by Charles F. Lummis. First published 1920. University of Nebraska Press, 1982.

A Walk in the Woods, Rediscovering America on the Appalachian Trail by Bill Bryson. Broadway Books, 1998.

Into A Desert Place, A 3,000 Mile Walk Around the Coast of Baja, California, by Graham MacKintosh. W.W. Norton & Company Ltd, 1995.

A Walk Along Land's End, Dispatches from the Edge of California on a 1,600-mile Hike from Mexico to Oregon, by John McKinney. HarperCollins, 1995; republished Olympus Press, 2010

The Man Who Walked Through Time by Colin Fletcher. First published Alfred A. Knopf, 1968. Vintage, Random House.

A Thousand Mile Walk to the Gulf by John Muir. Written 1867, first published 1916. Sierra Club Books.

Where the Waters Divide, A Walk Along America's Continental Divide, Karen Berger and Daniel R. Smith. Harmony Books, 1993.

The Art and History of Walking

The Art of Pilgrimage, The Seeker's Guide to Making Travel Sacred by Phil Couisineau. Conari Press, 1998.

Wanderlust, A History of Walking, by Rebecca Solnit. Viking, 2000.

Walking by Henry David Thoreau. Many editions of this classic essay, first published after the great naturalist's death.

The Walker's Literary Companion, edited by Roger Gilbert, Jeffrey Robison and Anne Wallace. Breakaway Books, 2000.

The Winding Trail, A selection of articles and essays for walkers and backpackers edited by Roger Smith, Foreword by John Hillaby. Diadem Books Ltd, London, 1981.

Web Trails

Advocates for Hikers

American Hiking Society . . . . www.AmericanHiking.org

Conservation

Sierra Club. . . . . www.SierraClub.org
Leave No Trace . . . . www.lnt.org

Gear

Altrec. . . . . www.altrec.com
REI . . . . www.rei.com
Fogdog.com outdoor products . . . . www.fogdog.com

Gear Reviews

Gear Junkie. . . . . www.GearJunkie.com
Outdoor Industry News . . . . www.Snewsnet.com

Maps

Trails Illustrated Maps . . . . www.trailsillustrated.com
MapLink. . . . . www.maplink.com
Maps.com . . . . www.maps.com
Tom Harrison Maps . . . . www.tomharrisonmaps.com

Trails/Recreation Info

Trails.com . . . . www.Trails.com
Local Hikes . . . . www.LocalHikes.com
GORP . . . . www.gorp.com

U.S. Government

National Park Service . . . . www.nps.gov
U.S. Forest Service. . . . . www.fs.fed.us
Recreation One-Stop . . . . www.recreation.gov
Bureau of Land Management . . . . www.blm.gov

Walking

The Walking Connection . . . . www.WalkingConnection.com
American Volksport Association. . . . . www.ava.org

Acknowledgements

For their companionship and inspiration along The Hiker's Way, I thank Cheri Rae McKinney, Penny and Terry Davies, Bob McDermott, Bob Howells, Tim McFadden, Helen and Jim McKinney, Fotine O'Connor and Don Robinson.

I am forever grateful for my good start on the trail to the scout leaders of Troop 441 from Downey, California. Explorer Scoutmaster Harry Goldstein, along with his wife Clara Goldstein, was especially encouraging to me at a young age, as well as later in life when I made hiking a career path.

During my long tenure as the *Los Angeles Times* hiking columnist, I appreciated the enthusiastic support and deft editorial skill of a dozen editors. Travel section editor Leslie Ward was consistently encouraging about my hiking adventures locally and globally.

While helping to develop and teach a hike-leader training program, it was a pleasure to work with and learn so much from Tracy Roseboom, senior national campaign manager for Hike for Discovery, a program of the Leukemia & Lymphoma Society.

Thanks also to those who shared their expertise on various aspects of hiking: on our alienation from nature, Richard Louv and Emilyn Sheffield; on hiker medical issues, Dr. Bill Meller; on trails and advocating for hikers, Greg Miller and the staff of the American Hiking Society; on hiking vacations, Michael West, founder of The Wayfarers; on trail maps, Tom Harrison; on sharing hike experiences and social media, Andrew Dean Nystrom. My daughter Sophia and son Daniel, great trail companions, contributed their keen viewpoints to the book's advice about hiking with kids and teens.

I also extend my thanks and want to voice my appreciation for the many rangers and administrators of America's national parks, national forests, BLM lands, as well as various state and regional parks across America, who generously contributed knowledge and expertise along the way. Many equipment makers and outdoor retailers were very helpful to this project and the time they took answering my questions about hiking gear and apparel is greatly appreciated.

For some of the inspirational quotes used in this book, a big thanks to *Trail Quotes: From Advocacy to Wilderness,* Jim Schmid, editor, South Carolina Department of Parks, Recreation and Tourism, Columbia, SC. Another tip of the hiker's cap to Jim Schmid for the assorted trail definitions and terms he compiled in *A Glossary of Trails, Greenway, and Outdoor Recreation Terms and Acronyms.*

Index

Abbey, Edward, 165
accessibility, 131-132
acute mountain sickness, 230
aerobics, 59
aging, 49
altitude, 226-227
altitude sickness, 226-230
American Automobile Association, 144
American Diabetes Association, 42
American Heart Association, 42
American Hiking Society, 31, 42, 124, 130
American Lung Association, 42
Anderson, Lorraine, 67
arthritis, 48-49
Austen, Jane, 141
autumn hiking, 199-200,
autumn hiking, 211-212, 215

backcountry driving, 145
bars, 86, 257
Bashō, Matsuo, 59
Bay Area Ridge Trail Council, 120
bee stings, 191-192
Bennet, Arnold, 161
binoculars, 147
bird-watching, 235-236
black flies, 185, 189
blazes, 128
blisters, 183-184
BPA, 91
Brooks, Earle Amos, 117
Buddha, 49, 83

cairns, 128, 175
cameras, 266
Camino de Santiago, 60
Capilene, 106
cell phone, 146
Chase, Joseph Smeaton, 239
child-carrier, 251
children, 249-264
chocolate, 85, 257
Civilian Conservation Corps, 119
clothing, 78, 101, 256-257
CNN, 16
cold weather hiking, 213-216
Coleridge, Samuel Taylor, 56
companions, 239-243
compass, 77, 172-173, 255
Confucius, 240
Conrad, Joseph, 133

daypacks, 96, 99-101, 255
DEET, 185-186, 189-190
dehydration, 89-90, 227
depression, 49-50
diabetes, 48
Dialameh, Amir, 84
Dickens, Charles, 55
Dickinson, Emily, 235
discs, 129
dogs, 246-247
Douglas, David, 180
dried fruit, 85
ducks, 128
Dwyre, Bill, 65

Ecopsychology, 50
ecotones, 234
Eeyore, 21-22
elevation, 161, 201, 226-227
emergency plan, 182
Erhlich, Gretel, 204
falls, 221-222
Feng shui, 121
fire-starter, 81
first-aid kit, 78-79, 256
flash floods, 206-207
flashlight, 80-81, 146
Fletcher, Colin, 158
food, 77-78, 214
Francis, Saint, 51

Gandhi, Mahatma, 55, 155
gear, 95-113, 157, 255-256
gear philosophy, 95-98
Girl Scouts, 261
Goethe, 55

Google, 19, 144
Gore-tex, 105
GORP, 13, 86, 257
GPS, 97, 145, 168, 174-175
grade, 161-162
Great Hiking Era, 119
Green Exercise, 69
Green, 32, 36-38

Hammarskjöld, Dag, 226
Harrison, Tom, 167
hats, 103
hay fever, 195-196
headlamp, 80-81, 256
heart, 44, 47
heat, 210-211
hike
  difficulty ratings, 159-161
  planning, 141-153
  selection, 134-135
hiker
  biorhythm, 163-164
  definition, 15-18
  ethics, 198
  hygiene, 196
  myths, 197
  safety, 148-149, 181-182
hiking
  boots, 106-108, 256
  clubs, 242-243
  defined, 64
  estimating time, 162-164
  guidebooks, 161
  merit badge, 261
  mud season, 206-207
  snow, 225
  solo, 244-245
  speed, 156, 162-164
  sticks, 110-113
  uphill, 220
  with children, 249-264
Hilary, Edmund, 226
Hippocrates, 43
hot weather hiking, 209-210
Human vs. Nature, 68
hydration packs, 91-92
hypothermia, 216-218

insect repellant, 147
insects, 185-192

jerky, 85, 257
Jesus, 55-56
Jewell, Sally, 19-20

Kant, Immanuel, 55
Keillor, Garrison, 41

L'Amour, Louis, 175
land ethic, 71-72
laptop, 99, 269
layering, 101-103
Leopold, Aldo, 231
Leukemia and Lymphoma Society, 14
lightning strikes, 204-206
Lincoln, Abe, 13
lost, 176-178
Louv, Richard, 27, 249, 250
Lyme disease, 188

MacLaine, Shirley, 60
map-reading, 172-173
maps, 76, 97, 138, 144-145, 172-173, 255
matches, 80, 146, 256
McLeod, 123
mental health, 49-50
Miller, Greg, 31
Milne, A.A., 22, 83
monuments, 128
Morada, Rich, 83
Moses, 112
mosquitoes, 185-186, 188-189
mountain bikes, 129-130, 222
Mountaineers, The, 76
Mozart, Wolfgang Amadeus, 55
mud season, 207-209
mugwort, 193
Muir, John, 25, 69, 179, 244

National Park Service, 33, 41, 134
National Public Radio, 41
Nature Conservancy, 250
Nature Deficit Disorder, 250

nature films,. 231-232
Nystrom, Andrew Dean, 270-271

osteoporosis, 48
Owens, Glen, 128

pace, 156, 158-159
Pausch, Randy, 22
Pavese, Cesare, 269
photos, 265-271
pilgrimage, 59-60
pocket knife, 79-80, 256
poison ivy, 192-193
poison oak, 180, 192-193
polyester, 105
polypropylene, 104-105
precautions, 179-197
Pulaski, 123-124
Rails to Trails, 46, 139-140
rain, hiking in, 202-204
rainwear, 103-104, 203-204
REI, 19-20
rest step, 221
Rogers, Will, 55
Roosevelt, Eleanor, 141
sandals, hiking, 110

Scouts, 61, 79, 98, 260-261
scree, 223
Searns, Robert, 118-119
seasons, 137, 199-218
Seneca, 133
Shakespeare, William, 220
Shelley, Percy Bysshe, 56
Showers, Paul, 263
Sierra Club, 134, 139, 242, 251, 265
single file, 164
ski lifts, 139
snacks, 204
Snyder, Gary, 219
social media, 270-271
socks, 97, 109-110
Socrates, 55
solo hiking, 244-245
SPF (Sun Protection Factor), 194-195
spring hiking, 201-202
Stegner, Wallace, 165
stream crossing, 224
summer hiking, 209-210
sun protection, 80, 194-195, 210, 255
sunscreen, 147
Swaim, Will, 53
switchbacks, 29-32, 163-164
talus, 223
Teale, Edwin Way, 155
teens, 262
Ten Essentials, 23, 75- 81, 157, 217, 253, 255-256
Theroux, Paul, 75
Thich Nhat Hanh, 52
Thoreau, Henry David, 29, 55, 61, 69, 97, 213, 244
ticks, 185-187
Tigger, 21-22
toddlers, 263-264
topographic maps, 169-171
tourons, 34
Trail Days, 124
trail
  building, 117, 120-122
  erosion, 123
  foods, 257-258
  guidebooks, 133, 135-138
  maps, 166-172
  mix, 83, 87, 257
  promoting, 272
  signs, 127-128
  washouts, 164
  work, 122-123
trailhead
  maps, 144-145
  parking, 150-151
  safety, 149-151
  transport to, 147-148
trails, 117-132, 258
Transcendentalism, 55, 70
Triangulation Method, 173
T-shirt, 102
Twitter, 271

U.S. Army, 158
U.S. Forest Service, 160. 168
U.S. Geological Survey, 166, 170

urushiol, 192

Vorarlberg Institute, 41-42

walkabout, 241
walking sticks, 110-113
Walton, Izaak, 239
Watchable Wildlife Areas, 233-234
water, 77, 255
water bottle, 90-91, 97, 101
water treatment, 92-93
water, 87, 89-90
way marks, 175
weather, 101, 149, 259
Webster, Ron, 117
weight control, 47
Welty, Eudora, 266
West Coast Trail, 179
whining, 259
Whitman, Walt 244
wildlife watching, 212, 231-237
winter hiking, 213-216
wool, 105
Wordsworth, William, 41, 56

Young, Noel, 25

John McKinney is the author of twenty books about hiking, parklands, and nature, including *A Walk Along Land's End, Dispatches from the Edge of California on a 1,600-mile hike from Mexico to Oregon.* For eighteen years, McKinney, a.k.a. The Trailmaster, wrote a weekly hiking column for the *Los Angeles Times* and now writes articles and commentaries about nature and outdoor recreation for both print and online publications. A passionate advocate for the environment and our need to reconnect to nature, McKinney also shares his expertise on radio, TV, in the blogosphere and at www.TheTrailmaster.com.

www.ingramcontent.com/pod-product-compliance
Lightning Source LLC
Chambersburg PA
CBHW021046090426
42738CB00006B/211
9780934161381